Peace Psychology Book Series

Series Editor

Daniel J. Christie

For further volumes:
http://www.springer.com/series/7298

Ami C. Carpenter

Community Resilience to Sectarian Violence in Baghdad

Springer

Ami C. Carpenter
Joan B. Kroc School of Peace Studies
University of San Diego
San Diego, CA
USA

ISBN 978-1-4614-8811-8 ISBN 978-1-4614-8812-5 (eBook)
DOI 10.1007/978-1-4614-8812-5
Springer New York Heidelberg Dordrecht London

Library of Congress Control Number: 2013946313

Printed on acid-free paper

Springer is part of Springer Science+Business Media (www.springer.com)

Foreword

The phrase "victory has a hundred fathers and defeat is an orphan" is often attributed to the Italian diplomat Count Caleazzo Ciano, but the insight is a common one. US News and World Report correspondent Chitra Ragavan, reflecting on the war in Iraq, noted "Success has many fathers. The mess in Baghdad has a lot more."[1] Iraq is a complex endeavor, on a historical scale and its parental attribution is simultaneously clear and contentious. Some claim parenthood and assert success; others assert failure and seek to ensure that parenthood cannot be denied.

These arguments are both necessary, and unlikely to be resolved any time soon. But an exclusive focus on the role of international, particularly American, decisions in the origins and conduct of the war unfortunately obscures the equally important understanding of the Iraqi role in the evolution of the conflict. While some attention is paid to "The Awakening"—the Sunni rejection of Al Qaeda—less attention is paid to other Iraqi actors in the conflict's evolution, for example, Muqtada al Sadr. A variety of Iraqi actors played key roles in the evolution of the conflict. Their motivations and political agendas were diverse and often unclear—anti-occupation vocabularies frequently accompanied robust personal, criminal, and factional-political agendas—and historical work on these issues will take time to bring clarity. But at least these actors are visible.

Professor Ami Carpenter's book is unique, in that it highlights the efforts of ordinary Iraqis to resist the violence produced by the intersection of the American-led invasion and a diversity of local agendas. In Professor Carpenter's book the experiences, the efforts, the voices, of ordinary Iraqis seeking to cope with the war and to shape events so as to maintain their ordinary lives and their neighborhoods, are front and center.

Professor Carpenter's work focuses on resiliency, "the ability of social systems to cope, adapt, and reorganize in response to dramatic challenges." She develops, and through her research carefully examines, the four sets of factors shaping community resilience—social capital, economic development, information and communication resources, and community competence. Through well-developed

[1] "Who Lost Iraq: Success has many fathers. The mess in Baghdad has a lot more." US News and World Report, 11/19/2006. http://www.usnews.com/usnews/news/articles/061119/27iraq_10.htm accessed 23 June 2013.

theory and careful attention to the specific social context of individual neighborhoods in Baghdad she brings to light how these factors shape the evolution of conflict. In some communities, neighbors were able to maintain cross-cutting connections, employ the resources they had, and sustain an imperfect peace. In others, sectarian fear developed, communities polarized, and violence overtook these efforts. While the Iraq War, viewed from afar, may seem an event of grand scope and scale, and a blur of factions, sectarian tensions, and international and regional actors, it was in fact an intimate and local affair. Local dynamics shaped larger outcomes, all successes and failures, of any actor involved, were grounded in small-scale actions and events. At this scale, the actions of individuals and small groups matter, and Professor Carpenter carefully traces the interaction of these actions with wider social conditions and their impact on conflict within communities.

Whether the Iraq War was a war for oil, or for freedom and democracy; whether it was sadly misconceived or boldly and courageously crafted, are questions for political contention and historical assessment. What is clear is that it was a *war*, into which the people of Iraq were plunged, as individual and as communities, and with which they had to cope. Though some sought to participate in the conflict, the vast majority of them sought, or at least wished for, peace. Professor Carpenter quotes Adel Abdul Mahdi, the former Vice President of Iraq, who, writing this spring, saw the Iraqi people as hostages: "We all have become hostages…. The Sunnis are hostages; they cannot support the policies of authorities that weaken them in their regions and threaten them in other regions. The Shias are also hostages. They stand helpless before daily killings and menacing threats while they find themselves unable to discuss failing policies related to their security, politics and services."[2] Professor Carpenter's book reminds us, and shows us how, at least some ordinary Iraqis rejected the idea that they were hostages. The Iraqis whose efforts Professor Carpenter analyzes may not have fully succeeded in maintaining peace in their neighborhoods, but they refused to be hostages and struggled to build peace as they could. This is not a simple or heroic tale—it is social science, rather than a novel, after all—but the understanding Professor Carpenter develops can help all of us who seek to help develop a more peaceful and just world; the efforts of the ordinary Iraqis whose story she tells can inspire us.

Dana P. Eyre

[2] Mahdi [1].

Acknowledgments

This project would not have been possible without the invaluable assistance of Dana Eyre, Stefan Kabowski, S. S. Motlak, Ali Hassan, and Salman Salman. I am deeply, immeasurably grateful to all five of these extraordinary individuals. All helped me rewrite and de-jargonize my questionnaire to get the answers I really wanted. Dana and Stefan juggled insane travel schedules to participate in numerous conference calls about the project as it progressed, and to set me straight several times with seasoned advice on the methodology. Ali and Salman undertook the risky project of conducting interviews in the ten neighborhoods we chose to study. S. S. Motlak spent additional innumerable hours explaining the social and political intricacies of identity in Baghdad, regional tribal histories, and aiding my interpretation of our data.

I am deeply grateful that my brilliant colleague, Dr. Topher McDougal, joined the project team. He broadened and bettered our methodology, reminded us not to overlook or undervalue the contribution of economic variables in our analysis, and taught me much about the impact of trade and social networks on urban resilience.

I wish to thank Ibrahim al-Marashi for reviewing this manuscript before its publication, and for his supremely helpful inquiries, corrections, and encouragement. This book was certainly made better by his thoughtful critique and suggested revisions.

Last but not least, I would like to thank James Kohn for supporting me through the final stages of this project, for no small amount of proofreading, and for his invaluable emotional support.

Contents

1 **Introduction** ... 1
Al-Nil Raises a Question ... 2
A Subtle Difference ... 4
Resilience and Conflict ... 5
Methods ... 7
Research Sites ... 10
Multicultural Iraq ... 13
Amiriyya ... 13
Adhamiyya ... 14
Dura ... 15
Sadr City ... 16
Zafaraniyya ... 16
Bayaa ... 17
Palestine Street ... 17
Al-Dhubat ... 17
Karada and Kuraaiat ... 18
Overview of the Book ... 18
References ... 20

2 **Violence and Extremism: Sources of Sectarian Violence in Baghdad** ... 23
Constructivism, Identity, and Conflict ... 24
Identity Conflict Through a Constructivist Lens ... 27
Group Identities in Iraq: Religious and Tribal ... 32
Conclusion ... 36
References ... 37

3 **Conflict Drivers** ... 41
Global and Regional Levels ... 42
State-Level Sources ... 44
Elite/Individual Level ... 47
References ... 51

4 Conflict Escalation: The Sharpening of Sectarian Identity 53
Psychological Changes 54
Group Changes 55
Change in Communities 60
Conclusion 61
References 62

5 Resilience: Conceptual Foundations 63
What is Resilience? 64
Regime Characteristics in Baghdad Neighborhoods 68
Regime Resilience 70
Modeling Conflict Resilience 72
Conclusion 77
References 77

6 Social Capital 81
Defining Social Capital 82
Relations Between People 83
Crosscutting Bonds 83
Overlapping Ties 87
Relations with "the Community" 88
Sense of Community 89
Citizen Participation 90
Place Attachment 91
Conclusion 92
References 93

7 Information and Communication 95
Sources: Leaders, Media and Working Trust 96
Spaces for Information-Sharing and Communication 100
Narratives 102
Conclusions 103
References 105

8 Economic Resources 107
Socioeconomic Status 109
SES and Resilience to Violence 111
Mechanisms of Influence 113
Trade Networks 115
Conclusions 116
References 117

9 Community Competence 119
Psychological Components of Community Competence 121

Collective Efficacy 121
Inward Orientation 123
Behavioral Components of Community Competence. 124
Linkages Between Regime Characteristics and Community Competency 126
Conclusions. 128
References. 130

10 Looking Ahead 133
Structural Versus Relational Approaches to Resilience 135
Strengthening Community Resilience. 136
Spaces for Visioning. 136
Collaborative, Crosscutting Projects 140
Supporting Peace Leaders 142
Beyond Baghdad? 143
Concluding Thoughts 145
References. 147

Author Biography 149

Index. 151

Chapter 1
Introduction

Abstract This book is about how individuals and groups managed the dynamics of conflict escalation in Baghdad neighborhoods. This chapter introduces the concept of community resilience to violence and provides the background, context, and overview of this book. It introduces and explains key concepts including sectarian violence, resilience, conflict prevention, and "resilience thinking," and describes the research partnership and methodology used to conduct this research. This chapter describes the ten neighborhoods that served as research sites, six of which suffered the sustained presence of a militia (Amiriyya, Adhamiyya, Dura, Sadr City, Zafaraniyya, and Bayaa) and four of which prevented sectarian militias from setting up local operations (Al-Dhubat, Palestine Street, Karada, and Kuraiaat). This chapter concludes with an overview of the rest of the book.

Keywords Community resilience • Conflict resilience • Conflict escalation • Conflict resolution • Urban resilience • Sectarian violence • Conflict prevention • Resilience th inking • Iraq • Baghdad • Neighborhoods • Al Nil • Palestine Street • Kuraait • Karada • Kazimiyya • Adhamiyya • Dhubat • Bayaa • Sa dr City • Zafaraniyya • Amiriyya • In-depth interviewing (IDI) • YouGov

The oak fought the wind and was broken, the willow bent when it must and survived.

Robert Jordan

This book is about community resilience to sectarian violence. It is not about the war in Iraq, nor is it about Iraq's ancient and modern history, the inner mysterious workings of the Ba'ath party, or the ways—some clandestine and some obvious—by which neighboring countries influence Iraqi politics. I cannot do justice to these topics, as have scholars like Charles Tripp, Toby Dodge, Anthony Cordesman, Ali Wardi, Hamid Bayati, and others upon whose work I have heavily relied. This book touches on all these topics, but lingers on none. This book is about how individuals and groups managed the dynamics of conflict escalation

A. C. Carpenter, *Community Resilience to Sectarian Violence in Baghdad*,
Peace Psychology Book Series, DOI 10.1007/978-1-4614-8812-5_1,

in small communities, situated within a large city itself embedded in a country at war, and a region that is undergoing profound social changes. It is about places where SSunni and Shi'a residents lived together and prevented sectarian violence from taking root within their neighborhood during and after the escalation of sectarian violence and massive dislocation experienced in most of Baghdad.

The term "resilience" generally refers to the ability to cope successfully in the face of extreme adversity or risk. Resilience *to violence* is about preventing conflict escalation so as to prevent accompanying changes in how people think about themselves and each other, changes in the way groups of people behave, and ultimately changes in the larger community. Specific to Baghdad, resilience to violence is conceptualized as the capacity of a militant subgroup to operate relative to the power of a community to regulate its operations [1]. Communities wielded many tools and capitals to limit the formation of sectarian militants within their borders, prevent people from adopting sectarian ideologies and attitudes, and prevent violent attacks from outside groups.

Other studies of urban resilience use cities as the unit of analysis. This study takes an approach of looking deeply into the subareas of a city in order to understand local configurations of people, resources, relationships, and quality of life. I use the terms "neighborhoods" and "communities" interchangeably throughout this book. Communities are not just geographically or territorially defined spaces, as demonstrated by the variety of Baghdadi "neighborhoods" studied that ranged from simple alleyways to whole zones ranging several kilometers in size. Instead, they are places where people live, work, and address social problems. In other words, community is not simply urban space—it is what people *do* within that space. And it was a story I read about a particular Baghdad community that launched this entire project.

Al-Nil Raises a Question

In 2006, American news station CBS news ran a short story about Al-Nil, called "*A Baghdad Neighborhood without Violence.*" Since the American-led invasion in 2003, thousands of people had been killed and injured in Baghdad City, casualties of armed violence between US and Iraqi military forces and armed insurgents and (more significantly for the purposes of this book) in sectarian clashes. Reporter Randall Pinkston was surprised to find Sunni, Shi'a, and Christian neighbors still living side by side during the height of the sectarian violence, committed to protecting their neighbors and preventing the roving militias and death squads from entering their neighborhood [2].

> There, children play on the street, young men hang out and businesses open their shops not worrying about kidnappings, bombings or guns. "In this neighborhood," one Shi'a man says, "there're no problems. The evil will never reach here." In the Al Nil neighborhood, Shi'a, Sunni and Christian residents have lived side by side for decades—like family. And in some cases, they are family. "My son's wife is a Sunni," said one woman,

> "we are Shi'a, we love each other." When Abu Sayiff, a Christian, received a threatening letter, his worried son went to his Muslim neighbors. They told me, anything happens to you, happens to us," said Sayiff's son. The neighbors promised to protect his father's home, and they have. So far, no one has been kidnapped or forced to move out of a neighborhood that's close to the scenes of so many violent incidents. The question is: Why is Al Nil seemingly immune to the poisonous attitudes that fuel the violence here? One possible answer from Abdul Abdullah Muzban, a Shi'a who runs a security service: "We're close to each other and we like each other," he says. "Most of us have lived here 40 years, so we know each other."Many Iraqis say the Sunni-Shi'a divide isn't the only reason for the violence—corruption and foreign fighters pour fuel on it too. One man suggested that "the good people" should talk to "the bad people" to get them to stop the attacks.

Though intrigued by the story—and by the notion that the "good people" knew who the "bad people" were and could potentially open a dialogue with them—I was not completely satisfied with the explanations offered for why this community had chosen a course of non-violence. As a social scientist of conflict and conflict resolution, I had been very interested in places of this type for years and had familiarized myself with major cases and studies on the topic of what I call "conflict-resilient areas." One of my favorite case studies was a place called Jaghori District in Afghanistan. I originally wrote about Jaghori in 2006 in a white paper commissioned by the United States Agency for International Development (USAID) called "*Patterns of Resilience: Adaptive Capacity in Fragile States*." USAID was interested in the concept of resilience, and my task was to conceptualize what it meant in the context of weak states and international development strategies.

Jaghori was, and remains, a case study of considerable interest for scholars of violence and conflict resolution. Jaghori is, so far as is known, the only area in Afghanistan that proactively negotiated conditions for its surrender with the Taliban in the early 1990s. Instead of waiting for the Taliban to arrive and "take over," the community sent out delegations to meet with Taliban leadership and negotiate. They offered a peaceful surrender, promising that Jaghori fighters would not attack the incoming Taliban. In return, they insisted on protection of key social institutions including Shi'a Islam (the Taliban were Sunni), the *shura* (community-led governing body headed by religious leaders), and traditions of non-violence and participation in public life (including education) for both men and women. The Taliban eventually agreed to a minimal level of education for boys *and girls* and agreed to allow the *shura* to continue governing the community. In return, Jaghori kept its promise to surrender peacefully. Unlike neighboring communities, Jaghori did not suffer casualties or damage to physical infrastructure, nor were relationships damaged with surrounding Pashtun tribes [3].

Jaghori embodies what I mean by resilience to violence and carries within it many existing explanations for why particular areas are able to self-organize to protect a people and their way of life. For one thing, the relationships between people must already be strong, cohesive enough to weather toxic stories that begin circulating in times of political, social, and economic upheaval. These stories are often spread intentionally by "ethnic entrepreneurs" who, for a variety of reasons, *want* to incite people to behave violently and know full well that the best way to get former neighbors on board with a killing spree is to tap into deep fears and insecurities of "the other"—whomever that other group might be.

The relationship between community *leaders* and members, and the choices leaders make in crisis are both very important. "Relationship" and "choice" are both complex variables that influence each other. For example, choices made by leaders in crisis (and the outcomes of these choices) are encouraged or constrained by relational factors, including whether the community believes their leaders to be legitimate, and whether the leaders believe their community supports them, and what relationships between community members were like before the crisis began.

Other explanations for why some areas experience less violence than others are readily available from multiple literatures. Geospatial variables—like the structure of roads in and out of an area—have been shown to influence the behavior of warmongers or "ethnic entrepreneurs." If there are many ways to get in and out in of an area, then the area becomes difficult to control (depending on the capacity of the group to set up and operate multiple checkpoints, in addition to launching attacks and running other aspects of the armed organization). In these cases, ethnic entrepreneurs tend to scale down their violence and negotiate the terms of their presence with a given community. In addition to roads, which are highly valuable resources, geospatial variables also include other kinds of strategic infrastructure—oil pipelines, airports, and culturally symbolic places (i.e., holy shrines and mosques). Socioeconomic variables also influence levels of violence, because levels of economic well-being and human development influence the likelihood that people will support an armed group aimed at altering the status quo.

A Subtle Difference

Note, however, that when we consider the geospatial and economic explanations, the primary question has changed from "why a community has chosen a course of non-violence" to "why a community experiences less violence than others." They are similar inquiries, but differ in their underlying logics, or assumptions. The first question invokes the agency of community members—through individual and collective action—to actually choose a course of non-violence. The community's beliefs, actions, decisions, and capitals (whether social, technical, or institutional) are the main independent variables. The second question sets the community as a stage where violence is "played out" by militias or is "experienced" by people. Structural variables (like road and transportation networks) are the main independent variables in understanding a militia's inroads and behavior in certain communities.

Neither explanation is fully adequate and here enters the concept of resilience. Resilience refers to the ability to rebound, maintain, or strengthen functioning during and after a disturbance, or to cope successfully in the face of extreme adversity or risk. A wealth of research exists on community resilience to poverty, disasters, and chronic crime and violence. Like these hardships, communal or sectarian violence represents a major disturbance to the physical and economic survival of civilian populations, whether riots, gang wars, ethnic clashes, guerilla insurgencies, or rebellions. Larger than its individual perpetrators, sectarian violence is a contagion of destructive attitudes and behaviors that destroys not just human life but the communal basis of human life: social trust, local governance, and the ability to provide for and thrive in diverse groups.

Thus, the essence of conflict resilience is preventing conflict escalation, and given the complexity of any given community, people's individual actions in streets, markets, and community forums represent the ultimate absorptive capacity of a whole community. However, those individual actions—those choices people make—*are* constrained by structural variables, so we should pay attention to networks of all types that might influence decision-makers, whether these are road networks, trade networks, social networks, or some combination. And however easily manipulated are human beings in times of crisis to make antisocial choices, there are also inherent characteristics of communities—social psychological characteristics—that make proactive, pro-social choices more likely. Such communities are not "stages" so much as they are "sets" where multiple actors are performing agreed upon roles, most understand the rules of the job and feel empowered to act, and the director is on hand to encourage, manage, and oversee. What are the characteristics of those "sets," those conflict-resilient communities? That is the question that launched my study of Baghdad neighborhoods, like Al Nil that prevented the onset of sectarian attitudes and violence.

Resilience and Conflict

What makes resilience a useful conceptual and theoretical lens for making sense of the world? For one thing, resilience shifts our focus to conflict prevention[1] and the ways in which social systems will respond to future crises, including advanced planning protocols and early warning systems [4]. Short-term prevention of immediate violence and long-term efforts to reduce underlying issues that produce large-scale conflicts are situated more and more often within the conceptual framework of strengthening societal resilience [5].

Resilience at community level also focuses on conflict prevention. Of the three phases of preventive actions identified by Raimo Väyrynen—conflict prevention,

[1] Michael Lund's broad definition of conflict prevention has been widely accepted for over a decade: Any structural or intercessory means to keep intrastate or interstate tension and disputes from escalating into significant violence and use of armed forces, to strengthen the capabilities of potential parties to violent conflict for resolving such disputes peacefully, and to progressively reduce the underlying problems that produce these issues and disputes. Michael Lund, "Preventing Violent Intrastate Conflicts: Learning lessons from experience," in Searching for Peace in Europe and Eurasia, p. 117.

escalation prevention, and post-conflict prevention [6]—this study focuses specifically on the second. After all, "the greatest potential for conflict prevention lies in fostering the strength and resilience of local social and political networks and institutions that identify and mobilise constructive responses to tensions and stress factors" [5].

Resilience is also a useful lens because it shifts the focus from deficits to assets. "Resilience thinking" [7] is about harnessing strengths instead of fixing weaknesses. As this study highlights, those strengths in fragile states are often found at the *local* level where resilience "draws our attention to the inherent strengths of local actors, rather than their weaknesses [4, p. 6]."

> Resilience is a powerful metaphor to remind peacebuilders that successful outcomes for peace depend on local actors, to encourage the peacebuilding community to value prevention more, and to focus them on the long term and on peacebuilding at the local and not just national level [4].

The challenge for resilience research is to move beyond resilience as a metaphor or a lens and apply it as an analytical framework—a conceptual system of definitions and classifications of data—that includes specifying units and levels of analysis, and causal attributions. One modest contribution of this book is to attempt precisely that by focusing narrowly on resilience to extremism and sectarianism in Baghdad. The difficulty is that resilience is not a directly observable phenomenon. Jutersonke and Kartas put it well when they wrote, "It certainly can be studied, but perhaps not as a social fact in its own right. One way of expressing this is to say that resilience is part of the external observers vocabulary to make sense of what is being observed…but it is not really a term that can be included in the questionnaire of the next survey administered in [some] poor neighborhood [4, p. 4]."

Still, I propose that indicators of conflict resilience can be observed in three ways: (1) by looking at *regimes* (structural characteristics of communities); (2) by looking at *process capacities* (such as preventing the adoption of sectarian ideologies and limiting the formation and entry of sectarian militias); and (3) by looking at specific *outcomes* such as low levels of casualties, injuries, physical infrastructure damage, economic disruption, and intergroup violence as well as retention of local authority over law and order. The main question is, what accounts for community resilience to violence when and where it has occurred?

I did not begin this intellectual journey cold: an expansive review of literature in the fields of psychology, social psychology, economics, conflict and peace studies, political science, and sociology turned up a variety of explanations for resilience to violence, which I sorted into three broad categories: Political and Social Structure, Leaders and Community Organization, and Economic and Geospatial Infrastructure. The first set of explanations (Political and Social Structure) credited the impact of a community's regime—salient norms, social institutions and networks, the political system—on the capacity of people to resist the desire for revenge seeking and retribution. These explanations credit internal (or endogenous) governing institutions and suggest that they consist of cross-cutting organizations, democratic norms, and relational practices (such as intermarriage) (see Footnote 8).

The second set of explanations (Leaders and Community Organization) highlighted the crucial role played by leaders (trust-building, sense-making, managing conflict) and the related capacity of the community to self-organize in response to threat (see Footnote 9). These explanations suggested that people are actively engaged in multiple strategies to prevent violent behavior and attitudes and maintain those communal relationships. Religious and community leaders are assigned central importance because they can wield persuasive narratives of toleration and coexistence to reinforce social solidarity. In addition, organizations (like mosques, churches, unions, or peace committees) are essential forums for bringing people together in times of crisis.

A third set of explanations (Economic and Geospatial Infrastructure) credited regime resilience with external (or exogenous) factors that affect the likelihood that violent actors will target (and be able to dominate) a particular area. These include proximity to strategically important geospatial variables (i.e., oil pipelines, airports, universities) or the structure of transportation and trade networks [8]. For example, diffuse production networks—"the cardiovascular system" of local economies—provide incentives for non-state armed actors to use violence more discriminatingly than they would in more concentrated networks [8]. In addition, a community's external economic linkages to other communities (specifically production network concentrations and the ethnic identity of the traders engaged in production networks) have a positive influence on the propensity of communities to adopt and adhere to effective internal social governance regimes.

Taking all of that into account, I decided to gather local perceptions regarding which of these multiple factors were most relevant. I developed an instrument for in-depth interviews that contained twenty-nine inquiries about life prior to 2003 and how sectarian violence had evolved over time. They included questions about neighborhood political and social organization, particularly the ways in which social participation was organized through formal and voluntary organizations, friendship networks, and aspects of social control; leaders and leadership behavior; economic infrastructure, such as the number of markets, universities, schools, average income level; and geospatial variables including proximity to US bases, bridges, or oil pipelines [21]. Research partners and colleagues in Iraq (described further below) helped me refine this questionnaire, and we used it to conduct interviews with residents in Baghdad.

Methods

I employed a technique called in-depth interviewing (IDI) to collect personal histories, perspectives, and experiences about the spread of sectarian violence in Baghdad. IDI is a form of interviewing which researchers use to achieve a holistic understanding of the interviewee's point of view or situation. It is often conducted in the context of a relationship between the researcher and interviewee "sufficient for a genuine 'meeting of minds' and that enable a mutual exploration of the meanings the interviewee applies to their social world" [9].

Being a cultural outsider, I did not conduct these interviews myself. It was difficult enough for our respondents to speak candidly about the sectarian violence to fellow Iraqis. My operating assumption was that the veracity of their accounts was enhanced by virtue of the fact that they were talking to cultural insiders, Baghdad residents whose approach was ethnographic and who could conduct interviews in Arabic. Moreover, restrictions on access to the city since 2003 made carrying out my own fieldwork a rather difficult proposition. And even more importantly, as a female American, my very presence was likely to have endangered the lives of our respondents and my research partners in Baghdad. For all of these reasons, I partnered with an organization called *YouGov LLC*, a global research and marketing firm with an arm devoted to research on political and social issues. YouGov's political and social research team tracks public attitudes to governments and political parties and had been operating in Iraq since 2003.

My colleague and friend, Dana Eyre, introduced me to YouGov's director of special projects, Stefan Kaszubowski. Stefan aided me in setting up in-depth conversations over several months, beginning in June 2010. YouGov researchers identified one person in each of the ten neighborhoods (described later on in this chapter) who were willing to talk about their experiences during the period of sectarian violence. They purposefully sought out men whose residence in the area extended back to prewar decades and who (either by virtue of their education or "known character") might offer more nuanced answers to our sensitive questions (see Footnote 13).

Researchers contacted these individuals (referred to from here on as *respondents*) clandestinely and conducted interviews in secret. Security conditions at the time of research, particularly in areas that had suffered sectarian cleansing, prohibited the field team even from being seen with cell phones, which residents connected to affiliation with the US armed forces. The delicate nature of our interview instrument gave great cause for caution, both in the selection of interview participants, and the timing and location of interviews. YouGov translated the questionnaire into Arabic, conducted the interviews, and then back-translated and transcribed the focus group data. Interviews took about three hours to complete. We have kept the names and exact locations of our respondents confidential for security concerns.[2]

The partnership enabled me to leverage YouGov's large local network of highly trained and experienced moderators, facilitators, and field researchers. With security concerns in mind and a deeply contextual (and personal) knowledge of the

[2] The intent of analysis was to identify regime characteristics and coping strategies as described by the respondents. Open coding of interview transcripts, informed by the literature review, generated five categories of variables—governance, social capital, socioeconomic opportunities, leader behavior, geospatial infrastructure—with between one and ten indicators for each category (see Box I). In the second round of coding, I grouped indicators into two themes: "Stories about Conflict Escalation" and "Resilience Management & Regimes." I used a hybrid method of frequency analysis to highlight key indicators, coupled with my interpretive reading of the "thick narrative accounts" in the Geertzian tradition, of people's perceptions, of key events, conflict dynamics, and lived experiences.

sensitivity of our topic, these local partners helped guide the structure both of the research process and helped finalize the interview instrument. This particular study method is called *empirical microanalysis*, a technique proposed by Kathleen Jennings for studying life in conflict zones by exploring the relationships between armed groups, local elites, and residents [10]. I believed it would also be useful in order to document elements of adaptive capacity, which is basically a function of how individuals and groups manage communities. It has a great deal to do with their ability to imagine the future, to plan forward, to act collectively, learn, and incorporate new knowledge, and to resolve conflicts [11].

Giving voice to the opinions and perspectives of local people in conflict-affected communities is vital, because individuals directly affected by conflict often have insights and opinions that can inform peacebuilding policies. In 2012, two international NGOs, Saferworld and Conciliation Resources carried out an 18-month-long study with the aim of bringing the opinions of local people in fragile states to forums of international policymakers. "The project has provided European Union institutions with analysis and recommendations based on the opinions and experiences of local people in a range of countries and regions affected by fragility and violent conflict" [12]. Though much more modest in scope, my research goals were guided by the same general principle that people living in conflict often have the greatest insight into its causes, its prevention, and ideas for enhancing local resilience.

A common critique of studies that rely on information from a small sample size or (n) is that they lack statistical power. What can be generalized or predicted from 10 individual accounts? I fall into a category of researchers that question the traditional dogma of sample size to argue that we can learn a lot—"sometimes even with an n of 1" [13]—especially in studies that are probing new ideas. This study was not designed to look for statistically significant effects, but to gather accounts and insights of people living through conflict. The narratives contained within this book are not an "objective" accounting of events, as such accounts simply do not exist. Instead, they document people's explanations of their own behavior, their perceptions of other people's behavior, and how they made sense of what was happening around them. Their stories contain observations of both internal processes (structural changes and mechanisms of change in each neighborhood) and external processes relating to cultural and demographic changes. I analyzed these stories using a particular analytical framework, introduced in later chapters, to explore elements of resilience in each area.

In so doing, I have found it useful to triangulate respondent's subjective accounts with other sources of data: Iraq Body Count, Wikileaks, blogs, media accounts, and secondary research. Respondents' stories contained contradictions with regard to particular attitudes and events: ambiguities inherent in the relations between experiencing trauma, and processes of remembering and forgetting [14]. For example, one respondent lived on Ras Al-Hawash street in Adhamiyya, and early into the interview reported that his neighborhood was not necessarily stable; however, "there was no sectarian violence." Blog reports indicated the opposite; the clashes that erupted in Adhamiyya in 2006 following the Samarra bombing took place in areas of Ras Al Hawash areas close to the police station [15].

The reader must view critically people's perceptions about the "good relationships" between Sunni and Shi'a prior to 2003. On the one hand, Iraq is a society "where different ethnicities, cultures, religions, and sects have mixed and mingled for centuries, where people worked and lived side by side" [16]. Iraqis identified primarily by nationality [17] prior to the US invasion of Iraq in 2003. Perhaps up to one-third of marriages were mixed, and most of the country's tribes included members of both sects [16, p. 6]. On the other hand, although sectarian differences were not as strongly felt before the 2003 invasion as after, self-reports of interethnic relations prior to the US invasion were subject to exaggeration due in part to the sensitivity of our inquiries. Comments by the Iraqi researchers accompanying one set of transcripts read:

> You can see that people usually described the 'good things' in their neighborhoods before 2003 rather than the bad things; we think that this is expected and normal in human behavior for people to easily forget what was really difficult and stressful.

The majority of respondents expressed varying levels of disbelief about how sectarian relations unraveled, citing sharing celebrations, neighborhood cohesion, frequent interaction, and friendships. The research team had mixed opinions about the veracity of these accounts, but to me, truth was not in the veracity of the story but in the story itself. Many Iraqis share a narrative that sectarian differences were not important before 2003. Sunnis gave examples of participating in each other's celebrations, while Shi'as gave examples of playing on sports teams together. Both say they were friends with each other. But these narratives do not speak the whole truth—in fact, they may disguise it. I could not put it better than the resident of Zafaraniyya who told us,

> Sectarianism was both absent and hidden. There was a strong state. Any person who dared to talk about sectarianism would have lost their heads. So no, there was no sectarianism in the country.

Research Sites

We selected respondents from two "types" of areas to which, after much deliberation, I referred to in early write-ups as "Sectarian Militia Permitted" (SMP) areas and "Sectarian Militia Rejected" (SMR) areas [1] (After much less deliberation, I have decided not to use those acronyms anywhere else in this book. I simply refer to neighborhoods by their names and trust the reader to refer to Table 1.1 on the following page when needed). As I noted then, these labels are not aesthetically pleasing like "Resilient" versus "Vulnerable," or "Peaceful" versus "Violent"; however, they are accurate to the dynamics under study. Resilience to violence boils down to the capacity of a militant subgroup to operate relative to

Table 1.1 Research Site Selections

Research Sites	Sunni (Dominant)	Shi'a (Dominant)	(Mixed)
	Approximately greater than 70 % of neighborhood population	*Approximately greater than 70 % of neighborhood population*	*Two or more ethno-religious groups (Sunni, Shiite, Mandaean, Iranian, Christian) representing approximately 30–70 % of population*
Sectarian Militia Permitted *SMP areas*	Amiriyya Adhamiyyah Dura	Sadr city Zafaraniyyah	Bayaa
Sectarian Militia rejected *SMR areas*	Al Dhubat	Karada Kuraiaat	Palestine street

the power of a community to regulate the subgroup's operations. The word "permitted" referred broadly to areas where residents either willingly or unwillingly submitted to the operation of militant groups, joined their forces, or provided material and psychosocial support. The word "rejected" refers broadly to areas that withheld support and organized to prevent the sustained presence and activity of sectarian militias (while not precluding the operation of *non-sectarian* self-defense groups that operated in certain neighborhoods). Moreover, a neighborhood might have prevented the spread of sectarian sentiment and support for militias but experienced attacks nonetheless, deeming labels like "Peaceful" or "Non-Violent" unsuitable.

Along with the research team in Iraq, and my fellow colleague and economist Topher McDougal, we further differentiated these two "types" of neighborhoods by ethnic composition, using BBC maps created from International Medical Corps data to distinguish between Sunni dominant, Shi'a dominant, or mixed communities [22]. We thus ended up placing neighborhoods in one of six categories, indicated in Table 1.1. As shown, six neighborhoods suffered the sustained presence of a militia: Amiriyya, Adhamiyya, Dura, Sadr City, Zafaraniyya, and Bayaa. These areas were the unfortunate sites of heavy militia activity and violent incidents. Four neighborhoods prevented sectarian militias from setting up local operations and prevented residents from joining or supporting the militias: Al-Dhubat, Palestine Street, Karada, and Kuraiaat.

Map 1 of Baghdad before major sectarian violence shows the predominance of Baghdad neighborhoods where Sunni and Shi'a residents lived together. The map shows a general distribution of heterogeneous neighborhoods throughout the capital—with a few exceptions, such as Sadr City in eastern Baghdad. Six out of the ten neighborhoods suffered from the terrible sectarian cleansing campaign which resulted in thousands killed, and many more displaced. Map 2 shows the dramatic shift in living patterns after the worst of the violence in 2006.

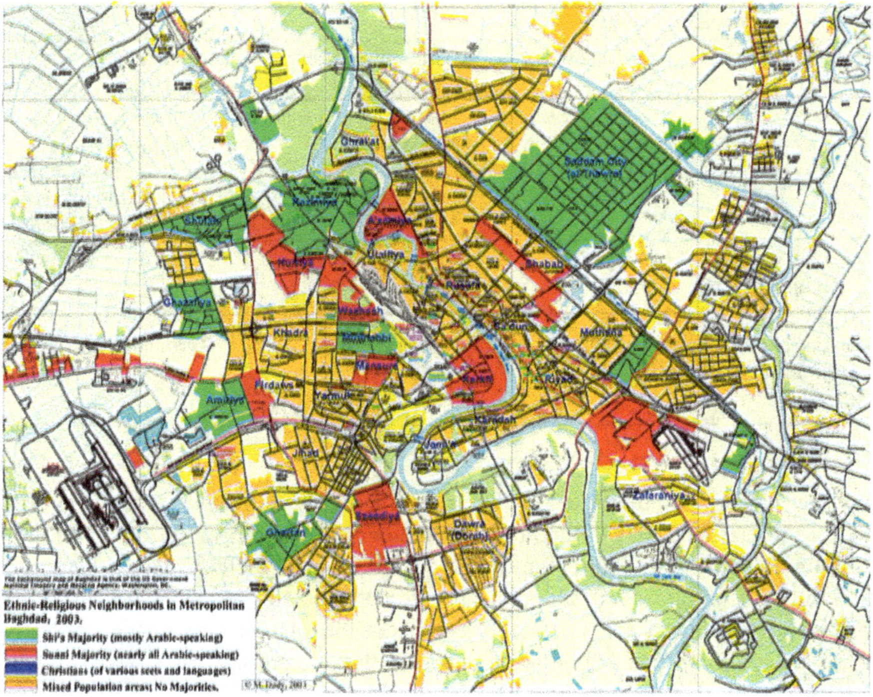
Saddam City (al Thawra)
Shabab
Zafaraniya
Ethnic-Religious Neighborhoods in Metropolitan Baghdad, 2003.
Shi'a Majority (mostly Arabic-speaking)
Sunni Majority (nearly all Arabic-speaking)
Christians (of various sects and languages)
Mixed Population areas; No Majorities.
© M. Izady, 2003

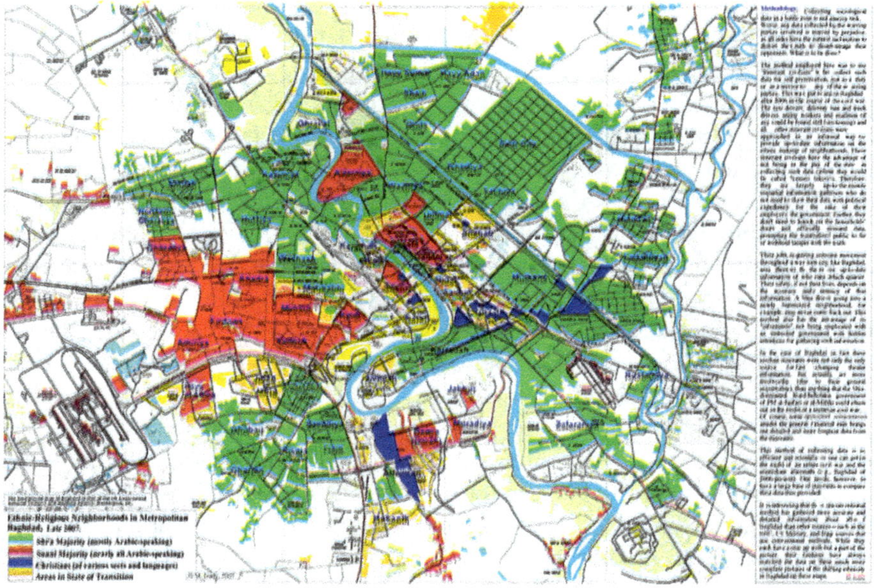
Ethnic-Religious Neighborhoods in Metropolitan Baghdad, Late 2007.
Shi'a Majority (mostly Arabic-speaking)
Sunni Majority (nearly all Arabic-speaking)
Christians (of various sects and languages)
Areas in State of Transition

Multicultural Iraq

Iraq used to be the most ethnically diverse country in the Middle East. The world's oldest empires either developed or conquered the lands of Mesopotamia, during which politics and culture emerged as twins in the cradle of ancient civilization [18]. Governance changed hands multiple times over the course of centuries, and each change brought new and diverse cultural influences under seven empires. I am compelled to whisk through centuries in a few paragraphs, if only to give a small sense of the sheer diversity of influences.

Early Sumerian city-states were first united into the Akkadian Empire, under which Sumerian art and literature continued to thrive in part because Akkadian leader Sargon understood that the legitimacy of his rule depended on how well he "fit in" to dominant Sumerian cultural expressions and practices. Subsequent empires included the Babylonian Empire best remembered for Hammurabi's introduction of the first system of law and the Assyrian empire's totalitarian rule and its "victory art" which celebrated warfare and slaughter of ethnic enemy "others." Absorption into the expansive Persian Empire brought a gentler, less violent form of governance. King Cyrus preferred to rule by granting autonomy to and religious freedom to religious and ethnic populations. Following the Persian Empire, the Seleucid Empire exposed Mesopotamia to the influences of Greek culture—arts, literature, theater, music, philosophy, architecture, and science—which became fused with indigenous cultures and local practices. Under the subsequent Parthian Empire, the Jewish community flourished alongside Hellenism. "By the time antiquity drew to a close, nearly every major empire, religion, and ethnic group had traveled through the streets and markets of the land of Iraq en route to ephemeral greatness, each leaving a unique legacy along the way [18]."

The sectarian segregation that occurred in Baghdad after 2003 had no precedent in Iraq's history of settlement patterns.[3] Iraq's capital of Baghdad dates back to the eighth century, when it was founded by the Abbasid Empire. "Spread along the banks of the Tigris river, the city boasts religious shrines, historical sites, and cultural artifacts [19]." The city is divided into nine districts and eighty-nine neighborhoods, which ranged from opulently rich to desperately poor residential areas, from gray industrial areas to colorful and bustling commercial thoroughfares. The last task left in this introductory chapter is to briefly present the ten neighborhoods we studied and sketch their basic demographics and characteristics.

Amiriyya

Amiriyya is an affluent and modern area located on the west side of Baghdad. It was constructed in the 1970s as a residential area for a professional class

[3] See Ref. [19]. Iraqis tended to reside in the same neighborhoods where their families had first settled when they arrived in Baghdad during Ottoman times.

(lawyers, doctors, engineers) and members of Baathist elite. The area enjoyed a high standard of living and was home to many wealthy residents including high-ranking Baath Party officials and army officers. Its residents originated from Anbar Salah al-Din, and Mosul. Amiriyya is geographically close to the suburban areas of Baghdad (including Abu Ghraib), and to Falluja and Ramadi in Anbar Governorate, which were heavily controlled by Al-Qaida in Iraq (AQI) after 2003. (Anbar Governorate is the largest in Iraq, and almost all of its inhabitants are Sunni from the Dulaim tribe, which will be discussed further in the following chapter.)

Though a majority Sunni area, Amiriyya was home to Shi'a families as well. They lived in a specific enclave of the neighborhood that might be designated "mixed" because both Shiite and Sunni residents lived in close proximity. Amiriyya is historically a "secular" area,[4] suggesting that residents were not likely to be initial supporters of extremist religious militias [20]. The area is also close also to Baghdad International Airport and just a few miles from one of the largest US military bases in Iraq. According to a member of the research team, the close proximity to Camp Victory accounted for

> …one of the frequently told stories by Shi'a, that Al-Qaida and its members are actually (as many people believe or like to believe) supported by the US; otherwise how can one explain this phenomenon of Al-Qaida operating next to the US base in the heart of Baghdad!

Adhamiyya

Adhamiyya is one of the oldest regions in Baghdad, dating back to the Abbasid Caliphate.[5] Its name means *al-Imam al-Adham*—the greatest Imam—and refers to the Imam of the Hanafi school of law, Abu Hanifa Al Nu'man, whose shrine lies on the east bank of Tigris (Dijla) river.[6] Adhamiyya *District* is a large residential area that includes both Sunni-dominant and Shi'a-dominant neighborhoods, while the area around the shrine is the old and original Adhamiyya city.[7] The shrine—the Abu Hanifa Mosque—lies just a few miles from its Shi'a counterpart in Kazimiyya, the shrine of Imam Musa Al Kazim. The Bridge of the Imams (*al-jisr al-aimma*) connecting the two areas was closed in 2005 as sectarian violence began to increase.

---

[4] Secular" or "civilian" and "religious" were terms used by Iraqi respondents to describe neighborhoods' character. These differences will be discussed at length further on.

[5] The Abbasid Caliphate was the third Islamic caliphate following the Umayyad caliphate. It was founded in 750 CE by the descendants of Muhammed's youngest uncle in Harran, an ancient city located in now modern-day Turkey. In 762, the Caliphate shifted its capital in 762 to Baghdad where it flourished for two centuries.

[6] The four traditional sub-Sunni sects are Al-Hanafi, Al-Shafii, Al-Hanbali, and Al-Maliki.

[7] According to local research team.

Adhamiyyah was a generally wealthy area, home to many colleges and universities[8] and a high standard of living.[9]

> Well, there are maybe two slums [with] narrow roads and you can find tens of families living there. The rest of my neighborhood has wide roads with large houses; most of the residents there are doctors and people of high social status.

The region was also home to many government and security officials and high-ranking members of the Baath party. An Iraqi researcher commented,

> Adhamiyya is known by Shi'a at least by being very loyal to Saddam and the Ba'ath party, and to have many sectarian people who disrespect and dislike Shi'a in many ways, that's at least what many Shi'a think…[10]

Adhamiyyah District was home to many prosperous Sunni before the invasion. As the battle for Baghdad unfolded, the district came under increasing attack from the Shi'a Mahdi Army (*al-Jaysh al-Mahdi*) as well Al-Qaeda Iraq (AQI). The Mahdi Army forced many Sunni residents out of the district, changing its ethno-sectarian makeup. The result was that Adhamiyyah District became predominantly Shi'a territory, even though the smaller Adhamiyyah neighborhood remained predominately Sunni.

Dura

Dura is a large residential area in Southern Baghdad where AQI carried out sectarian attacks against Shi'a and Christian families. Dispute exists over whether the area was Sunni dominant or Christian dominant prior to the invasion of 2003, and there exists no census to settle the score. For the purposes of this study, we designated it a Sunni-dominant area while acknowledging that its population was mixed to a greater degree than both Amiriyya and Adhamiyya. In particular, the Assyrian Christian community and percentage of Shi'a residents were both large. Prior to the Iraq war, Dura was home to the largest concentration of Assyrian Christians and Mandeans.

The second largest oil refinery in Iraq, after "Baiji purifier" in Salah al-Din, is located in Dura. Like Adhamiyyah, Dura was home to high-ranking officials from Saddam's regime. His relatives owned land there, including his wife Sajida, father-in-law Khairalla Tulfa, sons Udai and Qusai, and cousin Ali Hassan al Majid (Chemical Ali). ISAF (International Security Assistance Force—Nato's security mission) bombed these family residences in a failed assassination attempt in 2003 and continued carrying out operations against AQI operatives that had entered Dura from nearby rural Arab Jabur, an AQI stronghold on the boundaries

[8] Ibn Al-Haytham college, the Economy and Administration College & the Islamic University, Saddam's Islamic College.

[9] Interview, Baghdad 2010.

[10] Researcher feedback.

of Baghdad City. AQI's sectarian operations against Christian and Shi'a residents have been well documented. ISAF forces were unable to drive AQI out of Dura, and by 2010, Dura's ethnic composition was almost entirely Sunni.

Sadr City

Sadr City is a Shi'a-dominant community located on the eastern side of Baghdad. It was (and is) a marginalized area where the majority of people lived below the poverty line. Originally named Al-Thawra, or Revolution City, it was built in 1959 by Prime Minister Abd al-Karim Qasim and later renamed Saddam City after the late president took power in 1979. After Saddam's ouster in 2003, it became known as Sadr City. This unofficial title honors both Grand Ayatollah Mohammed Sadiq al-Sadr, the revered cleric widely believed to have been killed along with his sons by Saddam Hussein in the nineties, and Sadiq al-Sadr's sole surviving son Muqtada al-Sadr, who founded the Mahdi Army, and to whom many young men in its slums became supremely loyal [21].

At approximately 13 square miles, an area about half the size of Manhattan, Sadr City is one of the most densely packed communities in the Middle East. Sadr City is often referred to a slum or a ghetto, descriptors of the area's rampant unemployment, lack of basic services, and crumbling infrastructure. Sadr City is also often described as an area with a dual government in Baghdad, an infrastructure dominated by tribal and clerical leaders. The main administrative body is the Tribal Council, a 28 member legislative body. In 2004, it released an edict designed to restore public order. Enforced by the Mahdi Army, and punishable by death, the Edict banned street crime (kidnapping, hijacking, and robbery), political crimes (collaboration with the US government and terrorism), and moral crimes (sale of alcohol, prostitution). As recounted by Schwartz, "While many Iraqis are secular and oppose such laws, Sadr City is dominated by tribal leaders, clerics and citizens whose fundamentalist version of Islam supports such bans" [22].

Zafaraniyya

Zafaraniyya is a Shi'a-dominant suburb located in southeast Baghdad. It belongs to the wealthy Karada District, although residents' levels of economic and educational attainment are below average compared to other neighborhoods in the district. According to the resident we spoke to, the neighborhood had a secular character; in his words, "our neighborhood wasn't designated by a religious nature." Whether or not true in any real sense, the narrative of "being secular" served the residents of Zafaraniyya well considering that the neighborhood is the site of the Al-Rashid military camp, which was at one time charged with raiding Sadr City in the event of anti-regime uprisings. Zafaraniyya is surrounded by Sunni-dominant suburban areas in which AQI operated. Both the Mahdi and AQI carried out sectarian operations within its borders. Iraq Body Count recorded the first sectarian attack in Zafaraniyya on March 27, 2006. A rocket slammed into a house that supposedly belonged to the Shi'a militia al-Fadila al-Islamiyya,[11] killing 7 people.

Bayaa

Bayaa was a mixed, middle-class community on the southwest side of Baghdad, which sits along the Baghdad Airport Road. Bayaa was named after Ali Al Baiyaa who owned the land upon which the city was built. Sunni and Shi'a residents lived primarily in separate enclaves, although a few neighborhoods contained intermixed housing. Overall, residents had moderate to good levels of education and economic status. The area had an active economy; its hub was 20th street, lined with hundreds of retail and wholesale shops attracting people from the surrounding regions. Bayaa had many of the trappings of a modern, middle-class neighborhood including health centers, a police station, clubs, and a youth center. Unfortunately, both Mahdi Army and AQI carried out operations in Bayaa, as did ISAF as they hunted insurgents from both militias.

Palestine Street

Palestine Street belongs to Sadr City as an administrative division, but differs from the latter in significant ways. It is a well-known commercial area like Karada—a place where "people go to hang out and do shopping or go to restaurants."[12] Palestine Street is also home to the second largest institution of higher education in Baghdad, Al Mustansiriya University. Many residents have good economic status and are well educated. Buildings were in good condition, and home sizes were generally large. Despite being bounded by Sadr city regions, Palestine Street did not experience "in many parts of it" the same influence by Mahdi Army and remained "relatively" safe and non-violent.

Al-Dhubat

Al-Dhubat was the only nonviolent Sunni-dominant area identified by the field research team, where Shi'a and Christian residents also live. Al-Dhubat, whose name means "The Officers", is located within the otherwise violent Zayouna

[11] Iraq Body Count Database. Retrieved from http://www.iraqbodycount.org/database/incidents/k2791.

[12] Email correspondence, YouGov researcher.

district, a residential area in Baghdad whose residents earn above average income. Residents of Zayouna, and Al-Dhubat in particular, include a large proportion of high-ranking Iraqi army officers. Although Al-Dhubat prevented the sustained precense and activity of a militia, the area did suffer attacks. IntelCenter reported that on February 24, 2005 gunmen attacked a bakery, injuring two employees [23].

Karada and Kuraiaat

Karada and Kuraiaat were Shi'a-dominant areas. Karada neighborhood located in Karada district, a relatively large area on the east bank of the Dijla river, was also home to many Sunnis and Christians many of whom had high levels of education, and moderate-to-high socioeconomic status. Baghdad University is in close proximity, and the region was home to many companies, nongovernmental organizations, restaurants, hotels, and wholesale stores. On the same (east) side of the Dijla river as Karada is historic Kuraiaat, a smaller area famous for its restaurants and bordered by Adhamiyya (described above). Diversity in socioeconomic classes wasreported in Kuraiaat, meaning that wealthy residents intermixed with poor residents who also tended to have a lower standard of education.

A key point suggested in these general site descriptions is that proximity to violent areas did not predict the spread of sectarian attitudes and behaviors. Both Zafarniyya, where Mahdi Army and AQI operated, and Karada neighborhoods, where militias were not permitted to operate, are located within the larger Karada district. Palestine Street is a subdivision of Sadr City, an area plagued by sectarian militias, attacks and counterattacks. Al-Dhubat neighborhood is located in Zayouna district, which was an extremely violent area of Baghdad. Clearly, we need a more complex explanation of why sectarian attitudes and behaviors altered the configuration of some neighborhoods and not others.

Overview of the Book

This book is about how individuals and groups managed the dynamics of conflict escalation in small communities. The story is necessarily complex and begins in Chapters Two and Three by exploring causes of sectarian violence. Resilience to sectarian violence is about managing, preventing, and mitigating its sources so we must understand those sources and dynamics before we can move on to discussing resilience itself. Chapter 2 provides a basic theoretical foundation about the causes of sectarian and ethnic conflict. Even though the vast majority of all human conflict is settled non-violently, sectarian and ethnic conflicts fall into the particular class of identity conflicts, defined by irreconcilable moral differences, high stake contests of distributional issues such as resources, power (however defined), and basic human needs. Chapter 2 explores the deep roots of sectarian conflict, focusing on the cultural context of the modern Iraqi state, including the history of relations between Shi'a and Sunni communities in Iraq and regionally, as well as the great intrasect diversity generated by class divisions, and the rural–urban divide.

None of these deep roots made the Iraqi civil war inevitable; its emergence can be traced to specific security and political conditions that developed after the US invasion. Chapter 3 guides our attention to a series of internal and external factors that drove the escalation of Iraq's civil war, the opportunity structures for extremist groups to emerge in the ensuing vacuum of power, and the strength of tribal and local support for Al-Qaida and Mahdi Army.[13]

I have defined conflict resilience as a process of managing conflict escalation so as to limit the formation of sectarian militants within bounded areas and at the same time prevent violent attacks from groups outside those areas. In order to understand what "managing conflict escalation" means precisely, Chap. 4 focuses on the specific processes by which conflict escalation occurs in general and in occurred in Baghdad more specifically. Chapter 5 then lays a conceptual foundation for the rest of the book. It introduces the concept of resilience in general and explains its relationship to the spread of violence through conflict escalation dynamics and exposure to accumulated stressors. Community resilience to sectarian violence uses the lens of systems resilience—"the ability of social systems to cope, adapt, and reorganize in response to dramatic challenges" [23]. I conclude the chapter by presenting an adapted analytical framework that represents community resilience as four sets of resilience resources—Social Capital, Economic Development, and Information and Communication, and Community Competence—around which the following three chapters are organized.

Chapter 6 focuses on the causal influence of social capital on conflict escalation over time. Some areas experienced large-scale displacement and a deep deterioration in Sunni–Shi'a relations, while others did not. All areas engaged in early intersect cooperation to protect neighborhood boundaries from "outside" groups. Chapter 6 addresses the role of social trust and cross-cutting networks in addressing why some communities ultimately succeeded, while others did not.

Chapter 7 extends this basic inquiry to the roles played by information and communication resources in Baghdad neighborhoods. This chapter addresses three interrelated enablers of adaptation related to information and communication at the local level: *sources of information* such as clerics, neighbors, and news media; *spaces for communication* such as mosques and neighborhood councils; and *narratives* or collective interpretations of events that determine how people cope with them. This chapter also explores the influence of physical neighborhood infrastructure on communication and social relationships.

Resilience to violence begins with the ability to withstand certain psychological changes that commonly accompany conflict escalation. Chapter 8 explores the

[13] Al Qaida in Iraq (AQI) and Mahdi Army (JAM) were the two primary armed non-state actors (ANSAs) in Iraq during the period of study. Multiple other militias existed, including offshoots of AQI and Mahdi Army and other autonomous groups.

role of economic influences on individual vulnerability to the adoption of sectarian attitudes and behaviors. While this study was not set up to answer the broader question of the precise relationship between economic development and resilience to sectarian violence, Chap. 8 draws on a range of research relating to group mobilization and civil war, as well as individual propensity for violence.

Chapter 9 links the set of social, communication, and economic resources to community competence. Community competence is about organized action of people, communities and institutions to prevent, manage, and learn from crisis. Resilience to violence takes conscious planning, preparation, foresight, insight, communication management, and coordination. Chapter 9 links specific strategies used to prevent intracommunity violence, and protect people's security and community institutions, to key findings contained in the previous chapters. It also offers an integrative analysis by tying together the previous chapters and summarizing key perspectives on conflict resilience in Baghdad neighborhoods.

Chapter 10 applies the insights of resilience theory in general, and the findings of this study more specifically, to the question of strengthening resilience to violence in conflict-prone contexts. This chapter deals with this question in the context of Baghdad, which is still a divided city and (at time of writing) appears poised for another escalation of sectarian violence. This chapter looks beyond Iraq to reflect on what has become a sectarian civil war in Syria and identifies guiding principles for peacebuilding based on resilience thinking.

References

1. Carpenter, Ami. 2012. Havens in a firestorm: perspectives from baghdad on resilience to sectarian violence. *Civil Wars Journal* 14(2): 182–204.
2. Pinkston, R. 2006. *A Peaceful Iraqi Neighborhood*. Retrieved from http://www.cbsnews.com/video/watch/?id=2293833n.
3. Suleman, M., and S. Williams. 2003. Strategies and structures in preventing conflict and resisting pressure: a study of Jaghori District, Ghazni, Afghanistan, under Taliban control. Retrieved from http://www.necsi.edu/afghanistan/pdf_data/PreventingConflictinJaghoriDistrictGhaznAfghanistan.pdf.
4. Milliken, J. 2013. Resilience: from metaphor to action plan for use in the peacebuilding field. Retrieved from http://www.gpplatform.
5. Ganson, B., and A. Wennmann. 2013. Operationalising conflict prevention as strong, resilient systems: approaches, evidence, action points. Working paper No. 3. Retrieved from http://www.gpplatform.
6. Väyrynen, R. 1997. Towards effective conflict prevention: a comparison of different instruments. *International Journal of Peace Studies* 2(1).
7. Breen, P., and M. Anderies. 2011. Resilience: a literature review. Retrieved from http://www.rockefellerfoundation.org.
8. McDougal Topher L. 2011. Production and predation in a core-periphery model: a note. Peace economics. *Peace Science and Public Policy* 17(1).
9. Fielding, N. 2006. Ethnographic interviewing. In *The sage dictionary of social research methods*, ed. V. Jupp. Thousand Oaks: Sage.
10. Kathleen, J. 2007 The war zone as social space: social research in conflict zones. Retrieved from www.fafo.no/pub/rapp/20008/20008.pdf.

11. Holling, C.S., and B. Walker. 2003. Resilience defined. Entry prepared for the Internet encyclopedia of ecological economics. Retrieved from http://www.ecoeco.org/publica/encyc_entries/Resilience.pdf.
12. Conciliation Resources. 2012. It's good to talk: how listening to local people adds value to conflict analysis. Retrieved from http://www.c-r.org/news/peacebuilding-perspectives.
13. Bacchetti, P., S.G. Deeks, and J.M. McCune. 2011. Breaking free of sample size dogma to perform innovative translational research. *Science Translational Medicine* 15: 3.
14. Rogers, K.L., S. Leydesdorff, and G. Dawson. 2004. *Trauma: life stories of survivors*. New Jersey: Transaction Publishers.
15. Hawazin, A. 2006. Battle of Adhamiyya, live as LIVE can be. Retrieved from http://abbashawazin.blogspot.com/2006/04/battle-of-Adhamiyya-live-as-live-can-be.html.
16. Al-Khalidi, A., and V. Tanner. 2006. Sectarian violence: radical groups drive internal displacement in Iraq. Brookings Institute: 6.
17. Gairdener, D. 2012. Risk and violence in Iraq's new sectarian balance. Norwegian Peacebuilding Resource Centre. Retrieved from http://www.peacebuilding.no/Themes/Armed-violence-and-conflict-in-fragile-settings/Fragile-states-and-peacebuilding-in-the-new-global-context/Publications/Risk-and-violence-in-Iraq-s-new-sectarian-balance/(language)/eng-US: 2.
18. Braude, Joseph. 2003. The new Iraq: rebuilding the country for its people, the Middle East and the World. New.
19. Damluji, M. 2010. Securing democracy in Iraq': sectarian politics and segregation in Baghdad, 2003–2007. *Traditional Dwellings and Settlements Review* 21(2). 2013.
20. Cave, D. 2007. Amiriyya: walls and checkpoints bring hope and frustration. In assessing the 'surge': a survey of Baghdad neighborhoods. New York Times.
21. Cole, J. 2007. Shi'a Militias in Iraqi politics. In *Iraq: preventing a new generation of conflict*, eds. Bouillon, M., D. Malone, and B. Roswell. Boulder, CO: Lynne Reiner.
22. Schwartz, M. 2005. Iraq: Guerilla warfare in Sadr city. Retrieved from http://www.solidarity-us.org/node/1136.
23. IntelCenter Terrorism Incidence Reference. 2008. *Tempest Publishing*: 291.
24. Menkhaus, K. 2013. Making sense of resilience in peacebuilding contexts: approaches, applications, implications. Platform paper 6. Retrieved from http://www.gpplatform.

Chapter 2
Violence and Extremism: Sources of Sectarian Violence in Baghdad

Abstract This Chapter integrates multiple empirical explanations about the causes of sectarian and ethnic conflict and settles on constructivism as the "middle-ground" theoretical framework for introducing the nature of religious and tribal identity in Iraq. This Chapter explores several deeply rooted causes of sectarian conflict in Iraq including the nature of religious and tribal identity and the Sunni–Shi'a fracture to which many attribute sectarian violence. However, the Chapter concludes by pointing toward more proximate causes of violent conflict in Iraq: the cultural context of the modern Iraqi state, influential roles played by religious and political figures, and the structural, political, and economic sources of internal conflict present in Iraq prior to the US invasion.

Keywords Conflict • Violence • Extremism • Primordialists • Instrumentalists • Constructivism • Group identity • Sunni–Shi'a divide • Sectarian violence • Social construction • Social agency • Narratives • Psychocultural • In-group bias • Group dynamics • Prejudice • Religious identity • Tribal identity • Culture • Shi'a • Sunni

"Violence, even well intentioned, always rebounds upon oneself."

Lao Tzu

This Chapter provides a basic theoretical foundation about the causes of sectarian and ethnic conflict. Conflict refers to a situation in which people or groups of people perceive incompatible goals and interference from others in achieving what they desire. The vast majority of all human conflict is settled nonviolently. However, sectarian and ethnic conflict fall into the particular class of identity conflicts, defined by irreconcilable moral differences, high stakes, and intensely emotional contests over distributional issues such as resources, power (however, defined), and basic human needs [1]. Group conflict, or hostilities between different groups, is one of the most complex phenomena studied by social scientists today.

A. C. Carpenter, *Community Resilience to Sectarian Violence in Baghdad*, Peace Psychology Book Series, DOI: 10.1007/978-1-4614-8812-5_2,

What were the causes of sectarian conflict in Iraq? You might receive very different answers depending on whom you ask. "Every individual, whether a policy maker, a grassroots organizer, or a conflict analyst, has experiences and expectations that influence his or her interpretations of the conflict [1, p. 24]". Particularly those who have lived through violent encounters almost always have different interpretations of what happened [2]. It helps to make explicit the underlying theories or explanations of conflict from which analysis springs. Certainly, this is not a perfect enterprise. As Kriesberg and Dayton point out,

> We can say with some certainty that political regimes that inhibit political freedoms and exclude minority groups from participating in governance tend to 'conflict prone', but we have a harder time explaining why some of these societies spiral into civil war while others long remain relatively stable.

In this Chapter and the next, the task before us is not to settle the scores between different personal accounts of what caused sectarian violence in Iraq, but to integrate a variety of empirical explanations about why this kind of behavior, with all of its terrible consequences, emerged, and escalated. The following analysis of sectarian violence in Baghdad is theoretically grounded in constructivism, an approach to scientific inquiry that draws attention to the socially constructed nature of actors and their identities and interests, and the historically contingent and mutually constitutive relationships between social groups. Social conflicts are lodged in long-standing relationships, often characterized by animosity, perception of enmity, and deep-rooted fear. Social constructionists believe that the way we understand the world, whether in peace or in war, is a product of a historical process of interaction and negotiation between groups of people. Constructivism is also built around an appreciation of the power of communication (from words, to metaphors, to narrative forms) to create our sense of reality. The derivative conceptual bases of this study prioritize social identity, group dynamics, and language (discourse and narratives).

Constructivism, Identity, and Conflict

Constructivism is an approach to social research. It provides a theoretical lens, an analytical focus, and a set of conceptual tools [3]. The distinctive analytical approach of constructivism is based on three core concepts. First and foremost is the social construction of reality, or the notion that "the perceptions, identities and interests of individuals and groups are socially and culturally constructed, rather than existing outside of or prior to society [3, p. 175]". People's description of and interpretation of their world becomes truth (or reality) [4] and is a product of interaction and negotiation between groups of people.

> Related to this, constructivists point to the existence of social facts; unlike brute facts such as gravity or oceans, which exist independently of human agreement, social facts are wholly dependent on human agreement. Money, terrorism, sovereignty, anarchy and

> conflict, for example, are all social constructions that only exist so long as human agreement exists (Barnett, 2005 259). Importantly, when social facts are treated as objective facts…they become a constraint on behavior and thereby function as conditioning structures [4, p. 175].

Every human social system is based on sets of rules, codes of conduct, and institutions—invisible social structures that shape and guide human interaction. But actually, social structures are the rules and resources created through the actions (practices and routines) of individuals. We are both shaped by social structures and simultaneously shape those structures through our behavior, beliefs, and interactions [5]. Thus, a second core concept is that structures are interdependent with, and "co-constituted" by, human agency. "That is, agents produce structures through their beliefs, actions, and interactions, while structures produce agents by helping to shape their values and interests [5, p. 175]."

The term agent is intentionally used by social scientists to connote the capacity of individuals to act independently and make willful, intentional choices. Social agency refers to the fact that people are "deliberate, symbolic actors who act on the basis of their understanding and wants." Human actions are based on meaning—"they embody intentions, express emotions, are done for reasons and are influenced by ideas about value [6]." Anthony Giddens suggested that structural change comes about particularly due to the unintended consequences of action. While this is no doubt true in some cases, understanding why people take the actions they do, the central task of interpretive social science, requires a more detailed account of social agency [7]. Emirbayer and Mische argued that actors *can* "critically shape their own responsiveness to problematic situations" [8] using *purpose* and *judgment* and by considering the past, present, and future in determining courses of action.

As noted, this study begins with the observation that particular Baghdad neighborhoods chose a course of action that undermined the spread of sectarian attitudes and behaviors. Understanding this shift and the practices associated with it required a close look at individual agency, preexisting organizational structures, and forces external to the locality. In focusing on a specific aspect of social phenomenon[1]—namely how resilience to violence came about—I looked for mechanisms that link structure and action

A third core element of a constructivist approach is the emphasis placed on "ideas, language, symbols, and other discursive processes as constitutive of identities, interests, beliefs, and perceptions which in turn construct powerful normative structures." Constructivism holds that ideational factors (e.g., ideas, norms) have a causal effect on social action. For example, most people feel compelled to follow laws prohibiting shoplifting even when the clerk is not looking, or lowering the airplane tray table even when the flight attendants are already seated for takeoff. Likewise, states feel compelled to comply with agreed upon norms and rules, even when they have the incentives and the capacity to break them [9].

---

[1] Per Jeffrey Checkel's admonition that constructivist scholarship should focus on delimited aspects of the social world in order to generate 'middle range' theories of the actors and mechanisms bringing about change.

Because this "sense of obligation" operates independently of positive or negative sanctions, norms and rules demonstrate "a compliance pull of their own" [10]. Constructivists argue that norms exert effects on behavior by influencing the interests, identities, and policies of different actors. Moral values and norms "may provide the inspiration and motivation for foreign policy development and implementation" as in the increased incidence of humanitarian military intervention linked to wide acceptance of the human rights norm [11], or the impact of "moral vision" on foreign aid policies [12]. They also influence an actor's awareness and use of particular methods that can be used to achieve some objective (i.e., preventing violent conflict enhances the prospects for economic growth) [13]. And, as Kriesberg and Dayton have pointed out, when different groups share values and norms, they tend not to fight with each other [3].

Narratives also have effects for our identities, interests, and perceptions.[2] In particular, "narratives constitute crucial means of generating, sustaining, mediating, and representing conflict at all levels of social organization [16]." Narratives are basically stories that we develop about other people, just as other people develop stories about us.

> Our natural tendency is to make our stories as coherent and stable as possible. Given this dynamic, conflict can be seen as a system where information is being reduced. Information that would counter these storylines is restricted. We see best what will reinforce our stories [17].

Narratives derive from what Marc Howard Ross calls *psychocultural interpretations*. Psychocultural interpretations are "shared, deeply rooted worldviews which help groups make sense of daily life, and provide psychologically meaningful accounts of a group's relationships with other groups." According to Ross, they are "theories about the world, groups in it, and core assumptions about the motives of insiders and outsiders, and how they are likely to behave in particular situations" which order and influence people's beliefs and actions [18]. Narratives are psychocultural interpretations represented as stories, about a group's origins, history, and relationship with other groups. They frame how members of particular identity groups describe and make sense of all life situations [19].

Narratives play a causal role in conflict dynamics "by ruling certain political options either 'in' or 'out' for communal groups and for those who claim to advance their interests [19]." As documented throughout the book, narratives that promoted negative images of Shi'a and Sunni Iraqis aggravated communal tensions, but narratives that emphasized common Muslim identity and historically strong communal relationships characterized conflict-resilient neighborhoods.

> What is most crucial...about interpretations and narratives regarding conflict is the compelling, coherent account they offer to each group in linking specific events to that group's general understandings. Central to these accounts is the attribution of motive to parties

[2] The connection between language and social relations is often contested and is far too complex a topic to dwell on here. For differing perspectives on the question of whether language embodies or constitutes social relations (or both), see [14, 15].

> [which] makes it easy to "predict" another's future actions, and through one's own behavior to turn such predictions into self-fulfilling prophecies [1].

As the reader will see, my methodology relies heavily on narratives because, as Basso, Brenneis, and Herzfeld argued, "narratives of conflict provide privileged sites for reflexive examination of individual identities and the social order as a whole [20]." As an analytical tool, narratives tell us how people understand the nature of a particular conflict: their fears, their hopes, and what they value in the way of settlements. However, many conflicts are intractable precisely because narratives themselves do not match up, making it extremely hard to find solutions that satisfy the majority. The Iraqi research team I worked with was all too familiar with the conflicting narratives of Sunni and Shi'a participants in focus groups that they had been conducting since 2003.

> ...there is lack of real understanding of each other...Religious and more specifically sectarian attitudes determine to a big extent the course of such conversation, there is a clear and wide difference of opinion in nearly every political matter between Sunni and Shi'a. From our experience of living there and conducting many focus groups and listening to thousands of people, *I can now tell whether I speak with a Sunni or Shi'a Iraqi without asking him from the first minute of the conversation and I'm usually right in more than 90 % of cases...*

Identity Conflict Through a Constructivist Lens

Scholars disagree on the relationship of group identity to violent conflict and tend to fall into one of the three camps on questions about causation. In the *primordialist* camp are those who view ethnic conflict as driven primarily by enduring animosities between groups divided along ethnic or sectarian lines. According to this view, "ethnic groups lie in wait for one another, nourishing age-old hatreds and restrained only by powerful states. Remove the lid, and the cauldron boils over [20]." The underlying assumption is that identity-based conflicts are driven by persistent cultural differences and ethnic loyalties[3] that change little over time [20, P. 211]. Journalist Christopher Dickey assumes this much in his piece "*There's No Stopping Iraq's Bloody Cycle: Iraq's vendettas could haunt the West for years*". He wrote

> Iraq is in a class by itself: a breeder reactor where explosive hatreds were both incited and contained by Saddam Hussein's brutality, only to become an uncontrolled chain reaction after the U.S.-led invasion liberated both the country and its vendettas.

Social scientists who reject the primordialist view argue that it is based on three mistaken assumptions: "that ethnic identities are ancient and unchanging; that these identities motivate people to persecute, and... that ethnic diversity itself leads

---

[3] Robert Kaplan, in his dispatches for The Atlantic and in his Balkan Ghosts: A Journey Through History (New York: St. Martin's 1993), and (writing mainly on large-scale conflict) Samuel P. Huntington, in "The Clash of Civilizations?" Foreign Affairs 72 (Summer 1993): 22–49.

to violence [20].” According to those in the *instrumentalist* camp, ethnic identities are recent (not ancient) constructs that change over time. True, ethnic identity contains several components that make it easy to draw comparisons between “us” and “other” groups including belief in common ancestry, shared historical experiences, a shared culture, attachment to a particular piece of territory, and a sense of self-awareness [20]. True also is that social differentiation between “we” and “they” is a universal feature of human life in groups, along with the tendency to ascribe virtuous attributes to the “we” and negative ones to the “they” [22].

However, feelings of group superiority, or ethnocentrism, do not automatically lead to violence; after all the great majority of ethnic conflict—defined as a disputes about political, economic, social, cultural or territorial issues between two or more ethnic communities[4]—is *non*violent in nature. In addition, greater ethnic diversity is not associated with greater ethnic conflict [20]. Instrumentalists argue instead ethnic identities are manipulated by political elites for purposes of their own self-serving (political and economic) interests [21]. Ussama Makdisi has argued that sectarianism is too often dismissed as “an upswelling of primordial religious solidarities,” when in fact sectarian tensions are “actively produced.”

> With this in mind, it is clear that Iraqis, like people everywhere, have different aspects to their individual and collective societal identities: familial, professional, and geographic, as well as ethnic and religious. *A political situation and its history will determine which social identity will be most important to the individuals involved* [and become] the dominant vehicle for political mobilization (emphasis mine).

Yet beyond the political situation and its history, institutional deficits in fragile states open the opportunity for elites to manipulate identity. Bertochhi’s (2010) analysis of state fragility identified institutional deficits in democracy, rule of law, respect for human rights and fundamental freedoms [23] as the key drivers of state fragility. Her findings are in line with insights advanced in the 1980s by Lebanese scholar Edward Azar who argued that the relationship between identity groups and the state was at the core of protracted social conflict. In multi-communal societies, the domination by a single group or a coalition of groups that is “unresponsive to the needs of other groups in society…strains the social fabric and eventually breeds fragmentation and protracted social conflict” [24]. This theoretical framework cites the failure to address collectively expressed grievances by authorities as a precursor for violent conflict, and Azar was one of the first conflict theorists to conclude that reducing the incidence of violent social conflict meant not only increasing levels of development, but enhancing the role of the state to regulate, protect, and provide for the social good.

These structural factors kindle the flame of interethnic violence, but instrumentalists argue that opportunistic politicians fan the fire intentionally, using the mass media to aggravate ethnic tensions and provoke conflict in order to prevent domestic challenges to their power. “People do not kill mindlessly,” wrote Hugo Slim in 2008. “They have reasons to kill them. They become convinced by those reasons

[4] Brown (2001). Ethnic and Internal Conflicts.

and then convince others of them too. Reasons for killing and hurting civilians are mostly thought up by political leaders who decide that policies of mass killing, destitution, or terror are appropriate strategic and tactical responses to the problems they face [25]." And yet as Franke Wilmer observed, writing about the ethnic violence during the war in the former Yugoslavia, the machinations of opportunistic elites cannot account for the *brutality* of violence when it is carried out. Instrumentalist explanations shed light on "why leaders and institutional actors did what they did, but they do not tell us why the soldiers discussed whether to shoot or burn civilians alive, why they then lined up women and children, herded them into a house, and set the house on fire [26]."

The middle ground between these primordialist and instrumentalist camps is *constructivism*, which acknowledges the deeply rooted and meaningful basis upon which instrumentalist elites are able to construct particular identity discourses as suits their rational calculus. As Eriksen put it, "collective identities are constructed, consciously or not, but nothing comes out of nothing [27]."

> Ethnicity cannot be politicized unless an underlying core of memories, experience, or meaning moves people to collective action. This common foundation may include historical experiences, such as struggles against outsiders for possession of a homeland, or cultural markers, especially language, religion and legal institutions that set one community apart from others. Ethnic identities are also contextual, adaptable to and activated by unexpected threats and new opportunities…located on a spectrum between (primordial) historical continuities and (instrumental) opportunistic adaptations [28].

The constructivist view of ethnic identity pays close attention to "the social processes involved in the construction and destruction of political identities, the state, intergroup conflict, and the relationship between these processes and a psychosocial account of the self as a citizen of the polity [26, p. 82]." While enmity has many sources—struggles of political, economic, or ideological power—they have also psychological causes. Well documented by social and cultural anthropologists is the tendency of individuals and groups to experience strong negative emotions, including aggression, hostility, fear, and repulsion, toward "Others" perceived to be strange, unfamiliar, or different. Feelings of disgust or hatred combined with the threat of enmity "justifies actions that might otherwise be unacceptable or illegal [and] provide a contrast by which a person or nation can… inflate their sense of superiority".[5]

Such innocuous differences as age or appearance are enough to stimulate resentment toward other groups. Differences deeply connected to our individual and group identities, like religious beliefs, race, or culture, are even more likely to produce a dangerous "we–they" dichotomy that encourage "separation of particular racial, religious, ethnic, or cultural groups, positioning them as hostile and alien [29]." Sam Keen called this phenomenon our hostile imagination, full of distasteful images, and ideas about "others" [30]. We are hardwired to project those unsavory ideas onto other people, permitting us to construct (and dehumanize) enemies.

---

[5] Middens 1990.

Over the past three decades, social and behavioral scientists have increasingly emphasized the role of self and identity in the causes and consequences of intergroup hostility and harm-doing. For example, ample evidence supports the finding that "people like better, think more highly of, and discriminate in favor of" groups to which they belong, over other groups to which they do not belong.[6] Social psychologists call the *ingroup bias* "in which one thinks more highly of and discriminates in favor of the ingroup in comparison to the outgroup."[7] Studies show that human beings are psychologically motivated to think and behave this way because we have a universal and fundamental need for self-esteem, trust, and security [31] which is enhanced when we perceive the groups with which we identify to be superior to out-groups.[8]

This particular theory of human behavior (social identity theory) has been used most widely as an explanation for prejudice, defined as negative attitudes toward members of a group based solely on the fact that they are members of that group.[9] Prejudice toward a group involves a high reliance on stereotypes,[10] a tendency that emerges during intergroup conflict and results in members of each group viewing members of the other group as being "all the same". According to Hugo Slim, "intense collective thinking that resists seeing the individual inside the enemy group is ever present [32]."

This dangerous and powerful belief system can contribute significantly to the rapid escalation of violent acts toward "others" as occurred during the dissolution of former Yugoslavia between ethnic Serbs and Croats, in 1992 between Hutu and Tutsi Rwandans, in electoral clashes between Kenyan Kikuyu and Pokot tribes in 2007, and between Sunni and Shi'a Iraqis after US occupation. As Bartos and Wehr point out, "whenever individuals associate together, especially if they do so on the basis of shared characteristics that exclude others and make a distinction

[6] Pruitt and Kim 2004: 29. See also Gaertner & Dovido 2000; Tajfel and Turner 1979.

[7] Pruitt and Kim, 2004: 29, emphasis mine. Underpinning the division of people into 'us' and 'them' is the universal and biologically rooted tendency toward social categorization, a cognitive mechanism for dividing the world into separate categories so as to bring order to the enormous array of stimuli encountered. Thus, the process of designating someone as a member of one's own group (i.e., the in-group) or not (i.e., a member of an out group) is one that occurs almost automatically.

[8] Tajfel and Turner 1986.

[9] The importance of social identity is paramount in the study of human relationships, though social scientists lack cross-disciplinary agreement on its meaning. Well known to psychologists and sociologists is Tajfel's social identity theory (SIT) and accompanying definition of social identity as "that part of an individual's self-concept which derives from his knowledge of his membership in a social group (or groups) together with the value and emotional significant attached to that membership" (1981, 255).

[10] Stereotypes are cognitive structures that contain simplified and highly categorical information about a person, group, place, or thing. Although stereotypes aid our cognitive sorting system in perceiving, encoding, storing, and retrieving social data, they are highly simplified versions of reality that ignore the great variability that exists among people in any given group.

between 'us' and 'them', there are dangers of racism, ethnocentrism, xenophobia, and other acts of intolerance [which] can be expressed in tendencies to dehumanize [33]."

The study of group dynamics as distinct from "the study" of individuals can be traced back to early thinkers. The father of experimental psychology, Wilhelm Wundt, had a special interest in the so-called "psychology of communities" [34] and believed that researchers had to take a group or systems approach to studying their phenomena (religion, language, and custom). Emile Durkheim, the father of sociology, theorized that society is held together by "collective consciousness"—shared norms and beliefs that result in social integration [35].

> The totality of beliefs and sentiments common to the average members of a society forms a determinate system with a life of its own. It can be termed the collective or common consciousness [36].

These nonmaterial social facts include morality, cultural norms, and values that transcend individuals and exercise social constraint. Durkheim was one of the first scholars to appreciate culture as a "social fact" and to study the organization of human cultural relations [36]. Other key theorists included William McDougal, an early pioneer in social psychology who believed that a "a group mind" existed distinct from individuals [37, p. 103], Sigmund Freud whose crowd behavior theory posited that people in a crowd act differently than they would individually, and Gustave Le Bon's more precise studies of differences between the "psychology of the crowd" from the psychology of individuals within it. However, social identity theory has been criticized for its singular focus on how individuals perceive group membership, while neglecting the relational and situational influences on how that perception is constructed. Ideas, values, norms, and environmental factors influence the identities and interests of actors as has already been discussed.

Ultimately, social psychologist Kurt Lewin founded the movement to study groups scientifically and coined the term *group dynamics* to describe the system of behaviors and psychological processes occurring within and between social groups. Lewin defined groups in terms of interdependence between members. "It is not similarity or dissimilarity of individuals that constitutes a group," he wrote "but interdependence of fate" [38]. Societies are made up of different kinds of groups, all of which need each other. Iraqi society is like any other, a diverse mosaic of different groups built on social class, personal interest, professional and political association, tribal/familial ties, and more. The two social groupings of particular interest to me, within the context of this book, are religious and tribal groupings.

Iraq's ethnic communities coexisted for thousands of years, with communal conflict tied more often to explicit policies of the rulers. Both Sunni and Shi'a Muslims share the most fundamental tenants of Islam, including the interpretation of Sharia Law, and most Muslims do not distinguish themselves by sect, preferring to call themselves simply "Muslims". However, the Sunni–Shi'a divide is real, and its violent turn in Iraq is a reminder that modern communal tensions "can quickly take on the rhetoric and power of more ancient, even mythical, differences" [39].

Group Identities in Iraq: Religious and Tribal

A constructivist approach conceives of culture as framing the context in which particular conflicts occur. Culture refers to "the socially transmitted values, beliefs, and symbols that are more or less shared by members of a social group, and by means of which members interpret and make meaningful their experience and behavior (including the behavior of others)" [40]. Culture becomes context by stipulating what people fight over, and how. Specifically, culture indicates

> what sorts of things are subjects for competition or objects of dispute, often by postulating their high value and relative (or absolute) scarcity: honor here, purity there, capital and profits somewhere else. It does so by stipulating rules, sometimes precise, sometimes less so, for how contests should be pursued, including when they begin and how to end them [41].

All of this means that one must pay close attention to the cultural differences in order to interpret people's actions and motives.

The fracture between Sunnis and Shi'a dates back to the death of Muhammad and the ensuing dispute over who should succeed the prophet, assume the command of the community, and bear the title of Deputy of the Messenger of God (*khalifat rasul allah*) otherwise referred to as the "caliph." For Sunnis, the heir should be elected or chosen by consensus, "citing a tradition of the prophet Muhammad: 'My people will not unite on an error [42].'" Shi'a held that power should have been entrusted to one of the prophet's direct descendants. Ali, the prophet's cousin, had married Muhammad's daughter Fatima and their progeny were seen as the Prophet's anointed and rightful successors.

Abu Bakr's faction prevailed and Muhammad's father-in-law became the new caliph. However, the Party of Ali—Shi'a Ali in Arabic—did not waver in their belief that Ali was the rightful successor. Abu Bakr fortified his home bases in Basra and Kufa, but both of his immediate successors were assassinated, and in 646, Ali became the caliphate. As tensions rose into a civil war, Ali agreed to settle the conflict through arbitration. He lost, and returned to Kufa, defeated and under intense scrutiny and pressure for having agreed to submit his claim to a third party authority. If conflict resolution has limited purchase in the twenty-first century, non-violent methods were much less valued in the Arab tribal societies of Mesopotamia. In 661, one of the Ali's disciples murdered him with a poison-tipped sword.

Since then, Shi'as have considered the caliphate usurped and illegitimate. Ali's death marked "the beginning of an enduring tradition of mourning [42, p. 20]." Martyrdom and suffering is a dominant psychocultural narrative, memorialized annually in (what Howard Ross calls) the *cultural re-enactment* or Taziyya of the Battle of Karbala—which commemorates the death of Ali's son, Husayn. As with other oppressed minorities, a collective sense of victimhood has high symbolic meaning and Shi'a Muslims see themselves as constantly facing an existential threat. Shi'a Muslims are also a global minority[11] and minorities often see their own

---

[11] Although Shi'a Muslims are the majority in Iran and Iraq (and large minority communities live in Yemen, Bahrain, Syria, and Lebanon), 80 % of the world's Muslim population are Sunni.

history as a long series of persecutions, massacres, and forced conversions. Luomi notes that "The fact that the Shi'as have almost always been the oppressed and on the periphery of power in the Middle East is an important factor in the relationship between the two branches of Islam" with modern sectarian identities shaped according "to the rule that being Sunni or Shi'a defined "who has and who has not, who sits at the table and who does not" [43]. Proverbs like the following reinforce this collective sense of fear and victimization: "Me against my brother; me and my brother against my cousin; me, my brother, and my cousin against the Shi'a" [44].

In Iraq, Shi'a Muslims have usually been largely excluded from the highest executive positions of political life. Though the demographic majority, Iraq Shi'a population were largely denied government posts, needed special permission from the government to conduct religious celebrations, and were victims of state-sanctioned violence including disappearances, torture, and murder. As a result, some scholars have concluded that "Iraqi society is inherently divided and divisive—largely along sectarian (Sunni–Shi'a) and ethnic (mainly Arab–Kurd) lines" [45]. Others demur. Charles Tripp points out,

> This sense of exclusion has not led all Shi'a to see their identity and interests in terms of the reconstruction of the Iraqi state by clerics…On the contrary, many have looked to an Iraq in which all the excluded majorities—defined not in sectarian terms, but in terms of socioeconomic class, or in terms of the political rights of free citizens—are finally allowed to participate in the political life of the country. Meanwhile, others have [sought inclusion] in the kind of patrimonial regime that has thrived on kinship and tribal networks. Thus there is no more a single Shi'a narrative in Iraqi politic than there is an Iraqi one itself [46].

Culture is socially and psychologically distributed across many different kinds of "social groupings—regional, ethnic, religious, class, occupational [and] even members of the same social grouping do not internalize cultural representations or schemas equally [47]." As might therefore be expected, Shiites are divided into multiple followings that adhere to different religious doctrines and do not all answer to the same religious leader or Grand Ayatollah. One of the biggest differences, rooted historically in two distinct narratives, is the doctrine espoused by Grand Ayatollahs Ali Husain al-Sistani and Muhammad Baqir al-Sadr.

Al-Sistani supports a current of thought extending backwards for centuries termed "quietism" or "pacifism," according to which society is governed by the principles of Islam, but the Ayatollah neither demands political power for himself nor presumes to exercise control over it. This current of thought has always been dominant in the Iraqi city of Najaf. An alternative current of thought emerged during the Baath regime, one that opposed the repressive policies of the Baath Party's regime and stood in defiance of the pacifist Shi'as. The proponent of so-called "anti-establishment" thinking, Ayatollah Muhammad Baqir al-Sadr, was outspoken against the Baath's policies and advocated political power for clerics. This contrast between the leadership styles continues to date in post-Baath Iraq between the pacifist leadership of Ayatollah al-Sistani and the revolutionary leadership of Muqtada al-Sadr, the nephew of Ayatollah al-Sadr. The relationship between al-Sistani and Sadrists varies across southern Iraq, from tense coexistence as in Najaf, to armed confrontations in Basra and Samawa.

Ideological differences were also mirrored in tactical differences between the Mahdi Army and the Badr Brigades. The Badr Brigades are the armed wing of the Supreme Council for the Islamic Revolution in Iraq (SCIRI), recently renamed Supreme Islamic Iraqi Council (SIIC), and were founded by Iraqi exiles living in Iran. The two organizations did not get along and armed clashes between them were protracted, punctated by periods of cooperation (to which some of the stories below make reference). Tactical differences were just as dramatic—mainly that (1) Hakim welcomed US presence, while Sadr condemned it and (2) the Mahdi Army appealed for support to the working class, while SCIRI supporters tend to be well-educated members of the upper class. International Crisis Group assessed the rivalry as a class struggle "between the Shi'a urban underclass" and richer Shi'as in southern Iraq and in Baghdad. Journalist David Enders wrote the following in 2008:

> To ignore the class element of the Sadrist resistance is to fail to tell the story accurately. The differences are obvious at Buratha mosque, where Jalal al-Deen al-Saghir, one of the SIIC's leaders, preaches almost every Friday. While the Sadrieen pray in a dusty street than can burn your feet through a pair of tennis shoes, Buratha has air conditioners and a simulcast for those who cannot fit in the main prayer hall. The Sadrieen represent Iraq's traditionally disenfranchised, while SIIC represents the country's shrunken middle class and leaders who had the ability to leave Iraq during Saddam's reign…SIIC is careful not to engage the class issue. It prefers to paint Sadr's supporters as a bunch of hotheaded youths who don't know any better.

The bottom line is that "Sunni" and "Shi'a" have never been monolithic markers. In 2009, according to an informal study by Alan Silverman, the major division between Iraqis was "not over whether one should pray like a Sunni or a Shi'a or whether one was better than the other" [48]. The split was between Shiite fundamentalist parties that had lived the better part of two decades in Iran, and the groups that had remained in Iraq. These groups were the Sunni Awakening Council members and Shiite Sadrists, and both had lost blood and treasure resisting the US occupation. Thus, more important than sectarian identity was the perceived right to governance in post-Saddam Iraq. This makes perfect sense when considering that the oldest social structure in Iraq is not religious at all—it is tribal.

The tribe is an enduring social structure in Iraqi society and 75 % of Iraqis belong to one. Beginning with the founding of the Republic of Iraq in 1958, rural tribes have been significantly weakened by a series of land reforms and new laws designed to weaken the power of sheiks and free peasants from their landlords [49]. However, writing in 2007, in the heyday of international interest in Iraqi society, Jesmeen Khan observed that the tribal structure has endured through centuries "as the primary mechanism of societal organization" [50]. In many cases, tribal membership trumps ethnic or religious affiliation. Two of the largest tribes—the Jabur and Shammar tribes—have both Sunni and Shiite members. Adam Silverman, a social scientist who advised the US Army in Iraq from April to October 2008 and carried out a four-month long study of Iraqi tribes, had this to say:

> Virtually all the individuals we interviewed, whether sheikhs, internally displaced Iraqis, or average Iraqis, told us that tribes tended to be mixed religiously. Even if a tribe in Mada'in where we were conducting interviews was completely Sunni, it typically had a

branch elsewhere in Iraq that was Shiite. Likewise, the Shiite tribes had Sunni branches. Moreover, all the sheikhs indicated that their tribe's people intermarry with members of other local tribes regardless of sectarian orientation. When asked, about 2/3rds of tribal leaders insisted that "sectarian" conflict was really about resources. The remainder asserted that outside religious extremist influences (whether deriving from the Wahhabi form of Islam or from hard line Shiism) are to blame and that often that influence is used to manipulate Iraqis in order to usurp their resources [51].

The seminal work written on Iraqi society and culture is Ali Wardi's "*Understanding Iraq: Society, Culture and Personality*". Ali Wardi (1913–1995) was a US-trained Iraqi sociologist who explored the persistent historical roots of sectarian conflict in Iraq. He argued that this conflict was so deeply embedded in Iraqi society that four decades of national rule have proved ineffectual in fostering an overarching, cohesive national identity [52]. Even more than citizens of other Arab nations, Al-Wardi insisted Iraqis have long been divided along sharp lines of ethnic and tribal identity.

Wardi traced the strength of tribal institutions in the modern Iraq state to the near absence of governance under the Ottoman Empire, outside of major cities. "The result was a strengthening of indigenous tribal organizations and traditions, a factor reinforced by incursions of tribes, during the eighteenth and nineteenth centuries, as nomads from adjacent desert areas settled in the river valley [53]." When nomadic tribes left the desert and settled in rural areas, they faced "psychological and social pressures in their adjustment and in their ability to preserve the old nomadic values [53, p. 66]." For these reasons, Wardi drew a distinction between nomadic tribal societies and rural tribal societies.

Wardi theorized that Iraqi society was characterized by a deep split or conflict between culture and values of nomadism (*bedawa*) and urbanism (*hadara*). We encountered this split during interviews. In Adhamiyya, the old center of the neighborhood is governed by families, while settlers in the newer peripheral areas define themselves by tribe. Areas governed by families, whose leaders are called "old Baghdadis" or "wise old men" refer to a culture of "civilian identity," which (we were told) is different than tribal identity. "It is different to speak about culture that is tribal versus culture that is civil," noted a team member as we were interpreting our transcripts. "The most important difference is that the tribe orders and values do not play a role like it does in the tribal based society."

Tribal orders and values are hierarchical and patriarchal. The necessity for tribal affiliation led to the high value placed on conquest and revenge. Wardi wrote, "If a member of his tribe is killed by an outsider, the entire tribe would demand revenge. If the killer cannot be caught and killed, any member of his tribe would be subject to killing. This tradition gives strength and cohesion to the tribe as a whole [53, p. 17]." The blog site of a returning US soldier puts it similarly.

The tradition of "an eye for an eye" is so ancient and dangerously ingrained among the desert Arabs that 1,400 years ago the Qur'an called on good Muslims to forgo vengeance in order to expiate their sins. But the old codes of honor remained, and in the most troubled parts of Iraq today, increasingly, they prevail. When governments cannot or will not protect the people, then families, clans, tribes, gangs and militias will (Indeed, among the Shiites of Karbala, gang rule has a history as old and complex as the mafia in Sicily) [54].

The construction of masculinity in tribal society is tied to deeply held values of honor and loyalty to one's clan or tribe. Tribal identity can influence people to perceive defensive and retaliatory killings as perfectly acceptable. These values are part of the tribal worldview, psychocultural interpretations that proscribe honor as an object of conflict, and stipulate rules for waging defensive conflict. Indeed, both Sunni tribes and Shiite tribes have banded together on historic scales to battle sectarian militias and extremists since 2003. Wardi might have cast this as the contradiction between the tendency to "rob, attack, and kill" versus the tendency "to protect and assist," both of which were essential for Bedouin life. According to Khan (2007), these rules also take the form of tribal social and justice codes "which include the tradition of blood feuds (*al-tha'r*), protecting family honor (*'ird*), and exhibiting ones' masculinity in fighting (*al-mirowa*)" [55].

And yet, one of the most important contributions of constructivism is in pointing out that identity—ethnic, tribal, religious, national—is *socially constructed* and malleable, not fixed. The role that ethnic or religious identities play in particular cases of conflict escalation is highly contextual because "identity is defined by and reacts to the changing nature of society and crucially how a state seeks to interact with and control its population" [56]. Like other social identities, tribal identities in Iraq have shifted over time depending on the identity and relative power of different rulers.

> [Tribes and tribal sheikhs] have played various roles under different regimes, many of which have tried to fit them into their schemes for social control as key institutions to extend the power and reach of the center. Under such circumstances, [tribes] have formed characteristic elements of the narrative of the regime in question, even when these may be as different as those of Hashemite Iraq under the monarch or of the Iraq of Saddam Hussein…Similarly ethnic and sectarian categories such as 'Kurd' or "Shi'a' have not only meant different things politically over time, but have also been used in a variety of ways, by government and opposition alike [56, p. 3].

Conclusion

This Chapter has touched on several deeply rooted causes of sectarian conflict in Iraq, chiefly the nature of religious and tribal identity constructed through decades (centuries even) in prevailing "sociocultural discourses, national myths, and intergroup relations [56, p. 6]." The following Chapter guides our attention to more immediate proximate causes of conflicts: the cultural context of the modern Iraqi state, and the structural, political, and economic sources of internal conflict present in Iraq prior to the US invasion.

To conclude this Chapter, it is worth noting that prior to the invasion, perhaps up to one-third of Sunni–Shi'a marriages were mixed and most of the country's tribes included members of both sects. However, a cultivated culture of ignorance existed between sects, and I will return to this theme throughout this book. The "hidden and forbidden" nature of sectarian differences under the Baath regime was very damaging for Iraqi society. A resident of Baghdad since his birth, YouGov's research director was personally affected by this culture of silence and its lifting in

2003. I decided to close this Chapter with his commentary on sectarian relations before and after the bombs began to fall.

> People of different sects don't know each other at all. They live side by side, but if you don't discuss and debate this stuff, how would they know each other? The Shi'a were afraid to argue or debate any religious or political issue as they will be suspected of, or charged with "being sectarian" and working for Iran which meant death or at least jail and torture. Sunnis wouldn't sacrifice their privilege with the regime by raising such issue and they didn't feel the need to do so, they had more freedom in this field, but they were not interested in discussing issues, they obeyed the regime politically and supported it and they practice their religion freely and they don't touch political stuff.
>
> But after the fall of Saddam Statue on 9th of April 2003, I guess people started the conscious and serious thinking about who will rule now? Why and by which means? And here came the biggest dilemma for the Sunnis about how to accept and support and like the "new Iraq", where they will have much much less power and the Shi'a will have the major portion of power.
>
> There is also a great deal of ignorance and distrust [between] the brothers in the country. I believe that despite what people try to market as the "great" relationships and mutual respect between the two sects in Iraq, the unspoken truth is that there is a much greater degree of ignorance and distrust between the two. There was a balance of power for hundreds of years that determined the relationship between the two sects, the governments in Iraq and Sunni didn't need to think a lot about the "other", it was outside the equation all the way through. We lived with that and I did absolutely feel it at that time. There is also that kind of mutual ignorance of each other's sect, Shi'a know very little about Sunnis and Sunnis know less about Shi'a as a sect; what both sides know about each other are " the bad" and controversial things. I know this from my family experience too.
>
> It is amazing that people live together don't want to know about each other, they read what each sect is writing about the other sect so they know the other by the eyes of their own religious men who are in 99 % of cases will tell you the differences and will spend all their time and effort to prove that they are right and the "other" is wrong.

References

1. Ross, M.H. 2007. *Cultural contestation in ethnic conflict*, 24. Cambridge: MA Cambridge University Press.
2. Kriesberg, L., and B.W. Dayton. 2012. *Constructive conflicts: From escalation to resolution*, 23. Lanham: Rowman and Littelfield Publishers.
3. Jackson, R. 2009. Constructivism and conflict resolution. In *The SAGE handbook of conflict resolution*, ed. J. Bercovitch, V. Kremenyuk, and I. Zartman, 172–192. London: SAGE Publications.
4. Franklin, C. 1995. Expanding the vision of the social constructionist debates: Creating relevance for practitioners. *Families in Society: The Journal of Contemporary Human Service* 76(6): 395–407.
5. Giddens, A. 1979. *Central problems in social theory*. London: Macmillan.
6. Hollis, Martin. 2008. *The philosophy of social science: An introduction*, 144. Cambridge: Cambridge University Press.
7. Little, D. 1991. *Varieties of social explanation: An introduction to the philosophy of social science*. Oxford: Westview Press.
8. Mustafa, E.M., and A. Mische. 1998. What is agency? *American Journal of Sociology* 103(4): 971.

9. Henkin, L. 1979. *How nations behave: Law and foreign policy*. New York: University of Columbia Press.
10. Thomas, F. 1990. *The power of legitimacy among nations. Nations comply when rules are perceived as legitimate*. New York: Oxford University Press.
11. Martha, F. 2003. *The purpose of intervention: Changing beliefs about the use of force*. London: Cornell University Press.
12. Lumsdaine, D.H. 1993. *Moral vision in international politics: The foreign aid regime, 1949–1989*. Princeton: Princeton University Press.
13. Klowert, P., and J. Legro. 1996. Norms identity and their limits. In *The Culture of national security, norms and identity in world politics*, ed. P. Katzenstein, 463. New York: Columbia University Press.
14. Bourdieu, P. 1991. *Language and Symbolic Power*. Trans. Gino Raymond and Matthew Adamson. Cambridge: Harvard University Press.
15. Irvine, J. 1989. When talk isn't cheap: Language and political economy. *American Ethnologist* 16: 248–267.
16. Briggs, C. 1996. *Disorderly discourse: Narrative, conflict and inequality*. Oxford: Oxford University Press. 3.
17. Phelp, M. 2005. Transforming conflict narratives. Conference proceedings of the 2005 National Organizational Development Conference. Retrieved athttp://www.equalvoice.com/WelpODNConferenceProceeding.pdf.
18. MacGinty, R. 2013. *Routledge handbook of peacebuilding*, 96. New York: Routledge Publishing.
19. Ross, M.H. 2002. The political psychology of competing narratives: September 11 and beyond. In *Understanding September 11*, ed. C. Calhoun, P. Price, and A. Timmer, 303–320. New York: New Press.
20. Bowen, J.R. 1996. The myth of global ethnic conflict. *Journal of Democracy* 7(4): 3–14.
21. Brown, Michael. 2001. Ethnic and internal conflicts: Causes and implications. In *Turbulent peace: The challenges of managing international conflict*, ed. C.A. Crocker, and F.O. Hampson. Washington, D.C.: United States Institute of Peace Press.
22. Stein, J. 2001. Image, identity and conflict resolution. In *Turbulent peace: The challenges of managing international conflict*, ed. C.A. Crocker, and F.O. Hampson, 191. Washington, D.C.: United States Institute of Peace Press.
23. Bertochhi, G. 2010. The empirical determinants of state fragility. Retrieved from http://www.voxeu.org/article/determinants-state-fragility. This study found insignificant effects for economic determinants of state fragility (including per capita GDP (both levels and growth rates), investment, government expenditures, human capital, trade openness, and inflation) as well as geographic and historical variables related to colonialism.
24. Azar, E. 1990. *The management of protracted social conflict: Theory and cases*, 7. Aldershot: Dartmouth.
25. Slim, H. 2008. *Killing civilians: Method, madness and morality in war*, 123. New York: Columbia University Press.
26. Wilmer, F. 2002. *The social construction of man, the state and war: Identity, conflict and violence in the former yugoslavia*, 63. New York: Routledge.
27. Ashmore, R.D., L. Jussim, and D. Wilder. 2001. *Social identity, intergroup conflict and conflict reduction*, 66. New York: Oxford University Press.
28. Esman, M. 1994. *Ethnic Politics*, 14. Ithaca: Cornell University Press.
29. Merskin, Deborah. 2004. The construction of arabs as enemies: Post September 11 discourse of George W. Bush. *Mass Communication & Society* 7(2): 157–175.
30. Keen, Sam. 1986. Faces of the enemy: Reflections of hostile imagination. Bowker: 13.
31. Brewer, Marilynn. 2001. "Ingroup identification and intergroup conflict". In Social Identity, Intergroup conflict and Conflict Reduction.
32. Slim, Hugo. 2010. *Killing civilians: Method, madness and morality in war*. New York: Columbia University Press, 6.

33. Bartos, Ottmar, Wehr, Paul, 2002. Understanding conflict theory. Cambridge: Cambridge University Press, 131.
34. Hogg, M.A., and K.D. Williams. 2000. From I to we: Social identity and the collective self. *Group Dynamics: Theory, Research, and Practice* 4: 81.
35. Simpson, George. 1993. *Durkheim, Emile*. Trans. The Division of Labour in Society. New York: The Free Press.
36. Kenneth Allan, Kenneth D. Allan. 2005. Explorations in classical sociological theory: Seeing the social world. Pine Forge Press, 137.
37. McDougaall, William. 1920. The group Mind. New York: Arno Press, 1973 [©1920].
38. Lewin, K. 1948. Resolving social conflicts; selected papers on group dynamics. In ed. Gertrude W. Lewin, 165. New York: Harper & Row.
39. Kaufmann, Stuart, and Modern Hatreds. 2001. *The symbolic politics of ethnic war*. Ithaca: Cornell University Press.
40. Avruch, Kevin. 1998. *Culture and conflict resolution*, 10. Washington DC: United States Institute for Peace.
41. Avruch, Kevin. 2013. *Context and pretext in conflict resolution: Culture, identity, power and practice*, 12. Boulder: Paradigm Publishers.
42. Braude. 2003. *The New Iraq*, 19. New York: Basic Books.
43. Luomi, M. 2008. *Sectarian identities or geopolitics? The regional Shi'a-Sunni divide in the middle East*. Helskinki: Finnish Institute of International Affairs.
44. Rubin, M. 2006. Iran against the Arabs. The Wall Street Journal.
45. Stansfield, G. 2009. What were the causes and consequences of Iraq's descent into violence after the initial invasion? Submission to the Iraq inquiry, 1–9. Retrieved from http://www.iraqinquiry.org.uk/media/37048/stansfield-submission.pdf.
46. Tripp, C. 2009. *A history of Iraq*, 296. New York: Cambridge University Press.
47. Avruch, K. 2001. Culture and conflict. In *Conflict: From analysis to intervention*, ed. S. Cheldelin, D. Druckman, and L. Fast, 143. New York: Continuum.
48. Silvernman, A. 2009. Religion and politics in Iraq: What kind of sectarianism really exists? Informed comment. Retrieved from http://www.juancole.com/2009/08/religion-and-politics-in-iraq-what-type.html.
49. Baram, A. 1997. Neo-tribalism in Iraq: Saddam Husayn's tribal policies, 1991–1996. *International Journal of Middle Eastern Studies* 29: 1–31.
50. Khan, J. 2007. The Iraqi tribal structure. Perspectives on terrorism. Perspectives on terrorism 1(1). Retreived from http://www.terrorismanalysts.com/pt/index.php/pot/article/view/2/html.
51. Silverman, A.L. 2009. Religion and politics in Iraq: What types of sectarianism really exists? Informed comment: Thoughts on the middle East, history and religion. Retreived from http://www.juancole.com/2009/08/religion-and-politics-in-iraq-what-type.html.
52. Wardi, A. 2008. *Understanding Iraq: Society, culture and personality*, 115. New York: Edwin Mellon Press.
53. Marr, P. 2008. *The modern history of Iraq*, II. Boulder: Westview Press.
54. Mattingly, T. 2007. Arabs, tribes, Iraq and Islam. Retreived at http://www.patheos.com/blogs/getreligion/2007/01/arabs-tribes-iraq-and-islam/.
55. Jesmeen, K. 2007. The Iraqi tribal structure: Background and influence on counter-terrorism. Perspectives on Terrorism 1(1).
56. Tripp, C. 2007. *A history of Iraq*, 3rd ed, 3. New York: Cambrige Univeristy Press.

Chapter 3
Conflict Drivers

Abstract This chapter uses conflict analysis, a method of discerning the sources and dynamics of violent conflict, to assess key drivers of sectarian violence in Iraq following the US invasion. Violence did not erupt automatically, but rather was driven by a variety of factors at global, regional, and national levels of analysis. The most significant conflict drivers are found at the state level. Bad governance and poor economic conditions created a security dilemma for Iraqis so that for many, day-to-day governance revolved primarily around family members, tribes, religion, and the surrounding people of an area, and only secondarily toward the institution of the state. Additional primary factors included purposeful actions by internal and external actors to foment violence and a series of critical mistakes made by the US and Coalition forces.

KeyWords Conflict analysis • Conflict drivers • Sectarianism • Global War on Terror (GWOT) • Baathism • Al Quaeda in Iraq • Mahdi army • Security dilemma • Governance • Local/private authorities • Horizontal legitimacy • Vertical legitimacy • Elite strategies • Coalition Provisional Authority (CPA) • United States Agency for International Development (USAID)

Of war men ask the outcome, not the cause.

Seneca

Sectarianism according to the *Oxford English Dictionary* is "adherence or excessive attachment to, or undue favoring of, a particular sect or party, especially in religion". As Chap. 1 made clear, sectarian violence is no simple "upswelling of

A. C. Carpenter, *Community Resilience to Sectarian Violence in Baghdad*,
Peace Psychology Book Series, DOI: 10.1007/978-1-4614-8812-5_3,

primordial religious solidarities" [1]. Its causes are complex. As seminal conflict researcher Louis Kriesberg noted,

> The paths of large-scale conflicts are profoundly shaped by the structure of the relations between the opposing collectivities [including] differences in population sizes, economic resources, coercive capabilities, and cultural patterns of conduct. They also include the nature and degree of integration between adversaries in economic, social, and cultural domains [2].

Fortunately, frameworks for analyzing the causes of violent conflict have become increasingly sophisticated. Conflict analysis is a central method in the transdisciplinary field of conflict resolution, which studies the sources and dynamics of social conflict and applies research-informed methods to prevent and interrupt violence and build sustainable peace in post-conflict societies [3]. Conflict analysis involves assessing key conflict factors (structural, proximate, and triggering causes) at different levels of analysis (global, regional, state, local) and places a priority on understanding the actors involved—their interests, relational history, and capacities for violence or peace.

Oliver Ramsbotham, Tom Woodhouse, and Hugh Miall, authors of *Contemporary Conflict Resolution*, developed one of my favorite analytical frameworks. They mined the literatures on interstate war, civil war, environmental and resource conflicts, peace studies, global conflicts (i.e., Huntington's "clash of civilizations"), and international political economy to develop a comprehensive framework for analyzing sources of conflict. The framework invites analysis at five different levels—global, regional, state, group, and individual—and I have used it here to generate insight into the underlying tensions in Iraqi society before and directly after the US invasion.

Global and Regional Levels

Global forces are the furthest removed from the street battles that played out in Baghdad, and I touched on some in the last chapter, but they are worth reiterating. The Global War on Terror (GWOT) provided the narrative and conceptual rationale for the US invasion of Iraq, as part of a global military and political struggle against terrorist organizations and regimes believed to support them. The US has traditionally been concerned with Middle East security given Israel's political significance to the US, the economic importance of oil-producing nations on global economic markets, concerns over a nuclear Iran, and the pivotal role of Saudi Arabia in stabilizing global oil supply.

Another global source of particular conflicts including the Iraq war—though not the primary or only source—is a cultural gap between the Islamic world and the West. "Western leadership, especially in the United States, strongly plays down the reality of deep-seated cultural differences. The tendency is to see the other parties as thinking, valuing, and acting by the same customary rules we do. That assumption could not be further from reality and is rich in troublesome surprises" [4]. GWOT is an outgrowth of that gap and the cultural and economic hegemony of Western powers following the World War II. As Coates noted,

> …the end of WWI played a significant factor in bringing about hostility and conflict in Islam, since the post-war settlements usually involved arbitrary, unnatural geographic boundaries and the arbitrary imposition of governments. For example, the British forced a monarchy on Iraq…a more or less arbitrary form of government, with no popular support [4].

This set of conditions eventually led to, through a series of military coups, the rise to ascendancy of the Baath Party whose influence spread throughout the Middle East.

Baathism represented a regional force by itself. Exercised through particular leaders, the movement had regional consequences, the two most dramatic being the Iran–Iraq war and the Persian Gulf War. Knock-on effects of the Persian Gulf War included increased hostility toward the West and sympathy for Iraq as a nation seen as "standing up" to Western hegemony. Baathist ideology has also been the cause for conflicts between Iraq and Syria. "Ba'ath ideology—which calls for a sweeping renewal, rebirth and regeneration of the Arab world—does not lend itself to *two* centers of power any more than communism did. Baghdad and Damascus…have often attacked each other on ideological grounds, and their conflict has spread to other Baathist parties in other Arab countries" [5].

Iraq's external relations with other neighbors were a key reason for tensions with Western powers. Hussein had aided the Iranian dissident group Mujahadeen-e-Khalq and the Turkish separatist group called Kurdistan Workers Party (or the PKK). Iraq was also believed by the US to have supported the Islamist Hamas movement and reportedly channeled money to the families of Palestinian suicide bombers [6]. Neighboring Iran was perhaps the main regional source of tension. Iran supported both Shiite and Sunni militias, and even though their motives had more to do with finding proxies to fight the US than fomenting internal discord,[1] the operational support exacerbated relationships between Sunni and Shi'a Iraqis after 2003. Despite what many Sunnis in Iraq think, Shiite Iraqis view Iran with great suspicion. Iraq's Shiite majority identify themselves as Arab, whereas Iran's residents are predominantly Persian. Even Shiite militias supported by Iranians do not necessarily like or affiliate themselves with Iranians.[2]

Other regional actors supported non-state armed actors in Iraq's civil war. JAM's early recruits were reportedly foreigners recruited from Kuwait and Saudi Arabia and trained by Hezbollah operatives from Lebanon [7]. AQI's strategies were also driven and carried out by foreign fighters, primarily from Saudi Arabia, Libya, Syria, Yemen, and Algeria (see Footnote 2). The foreign fighters introduced the tactics of suicide bombing and beheading [7], financed the organization through extensive

---

[1] Ibrahim al-Marashi rightly pointed this out during an early reading of this manuscript.

[2] Wikileaks Cable, Iraq: Reference ID: 06BAGHDAD1570. ANTI-IRANIAN Shi'a CLERICS SPEAK OUT. Retrieved from http://www.wweek.com/portland/article-18361- iraq_anti_iranian_Shi'a_clerics_speak_out.html.

regional smuggling networks and access to global capital [8], promoted sectarian violence against civilians [9], and were guided by Zarqawi's radical goal of establishing and Sunni Islamist state, different from the goals of the local Sunni leaders who supported AQI to resist the foreign occupation.

State-Level Sources

Conflict drivers at the state level are related to the performance of domestic economic, political, and security institutions. "Most states which experience protracted social conflict tend to be characterized by incompetent, parochial, fragile and authoritarian governments that fail to satisfy basic human needs" [8]. Closed, authoritarian systems tend to generate significant resentment over time. "For many conflict analysts the unequal distribution of power, status, or access to goods and services or whatever else possible adversaries consider desirable and is widely regarded as one of the primary bases of social conflicts of all kinds" [9]. Changes in economic and social conditions serve as *mediating conditions* that "sharpen identity and prepare the terrain for violent conflict" [10], conflict that is particularly likely to erupt in states with a history of violent oppression and/or those undergoing a political transition.

Iraq certainly met these criteria before the invasion. Iraqis suffered under a dictatorship in which individual, civil, and human rights had no meaning, where resource allocation was based on who one knew and public services—healthcare, education, security, and waste management—were mismanaged, if managed at all. The economic sanctions imposed after the 1991 Gulf War further undermined Iraqi state capacity. Iraq's ability to export oil and further develop its oil fields was undercut; basic medicines and water purification technologies were banned, leading to massive upticks in disease and malnutrition. Sanctions forced factories to close and led to shortages in raw materials used in production, leading to spikes in unemployment.

States weak on these dimensions create what is called a security dilemma for groups living inside them. When groups do not trust the state to provide security and essential services, they typically find ways to provide it for themselves. This necessity, however, fractures larger communities (potential nations) into smaller collectivities (collectives). In situations of heightened insecurity, "people seek security by identifying with something close to their experiences over which they have control", and that unit of identity might be a clan, ethnicity, religion, or geographic affiliation [11]. Many Iraqis came to view the state as the enemy of the people, not a guardian the people's interests and welfare. As a result, people's felt solidarity went first towards family, tribe, religious institutions, and their community and only secondarily to the state [12].

Most of the people we talked to over the course of the study confirmed that "leaving the state out of it" was the smart thing to do. Internal governance existed in a variety of informal and local institutions in all areas. While all areas reported the presence tribal elders and other third parties, Shi'a-dominant neighborhoods seemed to rely seldom or not all on formal authorities like elected officials, police, or courts.

> *Dura*: I can't remember a single fight that the police or sheiks had to interfere to solve it. [Car crashes] were solved instantly without the need for the police…The police never played part in such things.

> *Kuraait*: Most problems are solved between the people; this is similar to the situation of electricity; it is much better and easier than resorting to the state. Traffic accidents are often solved between the people; traffic police often complicate the matter for you. I remember a child who was hit by a car in my neighborhood; they took the child to the hospital and he had a minor injury. They didn't ask for the intervention of the police.

> *Karada*: People in the neighborhood used to solve problems without returning to the state. They helped each others, particularly with regard to poor families. Members of the society informed the rich people about the presence of poor families. Rich people used to collect money to help the poor. Sometime a person dies or has to undergo an operation so the people used to cooperate to help them financially.

> *Palestine Street*: The people themselves solved most problems. A man in the neighborhood was detained for two years because a secret informer wrote a report against him. He was released recently; we told him that he should file a complaint against the secret informer so that he would get his right through the law. The man refused and he decided to solve the matter directly; he said that he will not get anything from the judiciary.

We cannot know whether this individual from Palestine Street was guilty and therefore happy to leave well enough alone, or whether he was innocent but so distrusted the government that he chose to forgo restitution through formal channels. However, the widespread inability to rely on formal channels for conflict resolution and justice described in other areas both reflect and reinforce weak societal-level institutions. In many of the stories, you will hear, "solving things directly" involved dialogues and local councils that were convened to resolve disputes.

Like many weak states, Iraq's internal political regime was so dysfunctional that private authorities emerged to provide public services. Most states exist in a state of negotiated sovereignty where "multiple authorities may exist, each sovereign in its own realm and continuously renegotiating the extent of its authority" [13]. However, Iraq's political system was dysfunctional enough to invite private authorities—tribal and familial rulers—to play major role in social and political life. Hussein's regime was low in what social scientists call horizontal and vertical legitimacy or cohesion. Vertical legitimacy or cohesion refers to levels of social inequity, and Iraqi society had extreme disparities. Social and economic privileges were bestowed narrowly on the Sunni-dominated Baath Party, as well as the tribes of Tikrit and most importantly on Saddam's own clan of *Albu Nasir*. The Baath Party maintained control of the country for more than 20 years, granting disproportionate economic, political, social, and cultural control to Iraq's Arab Sunni minority.

Essentially, the Ba'ath Party was an institution that functioned as the eyes and ears of the Hussein regime. The party essentially took over all major government systems: the military, police, state and local ministries, and professional associations. It even had the power to propose, approve, and disapprove marriages! [14].

Joseph Braude wrote bluntly about the brutality of political control by the Baath Party—detentions, interrogations, torture, executions "as well as the complex web of serial snitches whose reports helped label colleagues and neighbors 'enemies of the state'" [15]. A respondent from Shi'a neighborhood Kuraiit recalled a terrifying incident from his childhood:

> I lived in a poor area. Many young people of the neighborhood were detained during the tenure of Saddam. We were students when suddenly a number of cars stopped and civilians came out and caught us; one of them grabbed me and he asked about my name. Then they told me that I had to go with them and said "There is no problem, it may be just a mix up or confusion about my name". They were catching other individuals, but one of them escaped and they shot him, but he fled. They took us on foot till we reached a small door; they blindfolded us and guided us through the door. They put us in a small dark room; it was 2 × 2 m and they handcuffed us. We hear them joking about us and about prayer. They opened the door and said that we are wanted. One of them said that he has a list of names. He called the names and took the people mentioned in his list. Only four of us remained; the man said that he was sorry for the inconvenience, but that was part of his duty; he said that he apologizes for what happened because of the mix up in names. They were after a person called Ali Hussein Abid Ali; my name is Ali Hussein Jawad. The man asked an officer to drive us to the nearest location, but he told him to hide his rank. They drove us back from the Suspension Bridge and released us near Al Harriri High school.

It is highly probable that the preexisting relationship between Ba'ath Party officials and area residents influenced the onset of sectarian attitudes and behaviors. For one thing, informants and spies targeted poor Shiite neighborhoods. In Sadr City "Ba'ath dominated the region", our respondent told us. In Sadr City, informants operated with the impunity to arrest and torture ordinary people. According to a Sadr City resident, "The Ba'athists they were influential and they used to report on the people. A friend of my father was so close to us and one day he wrote a report against us. He said that we didn't defend the country and the president…No one loved them. They were responsible for the detention of many people." It is not surprising therefore that "nowhere perhaps was the party loathed as intensely as it was in Sadr City. 'Oh Baath Party' read some recent graffiti 'There is no place to hide'" [16].

In the wealthier Shiite neighborhood Zafaraniyya, the Baath Party did not seem to play as negative a role.[3] When asked why not, the respondent replied:

> All the people of the neighborhood were government employees. The Ba'ath Party was active in the poor neighborhoods. Ba'athists used to flex their muscles against poor people. They didn't have a role in other neighborhoods. They weren't capable of pushing us to join Nakhwa forces and things like that. Ba'athists easily controlled farmers and free lance laborers in the poor regions.

Socioeconomic conditions were significantly higher in Zafarinyya than Sadr City, even though levels of economic and educational attainment were below average for the otherwise wealthy Karada administrative division in which Zafaraniyya

[3] Interview, Baghdad 2010.

is located. In Karada, the respondent described the Baath in a somewhat more benign way:

> Ba'athists used to dominate the neighborhood; Certain Ba'athists had responsibilities: you go and stamp your papers from them, file complaints over water/electricity problems, things like that.

Iraqis joined the Ba'ath Party out of fear or to ascend the only social ladder in pre-2003 Iraqi society. "Like any ruling party, the Ba'ath attracted some of Iraq's best and brightest who joined for the same reasons that ambitious people everywhere are drawn to the locus of power and wealth" [17]. The Shi'a Palestine Street resident spoke of Ba'athists with this sense of forgiveness.

> People didn't really like the Ba'athists. The people of the neighborhood used to fear and respect those officials. Most of them were ordinary persons like us and the chance came for them to occupy important positions of authority. The neighborhood used to feel proud of those individuals because they were considered as the sons of the neighborhood and they helped the neighborhood by offering jobs, providing information about detainees, and by reenlisting the deserters to the army.

Ba'athists also were not feared in mixed Bayaa where, according to the respondent, "our Ba'athists were very different. They used to warn the deserters once or twice; they tell them to leave the neighborhood when they arrange raids. There was a high level of trust".[4]

Horizontal legitimacy or cohesion refers to the strength of the social glue that ties people together, on the assumption that feeling of togetherness matter tremendously to the long-term health of a society [18]. The history of relations between groups and their perceptions of each other (vis-à-vis cultural, political, and economic discrimination) influences the likelihood of violent conflict [19]. Chapter 4 has more to say about horizontal cohesion—for now suffice it to say the majority of Iraqi society pre-2003, while not fractured and divisive, were loyal to local organizations—clans, tribes, large families, and political parties. Hussein's overthrow created new political, social, and economic spaces in which "freedom" could be exploited by those local, preexisting organizations that had resources, networks, information, militias, and also legitimacy to become the new sovereign powers in the parts of the country in which they were based.

Elite/Individual Level

Finally, sources of sectarian violence can be understood at the individual level of elite strategies. Elite strategies are tactics used by opportunistic individuals or groups in times of political turmoil, who purposefully provoke ethnic conflict because it serves their purposes. Saddam Hussein engaged in this type of political maneuvering during his decades of rule. As already noted, many Sunnis held

---

[4] Field interview, Bayaa, Baghdad, July 2010.

privileged positions over other ethnic and religious groups in the Hussein regime including employment preferences and higher salaries. Shi'a and Kurdish populations were systematically targeted for violent repression, including the state-designed ethnic cleansing of the rural areas of Kurdistan in the late 1980s (the Anfal Campaign),and the brutal suppression of the southern uprising (*intifadah*) in 1991 (which had very distinctive Shi'a references), and the equally ruthless quashing of the Kurdish uprising (*rapareen*).

Elite strategies also refer to important blunders made by the US and Coalition forces. Whether intentional or not, key oversights and decisions by International Security Assistance Forces (ISAF) and the Coalition Provisional Authority (CPA) strengthened the sectarian divide as it evolved in post-2003 Iraq. Journalist and author Nir Rosen has argued that "sectarian identities did not become politicized until the Americans occupied their country, treating the Sunnis as the bad guys and the Shiites as the good guys" [20, 21]. Other early mistakes by the Coalition included "not sending enough troops to secure the country, the absence of a nation-building doctrine or transition plan, dissolving the Iraqi armed forces and purging the civil service of mid-level Ba'ath party members, among others" [22]. Further hampering efforts was a lack of accountability and mismanagement by the U.S. officials. One mistake that occurred early on and came to hinder reconstruction and contribute into support for the insurgency was the Coalition's reorganization of the Iraqi political system. Gareth Stanfeld concluded:

> In short—the unpreparedness of the Coalition was largely to blame for creating an environment that permitted insurgent activities and facilitated the consolidation of power into the hands of communal-based (whether sectarian, ethnic, tribal, or local) actors.... This misreading of Iraqi society and politics fed into the policy-planning process of the US and UK, resulting in some core assumptions being made. The inaccuracy of these assumptions would turn the Coalition from having proactive to reactive agency and create a situation in which the Coalition was always several steps behind insurgent groups, political actors outside the process mandated by the Coalition, and external actors pursuing their own interests [23].

In addition, a largely urban-based insurgency that was not easily recognizable and blended in with civilians led to a high degree of uncertainty surrounding identification of the enemy.[5] In turn, this led to "...a persistent trend for response with heavy firepower...leading to high civilian casualties" [24]. This contributed greatly to early support, not only because of the civilian casualties but also because of the effect this had on those who survived and were affected [25]. Indeed, the more people injured, the more individuals had a direct personal experience with trauma caused by the foreign-led Coalition. The ongoing killing of civilians and ongoing occupation continued to contribute to the insurgency over time.

Aid organizations also made blunders. Heather Coyne, Senior Program Officer at the U.S. Institute of Peace describes early and well-intentioned efforts that had adverse effects. An early objective was to reinstate the United Nations'

---

[5] I am grateful to Jon Conroe, my former student and a Navy Chaplain who served in Iraq, for pointing this out.

World Food Program, which supplied monthly food baskets to Iraqi families. Coyne recalled how the Ministry of Trade, WFP's partner in the Food Program, had approached the local USAID office with complaints that food warehouses had been taken over by local militias who refused to relinquish control.

> So we were assigned to reach out to the militias and restore control of the warehouses to the Ministry of Trade. But once we started talking to the militias, it turned out that these vigilantes were actually volunteers…a well organized Islamic organization who had stepped in when they saw the looting, and organized themselves to guard the food stock sites and very effectively too…. These folks were proud of their role, how they had run off the thieves and looters, and made sure that the food was distributed to the community during the crises…the Shi'a militia leaders were telling us that the Ministry of Trade wasn't being fair in how it handled the resources…some Shi'a had been excluded from ration lists under Saddam and weren't able to get back on, a local community was passed over for jobs and warehouses in Shi'a neighborhoods, the food agents in some areas were corrupt and cheating people…so the militias had taken over what looked like to us a security role, but what they were really concerned about was governance.

USAID struck a deal with the militia leaders, promising to hold the Ministry of Trade accountable for equity and food quality if the militias would return control of the warehouses. Unfortunately, it was an impossible promise to keep; for one thing, it required too many tasks: checking on food rations, checking whether particular families had been reinstated to the list, checking on food welfare facilities and investigating complains about food agents, equality, and corruption. USAID field staff could not keep track of all the parties and whether they were keeping up their end of the bargain. "We shouldn't have tried to fix the *outcome* of governance," Heather reflected in her podcast, "but the *process*. The real key was to connect [the militias] to the new councils, the new local governance structures so that they could pursue their issues over time within the context of a democratic system rather than relying on us to solve problems in a way that we couldn't sustain for very long." When USAID could not follow through with their promises of equity and accountability, the militia leaders became even more disenchanted with the ministry, the government, and with USAID. According to Coyne's account, "even though they no longer physically controlled the warehouses, they started exercising their own parallel control over what was happening in the community. And there was the beginning of the Mahdi Army."

Of course, the Mahdi Army did not coalesce primarily due to disenchantment with USAID and the Ministry of Trade. Non-state elites like Muqtada al Sadr played definitive roles in bringing together armed militias under one banner. The Mahdi Army was the first armed group to form following the end of Saddam Hussein's regime and was established in April 2003. Al-Qaida in Iraq (AQI) was not far behind, led by Zarqawi, a Jordanian who adapted the Jihadist organization to which he belonged—Tawhid wal-Jihad—to the Iraqi context.

Zarqawi's early goals included armed and ideological opposition to the U.S. and foreign involvement in Iraq. Sadr's goals were similar; he opposed opposition forces and distrusted their involvement in the formation of the provisional government. JAM's first major attack was launched against Coalition forces a year later, on April 4, 2004. Later that year in November, the Mahdi Army battled Coalition forces in Najaf for three weeks, during which hundreds of people were killed. The first *sectarian* attack appears to have been in 2006 when, according to the National Counterterrorism Center, JAM attacked several neighborhoods in Sadr City.

However, Zarqawi's goals included the overthrow of the new Iraqi government and establishment of an Islamic caliphate. Early on, al-Zarqawi sought an alliance with Osama bin Laden's al-Qaeda organization after which (from late 2004 and into 2005) AQI's strategy shifted from attacking coalition forces to attacking Shiite civilians, first in western Anbar province and then in Baghdad's mixed sectarian and Shi'a-dominant neighborhoods. His explicit aim was to provoke sectarian violence, despite warnings from bin Laden's then deputy Ayman al-Zawhari that such a strategy undermined the overarching goal of ousting coalition forces and establishing a pan-Islamic state.[1] Zarqawi did not heed those warnings, and violence against Shiite religious leaders, mosques, religious gatherings, and civilians increased in 2005 "as part of [the] larger goal of using sectarian violence to provoke a civil war."

Attacks by AQI against Iraqi Security Forces (ISF)[6] also increased significantly toward the end of 2004, and in 2005, targeted political assassinations increased to "include local political and religious leaders, the heads of local police forces and ministry officials from Baghdad". These assassinations may well have been designed to disrupt the judicial and political process, and they intensified in the periods leading up to elections. But, Sunni Iraqis increasingly had an axe to grind. They had been systematically targeted by Iraqi Security Forces (ISF) in Diyala Province, where the Iraqi Army had conducted two widespread detention operations, for which there was no intelligence or evidence. During those operations, they detained 900 individuals of which 898 were Sunni. A report for the Institute for the Study of War concluded that the sweeps led to the impression of the Army as a sectarian organization [26].

Moreover, then Interior Minister Bayan Jabar incorporated the Wolf Brigade, a Badr Corps organization with a reputation for sectarian cleansing (previously discussed) into the National Police Force that operated in Diyala.[7] These early actions created a perception that the Iraqi Army and Iraqi Police operated with a sectarian bias, beliefs that fueled support for al-Qaeda. Perception became reality when the U.S. forces discovered a torture chamber and 173 severely abused (mostly Sunni) detainees in a facility administered by the Interior Ministry of the Shiite-led government.

---

[6] Iraqi security forces is a U.S. Department of Defense term for all security forces of the Federal government of Iraq including the Ministry of Defense (which oversees the Iraqi Armed Forces—Army, Airforce and Navy) and the Ministry of Interior (which oversees Police, Facilities Protection, and Border Enforcement.

[7] The Badr Corps is an example of one organization that was believed to operate according to Iranian interests; the Shi'a organization had been exiled in Iran for two decades during Saddam Hussein's rule. Several of the stories below make references to Iranian support for Shi'a militias, evidence for which is documented in the War Logs, a cache of classified documents released by Wikileaks containing military intelligence reports that Shi'a Iraqi militias received training and weapons from Iran's Revolutionary Guards.

In 2005, al-Zarqawi called for a comprehensive war against Shi'a Iraqis "wherever and whenever they are found" [27]. Although al-Sadr called for restraint, interviews performed by the International Crisis Group show that "the calls against Sunnis started to get louder as the ferocity of suicide bombings and the number of casualties increased" [28]. The bombing of the holy Shi'a il-Askari (Golden) shrine, February 22, 2006, represented the tipping point in sectarian violence [15]. However, it was the al-Askari Mosque bombing (also referred to as the Samarra bombing) that triggered the greatest uptick in sectarian violence. The bombing was followed by retaliatory violence with over 1,000 people killed in the days following the bombing—by some counts, on the first day alone [29].

References

1. Ussama, M. 2000. *The Culture of Sectarianism: Community, history, and violence in nineteenth-century ottoman lebanon*, 52 Berkeley: University of California Press.
2. Kriesberg, L. 2003. *Constructive conflicts: From escalation to resolution*. Lanham, MD.
3. Berkovitch, J., V. Kremenyuk, and W.I. Zartman. 2009. *The sage handbook of conflict resolution*. New York: Sage Publications.
4. Coates, J.F. 2004. The roots of conflict between the United States and Iraq. In *Trade Towers War Clouds*, ed. Shostak, A, 5. New York: Chelsea House Publishers.
5. Cordesman, Anthony. 1997. Iraq: Sanctions and beyond, 195–196. Boulder, CO: Westview Press. Emphasis mine.
6. Council on Foreign Relations. 2005. Terrorism Havens Iraq. Retrieved from http://www.cfr.org/iraq/terrorism-havens-iraq/p9513.
7. Roggio, B. 2008. Mugniyah behind establishment of Mahdi army. *The Long War Journal*. Retrieved from http://www.longwarjournal.org.
8. Ramsbotham, O., T. Woodhouse, and H. Miall. 2008. *Contemporary conflict resolution*, 86. Cambridge, UK: Polity Press.
9. Kriesberg, L., and B.W. Dayton. 2012. *Constructive conflicts: From escalation to resolution*, 37. Lanham, MD: Rowman and Littlefield Publishers.
10. Stein, J.S. 1996. Image, identity and conflict resolution. In *Managing Global Chaos*, eds. Crocker, C., Hampson, F., and Aall, P., 93–111. Washington, D.C.: United States Institute of Peace Press.
11. Lederach, J.P. 1997. *Building peace: Sustainable reconciliation in divided societies*, 13. Washington, DC: United States Institute of Peace.
12. Dodge, T. 2005. *Iraqi transitions: From regime change to state collapse*, Third World Quarterly 26 (4–5):705–721.
13. Lake, D. 2013. Practical sovereignty and post-conflict governance. In *Conflict management and global governance in an age of awakening*, eds. P. Aall, C. Croker, and F. Hampson. Forthcoming, cited with author's permission.
14. Sassoon, J. 2012. *Saddam Hussein's Ba'th Party: Inside an authoritarian regime*. Cambridge, MA: Cambridge University Press.
15. Braud, J. 2003. *The New Iraq: Rebuilding the country for its people, the Middle East, and the world*, 57–58. New York: Basic Books.
16. Wilson, S. 2003. Iraqis Killing Former Ba'ath Party members. *Washington Post*.
17. Braud, J. 2003. *The New Iraq: Rebuilding the country for its people, the Middle East, and the World*, 61. New York: Basic Books.
18. Kaplan, S. 2012. *Fixing Fragile States: A new paradigm for development*. Westport, CO: Praeger.
19. Brown, M. 2001. Ethnic and internal conflicts: Causes and implications. In *Turbulent peace: The challenges of managing international conflict*, ed. C. Crocker, and F.O. Hampson, 211. Washington, D.C.: United States Institute of Peace Press.

20. Rosen, N. 2006. Anatomy of a Civil War. *Boston Review* 31. Retrieved from http://bostonreview.net/BR31.6/rosen.php.
21. Papagianni, K. 2007. State building and transitional politics in Iraq: The perils of a top-down transition. *International Studies Perspectives* 8(3): 253–271.
22. Gairdner, D. 2012. *Risk and violence in Iraq's new sectarian balance*. Norwegian Peace building Resource Centre, 3. Retrieved from http://www.peacebuilding.no/Themes/Armed-violence-and-conflict-in-fragile-settings/Fragile-states-and-peacebuilding-in-the-new-global-context/Publications/Risk-and-violence-in-Iraq-s-new-sectarian-balance/(language)/eng-US.
23. Stanfeld, G. 2007. What were the causes and consequences of Iraq's descent into violence after the initial invasion? Submission to the Iraq Inquiry. Retrieved from http://www.iraqinquiry.org.uk/media/37048/stansfield-submission.pdf.
24. Rogers, P. 2005. The Iraq Impasse. *Oxford Research Group International Security Monthly Briefing*, 128. Retrieved from http://www.isn.ethz.ch.
25. Rogers, Paul. 2005. The Iraq Impasse. *Oxford Research Group International Security Monthly Briefing*, 140. Retrieved from http://www.isn.ethz.ch.
26. Kagan, K. 2007. Iraq Report. *Institute for the Study of War*, 3. Retrieved from http://www.understandingwar.org/iraq.
27. Fishman, B. 2008. *Bombers, bank accounts and bleedout: Al Qaeda's road in and out of Iraq*. West Point, New York: Combating Terrorism Center.
28. International Crisis Group. 2003. Iraq's Shi'as under occupation. Retrieved from,www.crisis group.org.
29. Knickmeyer, E. 2011. Blood on our Hands: What Wikileaks revealed about the Iraqi Death Toll. Foreign Policy. Retrieved from http://www.foreignpolicy.com.

Chapter 4
Conflict Escalation: The Sharpening of Sectarian Identity

Abstract This chapter describes the ways in which conflicts escalate through increases in the intensity of conflict and severity of tactics used to wage it. Escalation is driven by and reinforces three enduring changes: in people's psychological states, in the way groups function—both internally and vis-à-vis each other—and in the structure and function of the larger, heterogeneous community. This chapter integrates first-hand accounts by Iraqi residents with the rich empirical literature on conflict escalation dynamics to map the trajectory of violence of Baghdad's neighborhoods. It lays the conceptual groundwork for understanding conflict resilience as a process of managing conflict escalation, thus limiting the formation of sectarian militants within bounded areas, and preventing violent sectarian attacks from militant groups outside those areas.

Keywords Conflict escalation • Violence • Psychological changes • Hostile attitudes • Dehumanization • Deindividuation • Perceptual bias • Group identity • Zero-sum perceptions • Group polarization • Group cohesion • Community polarization • Self-defense groups • Sectarian militias • Al Qaeda in Iraq • Mahdi army • Civilian casualties

"You cannot simultaneously prevent and prepare for war."
Albert Einstein

I have defined conflict resilience as a process of managing conflict escalation so as to limit the formation of sectarian militants within bounded areas, and at the same time preventing violent attacks from groups outside those areas. In order to understand what "managing conflict escalation" means precisely, this chapter focuses on the specific processes by which conflict escalation occurs.

Escalation refers to an increase in the intensity of conflict and severity in tactics used [1]. It is accompanied by a series of transformations; for example, the number of issues in contention increases, each party becomes increasingly absorbed in

A. C. Carpenter, *Community Resilience to Sectarian Violence in Baghdad*, Peace Psychology Book Series, DOI: 10.1007/978-1-4614-8812-5_4,

and committed to the struggle, specific issues turn into grandiose positions, and motivation shifts from wanting to meet goals, to wanting to win over the other, and finally to a generalized desire to inflict pain [2]. Conflicts involving violence are particularly prone to increases in the use and severity of violent tactics [3].

A common model of conflict escalation is a "life cycle" metaphor, which proposes that conflicts escalate through stages. Early stages involve awareness of social tensions and differences between parties. The issues in contention become defined, and people begin to take sides. As the situation worsens, parties express open hostility—"we" and "they" become enemies to each other, and violence enters the relationship. Stages of de-escalation are marked by cessation of violence and movements toward resolution of settlement. The life cycle is sometimes depicted as a bell curve, the slope of escalation rising upward from low levels of tension to its peak at the height of open hostilities, and down again as conflict is resolved.

Unfortunately, this view is overly simplistic. The life cycle model of conflict escalation implies an unrealistically linear sequence of escalation phases and "neglect[s] the fact that civil wars and inter-ethnic disputes are made up of a multiplicity of embedded conflicts, which might exhibit properties of several escalation or de-escalation stages simultaneously" [4]. Escalation is a more complex phenomenon that is associated with specific stressors—aversive circumstances that threaten the well-being and functioning of people, groups, and whole communities. It is driven by and reinforces three enduring changes: (1) changes in people's psychological states, (2) changes in the way groups function, and (3) changes in a larger heterogeneous community. These three structural changes reinforce each other in a cyclical and destructive pattern, driving adversarial behavior to increasingly irrational and destructive ends. Perhaps the most destructive community-level change is polarization between large identity groups, such as created Baghdad's ethnic enclaves [5].

Psychological Changes

As happened in 2003 in Iraq, economic and political instability can produce psychological (cognitive and emotional) changes that mark the beginning of intergroup conflict escalation [5]. Two changes in psychological state include (1) emotional changes and (2) hostile attitudes, perceptions, and goals. Emotional changes include enhanced feelings of blame, anger, fear, and perceived threat to image, reputation, or adequacy. Exposure to violence (both potential or actual) triggers these emotional changes by making it easier to blame and to misconstrue benign or good intentions [2], and by skewing the perceived cost-benefit ratios of risky, conflict provoking behaviors [6]. While these are temporary changes, they exert a powerful effect on individual and group behavior.

Hostile attitudes, perceptions, and goals are longer-lived psychological changes that affect the long-term relationship between groups. Pruitt and Kim describe seven effects of hostile attitudes and perceptions: They make it easier to blame the "Other" for ones negative experiences; they lead to one to interpret ambiguous behavior in the worst possible light; they diminish inhibitions against aggressive behavior; they block communication; reduce empathy; foster zero-sum thinking; and "finally, when hostile perceptions grow really severe, Other comes to be viewed as a diabolical enemy" [2, pp. 108–109]. A Bayaa resident described the effect of psychological changes on behavior by Shiite militias.

> Shiite gunmen started to plunder Sunnis, you ask them why, and they tell you "they are damn Sunnis." They took their cars and their money; they killed them most of the time.

In contrast to the complex identities described in Chap. 1, Baghdad residents became simply "Sunni" and "Shi'a" in the eyes of their attackers. The clinical term for this psychological phenomenon is *deindividuation* or the reduced capacity to view people within a particular group as individuals. Deindividuation can also refer to a diminishing of one's *own* sense of individuality and personal responsibility, further loosening the reigns on antisocial behavior.

Dehumanization—the denial of humanness to others—also drove the increasing brutality of violence by sectarian extremists. Dehumanization permits belligerents to put certain people "outside [their] moral community," so that they no longer elicit compassion. The attackers described in the story below were impervious to attempts by their victims to relate as fathers and husbands.

> Once I heard two Mahdi Army members talking. One asked his colleague "How many Sunnis did you kill?" The man replied "six." The other man said "Well, I killed more, I killed seven…He said "We took them from their homes. They begged not to be killed, they even kissed our feet; asked about our wives and children."

The mass killings that occurred in Baghdad cannot be reduced "to a collection of individual tragedies [because] it is culture itself, the possibility of social life, that is under attack." Hostile goals emerge alongside hostile perceptions and attitudes—"to look better than, punish, discredit, defeat, or even destroy Other." These psychological changes lead inevitably to changes in groups, with revenge-seeking is perhaps the most dangerous hostile goal, an urge so powerful that it overrules other rational interests [2, p. 10]. Not only does revenge beget revenge in a vicious cycle, but "those seeking revenge can feel entitled to strike back even harder… committing atrocities which may be much greater than and hugely disproportionate to the original crime against them" [7, p. 139].

Group Changes

Once triggered, the cognitive and perceptual mechanisms described above can generate social tensions that support change in how groups behave. Of particular significance to these scholars are the conditions under which group identities come to be understood in zero-sum terms. Negotiation scholars use the term "zero-sum" to refer to characteristics of situations in which the involved parties perceive their goals to be in complete opposition, such that there can only be a winner and a loser. If threat to the group is understood to be the source of conflict—Serbs versus Croats, Hutu versus Tutsi, White versus Black—then people believe their goals to be *non-negotiable* and *diametrically opposed.*

When group identity is perceived in zero-sum terms, group narratives emerge that deny any common ground and promote existential threat. Even when group *identity* is not seen in zero-sum terms, group *safety* may be. According to this logic, "If they exist, we are not safe." Histories of marginalization and oppression can generate the seedbed for the emergence of this narrative, but so can immediate threats. In both cases, people believe and speak about themselves as victims that either have been (or are certain to be) exploited—or both. One of the people we spoke to during this research described why people in his neighborhood were motivated to support AQI.

> People would never fight them at that time or even speak up, not because they were too afraid to do so, but because the fighters were protecting them and if it wasn't for them, the people in my neighborhood would be dead by now. The government of Al-Jafari was the major enemy for Sunnis so my people in the neighborhood really needed the protection of these organizations.

When two groups in proximity have mutually exclusive, incendiary perceptions of each other—zero-sum perceptions of each other—conflicts can escalate very quickly. Pruitt and Kim describe several changes in groups that contribute to conflict escalation. One is group polarization meaning people on each side become more and more hostile toward each other, in part because of ordinary group discussion. "Research shows that when group members share any view (any attitude or perception) and discuss it with one another, that view becomes stronger" [7, p.116].

A second change is that groups may also experience an enhanced sense of group identity and cohesiveness, and choose to separate from each other along communal lines [8]. "Groups cohesion increases parallel to the extent that their members find them attractive" [2, p. 117] and the attractiveness of ones identity group increases parallel to perceived threat. Activation of identity is situational[1] and intensifies when social, economic, or political futures become uncertain. Thus, sectarian identities became especially salient following the invasion. A resident of Dura told us:

> I remember that my best friend was Shiite. We didn't care about that before 2003 but after 2004, he started to become sensitive from my opinions; like he might get upset or even fight with me if I said something about his sect. He was never like this before 2003. I witnessed gradual alienation between groups.

Cohesiveness affects group behavior by encouraging particularly vigorous conformity to group norms. In addition, "members of cohesive groups are particularly convinced of the rightness of their cause and the effectiveness of their intended actions" [2, p. 117]. Unfortunately for the "rightness of their cause," a third

---

[1] Stein, Janice (1996), Ibid:192.

change is that groups can develop *contentious group goals* in line with those of individual and vocal members [2, p. 116].

> Both sides, Shiites and Sunnis, started spreading hateful messages. Al-Qaida spread in Sunni neighborhoods and militias spread in Shiite neighborhoods. They told the people "The other side will eradicate you. They will slaughter you, they want to finish you."

One of the clearest indicators of changes between groups signaling conflict escalation is the emergence of militant subgroups and leaders who fomented contentious group goals. This study distinguishes between two types of subgroups: self-organized, neighborhood defense groups, versus offensive sectarian and criminal militias. Neighborhood defense groups aimed to prevent conflict escalation. However, the militant groups engaged in attacks and counter-attacks, a form of escalation called a conflict spiral. When caught in a conflict spiral, parties react to aggressive tactics from the other party in an attempt to reassert their power and to enact revenge. The spiral drives contentious group goals along a continuum from *wanting to do well*, toward *wanting to win*, graduating to *wanting to hurt the other*. Experiences in Bayaa offer a case in point. Below, the respondent describes how the goals and identity of armed groups shifted from self-protective (*wanting to do well*) to sectarian (*wanting to hurt the other*) after two conflicts in Najaf drew fighters from Baghdad, many of whom did not return.[2]

> The people joined the armed groups to protect their houses…We started to arrange lots of patrols on the borders of the neighborhood. Even old men participated in protecting the neighborhood. Those groups became more organized and with time they became part of Mahdi Army. Many members worked for free. They only wanted to protect the neighborhood, but most of those honest members of Mahdi Army were killed or detained in the events that occurred in Najaf.

After those battles, the membership of Mahdi Army in Bayaa changed from older men to younger men. Below, the respondent used the word "children" to describe the age and behaviors of new, younger members.

> With time other members of Mahdi Army, who were children, wanted to take advantage of their positions, took the houses of the Sunnis that they liked; some of them rented them for 100,000 Iraqi Dinars. They started to extort the shop-keepers telling them "You have to pay us because you are working in the neighborhood under our protection"…It reached to a stage that they took monthly rentals from people living in their own houses; they wanted 100,000 Iraqi Dinars per month from them in return for protection.

The devolution of armed groups in Baghdad has been widely documented. After the US invasion in 2003, a variety of armed groups formed with the aim of forcing out US and allied forces. Indigenous Sunni groups included the Islamic Army in Iraq (IAI), the 1920 Revolution Brigades (a militia of former members of the disbanded Iraqi army), and Ansar al-Sunna (a militia opposed to the Shi'a-led government). The explicit goal of these organizations was to expel foreign troops, not to incite sectarian violence. AQI's motivations were different, as we have read.

[2] The Najaf conflicts occurred in 2004, the first of which began when Coalition forces shut down al Hawza, the main Sadrist newspaper, and the second after Mahdi Army fighters attacked a US Marine patrol that they thought was on its way to arrest Muqtada al-Sadr.

Its entrance into Iraq coincides with the first attack of a sectarian nature on August 29, 2003,[3] a suicide car bomb outside the Shiite Imam Ali Mosque[4] in Najaf that killed over hundred people.[5] AQI was widely suspected of having orchestrated the 2003 attack in line with al-Zarqawi's goal of fomenting sectarian civil war, and outright claimed responsibility for the next major sectarian attack in March 2004 that killed 181 people celebrating Ashura festival in Baghdad.[6]

In early years, most indigenous Sunni insurgent groups had some connection with AQI and together formed a loose coalition of groups. The groups together were referred in the singular as "the Sunni insurgency" although analysts grasped that the insurgency did not refer to a single movement.

> The Sunni part of insurgency has become the equivalent of a distributed network: a group of affiliated and unaffiliated moves with well-organized cells. It is extremely difficult to attack and defeat because it does not have unitary or cohesive structure or a rigid hierarchy within the larger movements. The larger movements seem to have leadership, planning, financing, and arming cadres kept carefully separate from most operational cells in the field. Accordingly, defeating a given cell, regional operation, or even small organization does not defeat the insurgency although it can weaken it.[7]

This constellation of armed actors grew increasingly complex. As Phil Williams has noted, efforts to identify and classify the number, type and size of armed organizations within that constellation were stymied by ineffective policing, reporting, and incomplete or classified information [5]. He nonetheless produced a basic typology of armed actors which I found useful to distinguish among the variety of groups described in the pages below: traditional criminal enterprises; tribal-based criminal organizations; foreign jihadi groups; and militias which include splinter or rogue factions. According to William's later inquiry in 2009,

> … the analysis here distinguishes between different groups within the insurgency rather than treating it as monolithic. First, the insurgency has changed over time. Initially composed of former regime elements and Ba'athists, it soon extended to include other members of Sunni tribes whose objective was primarily to eject foreign occupiers. As former regime

---

[3] BBC Timeline: Iraq after Sadaam.co.uk. 2005. http://news.bbc.co.uk/2/hi/middle_east/4192189.stm.

[4] The Imam Ali Mosque is the third holiest site for Shi'a Muslims Imam Ali Mosque holds the remains of Ali ibn Abi Talib, cousin of Muhammad and first Imam according to followers of the Shi'a branch of Islam.

[5] Included among the victims was Ayatollah al-Hakim, leader of the Supreme Council for the Islamic Revolution in Iraq (SCIRI), which would become one of Iraq's most powerful political parties.

[6] The day of Ashura on the 10th day of Muharram (the first month in the Islamic calendar) is a day of mourning for Shi'a Muslims commemorating the death of Muhammad's grandson Husayn ibn Ali at the Battle of Karbala, and Sunnis have traditionally taken part in the days rituals, which include cooking and distributing food.

[7] Anthony Cordesman, Iraq's Sectarian and Ethnic Violence and its Evolving Insurgency: Developments Through Spring 2007 (Washington DC: Center for Strategic and International Studies, April 2007), online at www.comw.org/warreport/fulltext/0704cordesman.pdf, accessed July 2010.

elements became more concerned with the resettling of their families and maintaining them in the style to which they had been accustomed during the Hussein years, the tribes along with the foreign jihadis increasingly drove the insurgency… [5, p. 22].

Respondents made reference to these changes in the goals and tactics of groups within "the insurgency." Some respondents took care to distinguish between foreign jihadi groups (of which Al Qaeda in Iraq is one) and local militias, as well as the "splintering off" of specialized factions; for example, kidnapping operations carried out by specific cells affiliated to AQI. In Adhamiyya and Amiriyya, Sunni militias graduated from targeting US and Coalition forces, to viewing anyone affiliated with the new government as a legitimate target.

Before that they used to kill the Americans then the Federal Police then Iraqi Police and the Iraqi Army and whoever worked with them. I remember that one day they followed a Sunni man just because he was in the National Guard! Even though he ran away from them, they followed him till he reached his house then they shot him dead there…

Escalation also drove changes in the goals and tactics of the Mahdi Army. Respondents distinguished between early years (2003, 2004) when Mahdi Army members provided needed security, and later years when sectarian operations replaced protective operations, and criminality took hold. As early as 2005, Mahdi Army devolved into multiple groups, often operating independently from each other.

Killing became everyday news and everyone became a walking target at that time, even the unemployed rich men just because they were rich; they'd kidnap them, take the ransom and then kill them.[8]

Muqtada al-Sadr himself encouraged this when he issued a statement in May 2003, saying that "looters could hold on to what they had appropriated so long as they made a donation (khums) of one-fifth of it value to their local Sadrist office" [5].

According to Roggio, a popular perception was that Mahdi Army had split into "the noble Mahdi Army" which offered protective and social services (and eventually obeyed the Sadr's order for a ceasefire) and the "rogue Mahdi army" which operated as a set of criminal gangs, killing indiscriminately and embezzling people and businesses. The reality was more complex, according to the Institute for Study of War.

10 Mahdi Army groups operated criminal rackets in Shi'a neighborhoods across Baghdad to generate funding, intimidate the local population, and maintain power. The rapid growth in the movement from 2004 to 2006 and the subsequent emergence of a mafia-like system undermined Muqtada al-Sadr's control over his commanders. As local commanders grew more powerful and financially independent, they became less likely to follow orders from Muqtada al-Sadr and the clerical leadership in Najaf [9].

The bombing of the holy golden domed Shi'a al-Askari shrine, February 22, 2006, represented the tipping point in sectarian violence. Civilian casualties mounted each month through August 2007 and Baghdad became divided into Sunni and Shi'a enclaves as 80 % of Baghdad's households fled their formerly multiethnic neighborhoods.

[8] Interview, Baghdad 2010.

Change in Communities

Community polarization is the third and most lasting change when conflicts escalate. It serves as a feedback loop, both produced by earlier escalation and contributing to its perpetuation [2, p. 118]. "Community polarization contributes to further escalation for two reasons. One is that new supports and recruits give added strength to the individuals or groups on either side.…The other is that polarization divides a community into two opposing camps. The bonds within each camp become stronger while those between camps deteriorate" [2, p. 118]. Ultimately impacted is a community's intergroup "transactional capacity," a term Richard Ricigliano uses to describe "how people work together to make decision, build interpersonal relationships, and solve problems effectively" [10].

One of the most important factors in conflict escalation was whether or not local self-defense groups became "occupied" by a sectarian militia. A member of the local Iraqi research team explained the tough decisions that individuals faced:

> One guy worked in some of what we call "community watch groups" which were formed by people to protect themselves when the government was so weak and people found it important to organize such groups. Some of these groups remained doing the good job and didn't engage in any sectarian actions; other groups were "occupied" by Mahdi Army when they got active in these regions and so the members of these groups either work with Mahdi Army or they had to leave these groups and service…

Interviews suggest that physical entry of offensive, sectarian militias into a neighborhood was the determining factor in conflict escalation. Earlier, we learned that response diversity is an important source of community resilience. Threats and acts of violence by militias reduced response diversity—the range of possible responses by residents—to active or tacit cooperation [11, 12].[9] A resident of Dura described how this had taken place.

> Some clerics went along with the groups. The Imam in the mosque, he would never have been able to protect his neighborhood because if he criticized them or objected to their acts, they might have killed him. Having good relations with the fighters had provided protection for the Imam.
>
> Another Imam refused cooperating or having any connections with them, refused using the mosque as an ammunition stash and as a distributing site for kerosene and cooking gas. He tried to help a Shiite man who was chased, and he [the Imam] was shot.

A militia's physical presence in a community also boosted the ability to recruit from within those areas because it was easier to communicate with local populations, and rally a following. Weine and Ahmed (2012) found that the proximity of extremist groups influenced the perceived legitimacy of extremist violence[13]. Studying the phenomenon of violent extremism in the Somali communities of Minneapolis, they traced contact with "recruiters" to the "perceived social legitimacy of violent extremism," both of which facilitated involvement in acts of

[9] Communities with low response diversity are less able to cope with change because they lack multiple, redundant ways to solve problems.

violent extremism. Thus, when community members, either willingly or unwillingly, allowed sectarian subgroups to operate, joined their forces, or provided material and psychosocial support, structural changes in the community occurred that both signify—and reinforce—a high level of escalation.

Conclusion

"Tumult is asleep; he who awakens it shall be cursed" reads an old Arab proverb. Conflict was asleep in Iraq, suffocated under the brutal authoritarian rule of Saddam Hussein and the Baath party. Sectarian conflict, however, was carefully cultivated. It was not awoken so much as created and forced to life. Sectarian violence did not represent an eruption of ancient tribal or ethnic hatreds. The analysis thus far points to four underlying sources or drivers of tension in pre-2003 Iraqi society: ethnic and sectarian discrimination, weak state institutions, a history of intergroup politics, and manipulation of religious identities by political elites. Sectarian and ethnic divisions were not so pronounced prior to the US invasion in 2003, as described by residents further in the book. Therefore, the ongoing conflict in Iraq cannot be blamed simply on ethnic and religious divisions and historical tensions.

Specific to the study of sectarian conflict in Baghdad, positive or "conflict resilience" is conceptualized as a process of managing conflict escalation so as to limit the formation of sectarian militants within bounded areas, and at the same time preventing violent sectarian attacks from militant groups outside those areas. The areas of Baghdad that piqued my interest were those places where Sunni, Shiite, and Christian residents still lived in the same area and had prevented sectarian violence from taking root within their "neighborhood" during and after the escalation of sectarian violence and massive dislocation experienced in most of Baghdad (See Footnote 4).

During civil strife, neighborhoods are incubators either for street warfare or community resilience based on their institutional setup, the strength of interpersonal relationships and ability to organize across faith, ethnic, or racial divides. The variance in these characteristics makes neighborhoods either vulnerable to or resilient to violence. Yet though the focus is on the neighborhood or community level, neighborhoods are situated within different *regions* of cities that have varying levels of access to the economic, political, and social resources controlled by city and tribal governments.

Neighborhoods in West Baghdad were connected to rural tribes to a higher degree than neighborhoods in South Baghdad, and this proved significant for how sectarian violence spread. In addition, neighborhoods close to the city center offered greater opportunities to approach or enter (to access) jobs markets, educational centers, health services, and social service providers. However, the relationship between socioeconomic level and resilience should not be overstated. Experience has shown that even in areas of sheer desolation, social life, and organizational systems can readily re-emerge within community networks [14]. Resilience to violent conflict has much to do with belief systems, which socioeconomic resources sometimes affect and sometimes do not. To explore this phenomenon in greater detail, the following chapter fleshes out the concept of resilience and its importance for the growing attention has paid in recent years to the adoption of community-based approaches in conflict-affected and fragile contexts.

References

1. Kriesberg, L. 1998. Intractable conflicts. (Ed.) In *The Handbook of Interethnic Coexistence,* ed. Weiner E., 334. New York: Continuum Publishing.
2. Pruitt, D., and S.H. Kim. 2004. *Social conflict: escalation, stalemate and settlement*, 3rd ed. Boston: McGraw Hill.
3. Lund, M. 1996. *Preventing violent conflicts: a strategy for preventive diplomacy*, 134. Washington: United States Institute of Peace.
4. Dudouet, V. 2006. *Transitions from violence to peace: revisiting analysis and intervention in conflict transformation.* Berghof Research Center for Constructive Conflict Management. Retrieved from http://www.berghof-conflictresearch.org/documents/publications/br15e.pdf.
5. Williams, P. 2009. Criminals, militias and insurgents: organized crime in Iraq. Strategic Studies Institute. Retrieved from http://www.strategicstudiesinstitute.army.mil/pdffiles/pub930.pdf.
6. Loewenstein, G. 1996. Out of control: visceral influences on behavior. *Organizational Behavior and Human Decision Processes* 65(5003): 272–292.
7. Slim, H. 2008. *Killing civilians: method, madness and morality in war*, 139. New York: Columbia University Press.
8. Kahl, C.H. 2008. *States, scarcity, and civil strife in the developing world.* Princeton: Princeton University Press.
9. Cochrane, M. 2009. The fragmentation of the sadrist movement. Iraq Report 12, Institute for the Study of War. Retrieved from http://www.understandingwar.org/report/fragmentation-sadrist-movement.
10. Ricigliano, R. 2012. *Making peace last: a toolbox for sustainable peacebuilding*, 35. Boulder: Paradigm Publishers.
11. Bourdieu, P. 1985. The forms of capital. In *Handbook of Theory and research for the sociology of education*, ed. J. Richardson, 248. New York: Greenwood.
12. Adger, W. 2000. Social and ecological resilience: are they related? *Progress in Human Geography* 24: 347–364.
13. Stevan, W., and O. Ahmed. 2012. *Building Resilience to Violent Extremism Among Somali-Americans in Minneapolis-St. Paul*, Final Report to Human Factors/BehavioralSciences Division, Science and Technology Directorate, U.S. Department of Homeland Security. College Park, MD: START.
14. Pouligny, B. 2005. Civil society and post-conflict peacebuilding: ambiguities of international programmes aimed at building 'new' societies. *Security Dialogue* 36(4): 495–510.

Chapter 5
Resilience: Conceptual Foundations

Abstract Resilience is a conceptual framework used more and more often to study how communities cope with hardship, including war and violence. This chapter explains how resilience is conceptualized in different literatures—psychology, ecology, engineering—and settles on the lens of systems resilience for studying how human social systems absorb large shocks. The component parts of a social system (its "*regime*" Community Resilience) consist of prevailing institutional arrangements, the characteristics of which provide the resources and rules that characterize adaptive capacity. The Chapter concludes by introducing an analytical framework for analyzing regime characteristics according to their configurations of social capital, economic resources, and information and communication enablers.

Keywords Resilience • Regime • Conflict • Coping • Adaptation • Violence • Regime shift • Buffer capacity • Adaptive capacity • Transformative capacity • Iraqi tribes • Redundancy • Diversity • Robustness • Social capital • Information • Communication • Economic resources • Community competence • Conflict escalation • Stressors • Resilience management • Systems resilience

> *The ability to self-organize is the strongest form of system resilience. A system that can evolve can survive almost any change, by changing….*
>
> Diana Wright

In the past four decades, resilience has gained considerable traction in studies about how communities cope with war and violence. Of particular interest is positive resilience or "the condition of relative stability and even tranquility in areas recently or intermittently beset by violence" [1].

> Probably the most dramatic form of resilience is that evidenced by concerted or proactive efforts on the part of communities to actively wrest control of their daily situation in ways that could be considered a form of resistance to the power and influence of armed actors.

A. C. Carpenter, *Community Resilience to Sectarian Violence in Baghdad*,
Peace Psychology Book Series, DOI: 10.1007/978-1-4614-8812-5_5,

Specific to the study of sectarian conflict in Baghdad, positive or "conflict resilience" is conceptualized as a process of managing conflict escalation so as to limit the formation of sectarian militants within bounded areas, and at the same time preventing violent sectarian attacks from militant groups outside those areas. This definition builds on other contemporary definitions of community resilience; however, specific emphasis is placed on the capacity to adapt to episodic phenomena—the gradual escalation of sectarian violence—as opposed to sudden natural disasters or chronic violence. A resident of Kuraiit told us,

> Nothing occurred immediately after toppling the previous regime. A period of time passed before the spread of sectarian violence. People used to move freely at the beginning, but many sides interfered and this prevented Iraqis from reaching stability.

This Chapter lays a conceptual foundation for the rest of the book. I first flesh out the concept of resilience in general and then explain its relationship to the spread of violence through conflict escalation dynamics and exposure to accumulated stressors. Conflict resilience involves the capacity to adapt to episodic, cascading stressors that cause changes in people's psychological states, the way groups function and behave, and the efficacy of whole communities. Community resilience to sectarian violence uses the lens of *systems* resilience—"the ability of social systems to cope, adapt, and reorganize in response to dramatic challenges" [2].

The component parts of a social system—its "*regime*"—are crucial to the capacity to absorb large shocks and preventing large-scale social reorganization.

What is Resilience?

Generally speaking, resilience refers to the ability to rebound, maintain, or strengthen functioning during and after a disturbance, or to cope successfully in the face of extreme adversity or risk [3]. Resilience is both a metaphor for the durability, strength, or adaptive capacity of particular things (people, ideas, institutions, societies, or ecosystems) and a theoretical framework for studying *the dynamics* of this durability, strength, or adaptive capacity in relation to those things. Today, resilience is referenced on a wide range of issues associated with social and ecological systems, including disaster management, economics, community planning, urban renewal, and development. Naturally, each field conceptualizes resilience in different ways, which have led to a variety of definitions and understandings. Many of these definitions offer key insights into the specific concept of resilience to violence.

In material sciences, resilience refers to a property of materials to resume their original size and shape after experiencing stress. For mechanical engineers, resilience is the maximum energy per volume that can be elastically stored. Connoted in both is "the relationship of resilience to brittleness, which highlights that *flexibility is often a key quality of resilience*" [4].

Systems engineering proposed that diversity and redundancy (of functions) is a source of resilience leading to the related ideas that (1) social resilience depends on having multiple avenues for meeting needs or dealing with specific issues and (2) can itself be engineered into the way that an organization or society is organized.

Systems engineers also point out that the resilience of systems involves the interaction between engineered components and their environment [5]. For example, the resilience of an electrical grid depends on its having been designed to take into account its human environment (i.e., number of users) and geographic environment (i.e., susceptibility to earthquakes). In the same vein, psychologists maintain that resilience is an *interaction effect* regarding how particular variables moderate between risks and outcomes. Examples of moderating variables include hardiness (which enables people to reconceptualize the negative effects of events), collective self-esteem, or sense of humor [6]. Thus, even individual resilience under stress must factor in characteristics of communities and societies within which persons and families are embedded [7].

Psychologists have conceptualized resilience in other ways as well: as *outcomes* despite adversity (acquisition of social skills, emotional development, academic achievement, psychological wellbeing, self-esteem); as *sustained competence* under stress (coping skills, attitudes toward obstacles, environmental protective factors); or as *recovery* from trauma (resilience in relation to specific risk factors or events). In all these cases, the individual human is able to withstand or absorb adverse events without significant decreases to their well-being. A similar understanding emerged in ecology, where resilience was first conceptualized as "the capacity of a system to absorb disturbance and reorganize while undergoing change so as to still retain essentially the same function, structure, identity, and feedbacks" [8].

The paper *The Concept of Resilience: Understanding its Origins, Meaning and Utility*, McAslan [3], suggests that differences in its definition are not as wide as some literature may suggest. Regardless of its application, McAslan points out that the term resilience has a number of common characteristics such as "the ability to absorb and then recover from an abnormal event; being ready and prepared to face threats and events which are abnormal in terms of their scale, form, or timing; an ability and willingness to adapt to a changing and sometimes threatening environment; a tenacity and commitment to survive; and a willingness of communities and organisations to rally round a common cause and a shared set of values."

> Thus resilience is the ability of something or someone to cope in the face of adversity—to recover and return to normality after confronting an abnormal, alarming, and often unexpected threat. It embraces the concepts of awareness, detection, communication, reaction (and if possible avoidance) and recovery. These are essential features of the daily struggle for life and are founded in our basic instinct of survival. Resilience also suggests an ability and willingness to adapt over time to a changing and potentially threatening environment.

Building on these existing conceptual foundations, resilience to war and violence has increasingly come to refer to those mechanisms and capacities necessary to prevent conflict and promote peace [9]. According to Ryan, resilience in this context refers to "capacities to foster greater social and political cohesion and to address the causes of fragility" [9]:16. Fragility refers broadly to fundamental failures of a state to perform basic functions necessary to meet citizen's needs and expectations [10]. Causes of fragility include failures of state authority to protect people from violence, failures to ensure that all citizens have access to basic services, and failures of legitimacy wherein the state is not widely supported [11]. The previous chapter discussed these failures in Iraq.

But what does "capacities to foster greater social and political cohesion and to address the causes of fragility" actually mean? According to McAslan [3], a variety of assets, measures, relationships, and capabilities together define resilient communities. These enablers, so named because they enable a community to become more resilient, included physical enablers that provide basic requirements of human survival and security (e.g., water, electricity and gas infrastructure, food, transportation, and banking), procedural enablers for responding to disruptive events (e.g., action plans, strategies, local knowledge, and information) and social enablers (e.g., community cohesion and motivation) [12]. Resilient societies possess the capability for decision making that can avert violent conflict and enhance peace building through the capacity for dialogue and mediation.

> Lasting peace requires people, communities and leaders with the skills, capacities and opportunities to work together to reconcile political and sectarian differences. The absence of presence of these skills can make the difference between violence and stability on the one hand, and peace and growth on the other.

Routinizing or embedding processes of conflict management within common social practices and political culture greatly enhances *systems resilience* [2].

I will not belabor abstraction, but I encourage taking a systems view of resilience. Communities are highly complex and dynamic entities where different actors are interconnected by multiple relationships, interactions, and feedback loops. "This means it can be difficult to understand the impact of a particular decision or action may have on the overall system [and that] the emergent properties of a system cannot be understood by analyzing the components of the system in isolation" [13].

Simply put, the whole is greater than the sum of its parts. To take another example outside of Iraq, it is not possible to fully understand the war-resilient city of Tuzla by analyzing what various people did in isolation from each other. During the war that fractured the former Yugoslavia, Tuzla was the only Bosnian city that avoided major ethnic clashes *even though* it was also home to more internally displaced people than all of Southern Bosnia combined and faced the challenge of major housing, water, waste, and transportation difficulties. Studies have pointed to multiple causal factors: its history, culture, and democratic policies of multiethnic coexistence and opposition to oppression, "a close-knit and thriving intellectual population" [14], economic integration, intercommunal civic networks [15], and the presence of individuals and groups who actively promoted ethnic tolerance and good governance.

But these factors have to be considered together: Tuzla's resilience to ethnic violence was a property of the city *as a system*. In Joshua Weiss's words, "Whatever the exact reasons for the successful resistance of the war there is little doubt that it took the collective effort of almost the entire city to make it work" [14].

A collection of resilient individuals does not a resilient community make [16]. From these different parts or "sets of capacities," 130,000 people avoided descent into ethnic bloodshed and Tuzla as a whole adapted positively to the war around it.

In this book, I use the definition of resilience as *the ability of a social system to absorb disturbance while retaining its basic identity, function, and structure* [17–19]. This definition can be applied to the resilience of ecosystems, organizations, societies, and communities [3] but here refers to the ability of a neighborhood to absorb disturbance while retaining its ethnic composition, preexisting relations, and basic functions.

The very essence of systems resilience is the extent to which the component parts of a system can absorb shock so that the system does not collapse. Those "component parts" are called a system's *regime* [20]. Like resilience, the term *regime* has a variety of meanings deriving both from social sciences and material sciences. Material sciences define regimes as sets of physical conditions, particularly those of boundaries or physical phenomenon. For example, a river has a uniform regime when its flow (phenomenon) is equal at all the cross sections (boundaries). Social sciences also understand regimes as sets of conditions, most often those of political systems. Political regimes refer to the nature of political structures that make up a state. There are lots of ways to classify political regimes: limited versus despotic [21], autonomous versus heteronomous [22], and democracies versus dictatorships [23]. The NGO Freedom House uses a simple classification system either states are free, partly free, or not free.

These kinds of labels might suggest that regime refers to a state of affairs—dictatorships for example—but that would be incorrect. A regime is not an existing state of affairs, but the *components* of that existing state; its rules, boundaries, and types of control. A helpful definition from international relations defines regimes as "implicit or explicit principles, norms, rules, and decision-making procedures around which actors' expectations converge in a given area of international relations" [24]. They can also refer to "specialized arrangements" between certain members of the international community that address specific issues, activities, or regions [25]. Examples include treaties such as the Kyoto Protocol, which binds its parties to particular levels of emissions reduction, conventions like the Rights of the Child, a legally binding instrument which extended the full range of human rights to children, and monetary management arrangements like the Bretton Woods System which established the rules governing commercial and financial relations between countries.

Applied to communities, a regime consists of prevailing institutional arrangements, both formal (tribal or civic governmental organizations, laws, and political parties) and informal (social norms, traditions, and codes of honor). Regime characteristics provide the resources and rules that characterize adaptive capacity: institutions and networks that learn and store knowledge, creative flexibility in decision making and problem solving, and the existence of power structures that are responsive and consider the needs of all stakeholders [26]. These capacities are particularly important during political crisis because they support people to proactively engage and manage the dynamics of social violence.

Regime Characteristics in Baghdad Neighborhoods

In Chap. 2, I described the pervasive self-reliance of Baghdad residents on themselves, given their distrust of the central government. However, local governance and social norms differed in two important and probably interrelated ways between the ten Baghdad neighborhoods I studied. One difference was degree of reliance on tribes, relating to the schism between urban and rural peoples and culture discussed in Chap. 1. Regimes in all three areas—how people, organizations, resources, and processes functioned—rested on three pillars of institutional authority and social cohesion: the Iraqi state, tribes, and families who had lived for generations in a particular neighborhood.

State actors like police and district officials, though internal to Baghdad's governance structure, were often viewed as outsiders (and largely irrelevant) to life in a particular neighborhood. Tribal leaders were sometimes perceived as outside influences on a neighborhoods internal regime, and sometimes as important internal influences on governance.

Tribes played a large role in all the Shia-dominant neighborhoods: Sadr City, Bayaa, Palestine Street, Kardah, and Kuraiit. According to respondents, the underlying motivation was often to keep the state out of local affairs; however, the neighborhoods differed in their affiliation or loyalty to tribal leaders. In Sadr City, "tribesman used to solve problems between tribes and similar issues. They had a strong influence back then; they solved problems on the level of the province; problems related to murder, stealing and things like that."[1] In disputes (with car accidents being the most commonly mentioned), police were deferential to tribes.

> *Moderator: How were problems like car accidents solved when they occur between people of different neighborhoods?*
>
> *Sadr City*: Either through the state, particularly in regions that have a low tribal representation or through the tribesmen. The tribes of the south were among the largest. Even Christians and Mandaeans had to bring their tribes when a problem occurred.
>
> *Bayaa*:…if that ever happened, the police used to interfere; they detain both sides of the problem and if there was an injured person, he would go to the hospital. Tribes also interfere; they ask for the tribe of the other side and they try to reach an agreement. The state will discard the matter if the complaining side withdrew the complaint. Detained individuals were released then and they had to attend an ordinary tribal compensation session.
>
> *Palestine Street*: Conflicts between the people are solved between the tribes.
>
> *Kuraait*: There were no problems between sects, but there were problems between tribes and on property and those problems were often solved between the involved tribes or families. Most problems in my neighborhood were solved among the people without resorting to the government…. A person was killed or injured in a car accident or by a gunshot and the problem was solved through the tribes, tribal session for compensation. Sometimes similar problems were solved through arranging an agreement.
>
> *Moderator*: *And the state didn't interfere at that time?*

[1] Field interview, Sadr City, June 2010.

> The state wasn't informed about what happened. People said that they could solve the problem. They didn't want things to get complicated.

Narratives from Sunni neighborhoods were not necessarily as clear-cut. In Dura, tribal leaders lived outside of Baghdad; when a serious problem arose, they would travel to Dura to convene a meeting. "There were old sheikhs in my neighborhood," explained the respondent, "however they didn't have authority over anything except their own families." In Amiriyya, neighborhood leaders were described as "unofficial respectful old men" from the Kbeisat and Dulaymi families, who were among the first inhabitants of the neighborhood. During one conversation, the moderator asked "should they be tribal leaders and have positions in their tribes?" The respondent replied, "Yes, but the priority is to be the oldest family in the neighborhood."

In Adhamiyya, tribal authority bumped up against the older authority of the areas ruling families. Beginning in the 1960s, Hussein began relocating members of his family, tribe, and ruling party to Adhamiyya from Tikrit. This had the effect not only of changing the demographics of the area, but also its physical layout. Newer tribally affiliated residents settled in Adhamiyya's periphery, while the core continued to consist mainly of the "original" residents who defined themselves by the "civilian identity" of familial lineage. The individual with whom we spoke intimated the difference, as he described the nature of local leaders. He nods toward the presence of tribal leaders, but placed emphasis on familial governance.

> Families of Adhamiyya are big and well known like the Shakkuka…There are many well known tribes as well. Let's not forget that families have lived in this area for a very long time.

Also referred to "old Baghdadis," these can trace their families back thousands of years. Old Baghdadis identify themselves by family, not tribe, and are described as having a "civilian identity." "Ask where they are from, they will tell you by the names of their families (extending back) to the Ottoman Empire" (see footnote 9).

The reliance on tribes versus families is not the only difference in the character of local institutions: Iraqis also draw a distinction between so-called religious versus civilian or secular areas. "Civilian identity" is an Iraqi concept that tells us about the nature of local authority and culture. Iraqis who identify themselves as "civilian" have a broader set of social identities and do not see themselves as primarily Sunni or Shia, or as belonging to one tribe or another. In the Iraqi context, the term "civilian" does not mean people not serving in the armed services or police; instead, it literally means "urbanized" or "civilized."

> If you look at old Baghdadi areas, Rusafa, Adhamiyya, these old areas—there is no influence of the tribes. These areas because they were part of Baghdad for thousands of years, they were more urbanized, they have no connection to the tribes, they were known by families—it's a civilian rather than a tribal society."[2]

I will revisit the nature of governance structures in this chapter, in order to question their potential effects on regime resilience. *Regime resilience*, discussed in the following section, is the ability of dominant or reigning institutional arrangements (whatever they may be) to withstand internal and external shocks and risk factors for violent conflict.

---

[2] Interview with Dr. S. S. Motlak.

Regime Resilience

Across disciplines, scientists have converged on three basic models of regime resilience, each referring to different but interrelated capacities: buffer capacity, adaptive capacity, and transformational capacity. *Buffer capacity*, often highlighted in economic or country-level conflict studies, is concerned with the magnitude of shock that a system can absorb and remain in a given state, this being dependent on elements of the regime already in place [27]. Research on ecological systems generally tends to use the buffer capacity model, and studies of state resilience have also explained using this construct: for example Guinea's ability to absorb the impact of refugees and returnees [28], and Haiti's ability to cope with underdevelopment and political instability without social collapse or civil war [29].

The key insight of the buffer capacity model is that conflict-resilient communities have certain regime characteristics. Organizations, resources, and community processes are set up in ways that build and increase collective capacity for learning, adaptation, and self-organization. In ideal cases, they contain specific resources (or adaptive capacities) [27] "that are sufficiently robust, redundant, or rapid to buffer or counteract the effects of the stressor" [7]. These regimes can cope with external shocks and impacts and are characterized by diversity, redundancy, and positive feedback loops[3] to the sources of adaptive capacity. The resilience of systems is enhanced by diversity—of species, functions, and responses. In particular, response diversity depends on having multiple avenues for meeting needs.

Resilience thus refers in part to the ability of dominant or reigning institutional arrangements to withstand internal and external shocks and risk factors for violent conflict. When change is too sudden or overwhelming, a regime shift can occur. A *regime shift* means that the components of a system undergo a significant transformation, resulting in a different state of affairs. For Kinzig et al. [8],

> the seemingly stable states we see around us in nature and in society, such as woody savannas, democracies, agro-pastoral systems, and nuclear families, can suddenly shift out from underneath us and become something new, with internal controls and aggregate characteristics that are profoundly different from those of the original [8].

Violence, destruction, and war represent a regime shift. In Vivien Jabri's words, the altered regime "constitutes behavior which is unacceptable in times of peace… War breaks down taboos against killing and the deliberate and direct infliction of suffering against fellow human beings" [30]. Whatever tenuous distinction

---

[3] Feedback loops are patterns of interacting processes where a change in one variable, through interaction with other variables in the system, either reinforces the original process (positive feedback) or suppresses the process (negative feedback). Most of the main feedback loops in fragile states are positive (reinforcing fragility) such as entrenched corruption or horizontal inequality. There is much research that shows the cyclical nature of these patterns, which lead over time to greater and more instability.

between civilian and combatant breaks down and anti-civilian ideologies emerge that involve "the absolute rejection of the civilian idea."

> The fact that a person may be unarmed or be a child, a mother, a grandfather, a powerless workman, a doctor or a farmer is not important…she or he is [simply] a member of the group that has been defined as the main threat…

Peace and conflict researchers among many others, are very interested in the question of what prevents a regime shift from a state of coexistence to a state of violence between groups of people.

I will come back to that in a moment; first, let us move on to what happens when regime shifts do occur. When system failure takes place, reorganization takes place at an immense scale. Resilience as *transformational capacity* "refers to the ways in which the system may change its actual structure in order to continue functioning." Whatever shock has occurred, the existing system is untenable and must transform into a different one [20]. Had I chosen to focus on the *city* of Baghdad, I would have adopted transformational resilience as my lens for studying lives and livelihoods over the past ten years. The city became transformed into ethnic enclaves which, while permitting the city to continue functioning as a center of people and commerce, represented an immense change from the previous regime. But instead I am interested in smaller parts *of* the city, making adaptive capacity and buffer capacity my primary lenses.

Adaptive capacity is the capacity of a system to absorb disturbance and reorganize while undergoing change. This model is overtly concerned with people's actual behaviors (preparation, response, and recovery) [31]. For example, International Federation of the Red Cross and Red Crescent Societies defines resilience as a product of understanding the nature of possible natural disasters and taking steps to reduce risk before an event as well as providing for quick recovery when a natural disaster occurs. Bruneau et al. have defined earthquake resilience as "the ability of social units (e.g., organizations, communities) to mitigate hazards, contain the effects of disasters when they occur, and carry out recovery activities in ways that minimize social disruption, and mitigate the effectors of further earthquakes" [32]. Pfefferbaum speaks to "the ability of community members to take meaningful, deliberate, collective action to remedy the impact of a problem, including the ability to interpret the environment, intervene, and move on" [33]. Other fields use this construct as well. The resilience of cancer cells, for example, is explained as a function of their resistance to treatment.

The key insights of the adaptive capacity model are that individual actions—decision-making, predicting, planning, organizing, and cooperation—are key components in the capacity to absorb disturbance and prevent a regime shift. Particularly in situations of rising tensions, the ingredients of peaceful outcomes are micro-interventions consisting of people's conversations and actions [30]. For example, last year's seminal study *Urban Resilience in Situations of Chronic Violence* used a conception of resilience as *action*; specifically "those acts intended to restore or create effectively functioning community-level activities, institutions, and spaces in which the perpetrators of violence are marginalized and perhaps even eliminated" [34].

Resilience to conflict escalation involves the capacity to adapt to its episodic, cascading stressors. The stressors associated with escalating political violence accumulate over time, thus differ along the dimension of *surprise* from sudden disasters, and along the dimensions of *severity* and *duration* from chronic violence.[4] Firstly, conflict escalation toward intergroup violence is a gradual process involving changes in people's psychological states, changes in the way groups function, and changes in a larger heterogeneous community. Unlike responses to a sudden and surprising disaster, these changes are incremental, not sudden, and they are driven by the evolution of sectarian attitudes and behaviors over time.

Secondly, the level of exposure to violence (via severity and/or duration) varies between escalating conflict and prolonged periods of chronic violence. Chronic exposure refers to "situations in which violence is perceived to have become an overwhelming if not seemingly intractable feature of urban life, and in which the metabolism is constantly exposed to, and having to defend off, the stress factor" [20]. However, typologies of conflict escalation suggest that early stages in escalation spirals contain the *threat* of violence, but limited direct exposure to traumatic and stressful experiences related to war. These include direct experiences of violence such as violent assaults, torture, and rape, along with indirect experiences (no less traumatic) like seeing dead or mutilated bodies, and witnessing explosions or gunfire. Typologies of escalation differ, but each characterizes conflict escalation as a dynamic process in which early stages are characterized by tensions, low-level hostilities [35], and limited violence, while later stages are characterized by direct and repeated exposure to war traumas [36].

Not only are these phases different, but the "behaviors that precede a phase are distinct from those found when the [social] system is locked into single phase" [37]. In other words, resilience to violence during conflict escalation must be understood and studied in a different way than resilience in the context of chronic violence. The issue is *not* "how actors and institutions manage to cope, adapt, and ultimately self-organize in situations in which the dynamics of urban violence persist and when an immediate resolution to the problem is not foreseeable," but rather how actors and institutions cope and adapt and ultimately self-organize to prevent regime change in conflict situations of increasing intensity and severity. What culminated in sectarian violence was a gradual escalation of conflict dynamics, disturbances that some areas managed while others could not.

Modeling Conflict Resilience

Resilience to violent conflict, as opposed to earthquakes or tsunamis, suggests a particular theoretical and methodological approach [38] that places specific emphasis on the capacity to adapt to gradual social psychological changes. This

[4] Norris et al. define these dimensions of disaster.

theoretical approach emphasizes the capacity of a social system to withstand disturbance and maintain its stability. But primarily, I am interested in how local communities managed change so that systemic resilience was not lost.[5]

The discussion so far suggests that community resilience to conflict escalation in Baghdad neighborhoods may have boiled down to the capacity of a sectarian subgroup to operate relative to the power of a community to regulate the sectarian subgroup's operations. The "power to regulate" may be understood as (1) the capacity to withhold from outside groups access to a community (and the various supports that access provides); (2) the capacity to prevent internal self-protection groups from taking on a sectarian identity as they coalesce; and (3) the capacity to prevent psychological changes that motivate area residents to join outside groups with a sectarian character [39]. Communities lacking these capacities experienced increasingly competitive and retributive responses to threat, generating a further breakdown in community relationships, ultimately generating self-reinforcing cycles of violence [23].

In Kurait, Kazimiyya, Al-Dhubat, and Palestine Street, outbreak of violence close-by did not cause a transformation of the neighborhood regime [20]. Instead, these neighborhoods adapted to episodic, cascading stressors. If adaptation is a response to a stressor, adaptive capacity is the ability to mount the response: The difference, according to [47] is that

> The effectiveness of adaptation will be difficult to assess or measure until after a change (hazard, policy change or other event) has occurred. Adaptation can only be measured as a community's actual response to a change. A community's adaptive capacity [capacity for adaptation], on the other hand, can be assessed through the use of indicators.

Researchers sometimes conflate the two. For example, according to Adger, the following proxy indicators for social resilience can be observed in both temporal and spatial analysis (over time or across geographic space): conflict-resolving processes, capacity for collective action (networks, shared trust), and coping strategies. The first two (arguably) could be classified as adaptive capacities, while the latter is an example of adaptation or response.

My interviews turned up five indicators of adaptive capacity in communities with the power to regulate militant subgroups, which are relatively synonymous with those specified in a model developed by researchers at the Dartmouth Medical School in New Hampshire.[6] The Dartmouth researchers conceptualized resilience as consisting of four clusters of capacities—social capital, economic development, information and communication, and community competence [7]. These four clusters represent elements of both buffer (or regime) capacity and adaptive capacity as described above. However note that the Dartmouth researchers chose the term 'adaptive capacities' to describe the four clusters of resources. I also will use that term when I need to, which should not be confused with

[5] Adaptability is the capacity of actors in the social-ecological system to manage resilience—that is, to handle change so that systemic resilience is not lost.

[6] These five properties were social networks bonding Sunni and Shia, high socioeconomic status (SES), longevity of interpersonal relationships, integrated spatial configuration, and strong, inclusive neighborhood identity.

adaptive capacity as one of three models of resilience discussed earlier. Understandingly the distinction may be somewhat confusing, but thankfully our focus will henceforth be on the clusters themselves (and not what this or that social scientist chooses to name the lot of them). *Social capital* is about trust and cooperation. It has many formal definitions, some of which I will explore in the next chapter. The essence of social capital is connectedness between people and groups, which has a variety of positive functions for resilience.

Economic development is about alleviating poverty and making the general human condition better. For our purposes, it is worth noting that poverty is associated with greater vulnerability to violence; for example, young people who grow up in poor, overcrowded conditions have a higher incidence of anxiety, post-traumatic stress, and depression [40–44]. *Information and communication* has to do with how communities inform people about what is going on, and either encourage or constrain their responses to events as they unfold. The relation to social capital is clear; "high degree of interconnectivity within society facilitates the diffusion of information, lessons learned and the accumulation and recall of institutional memory" associated with resilience.[7] Finally, *community competence* is equivalent to human agency. Adaptable social systems are a function of the management of these systems by individuals and groups, and thus, community competence consists largely of collective action and decision-making processes.

Resilience is a function of these four adaptive capacities and the robustness of resources that they contain. Longstaff and colleagues write this relationship as resilience $= f$ (resource robustness, adaptive capacity). Resources are simply defined as "objects, conditions, characteristics, and energies that people value" and can be any number of things, because their value is highly contextual [38]. Two years ago, for example, a student of mine won a university grant to buy a tractor for farmers to share in his Ugandan hometown. The tractor was a valuable resource projected to increase the village's overall annual agricultural yields. But related resources required for the plan to work included time-sharing agreements among the farmers, knowledge of how to operate the tractor, an adequate supply of gasoline, and a way to get the tractor to the village. Unfortunately, most of these other resources were lacking, but I digress.

Resource robustness is a measurement of the performance, diversity and redundancy of a community's available resources.[8] *Performance* designates the capacity and quality of functioning. For example, corrupt city officials perform public service duties more poorly than ethical officials, and underfunded schools do a worse job producing learned graduates than adequately resourced schools. *Diversity* refers to availability of resources that perform the same function. For example, diversity in species and populations help maintain healthy ecosystem functioning,

---

[7] Longstaff, P., Armstrong, N, Perrin, K.A., Parker, W.M., Hidek, M. (2012). Community Resilience: a function of resources and adaptability. White Paper, Institute for National Security and Counterterrorism. Syracuse University, pp. 1–15

[8] Robustness has been defined in many ways. Norris et al. defined it as the ability of a resource to withstand stress without degradation. I chose Longstaff et al.'s more nuanced definition.

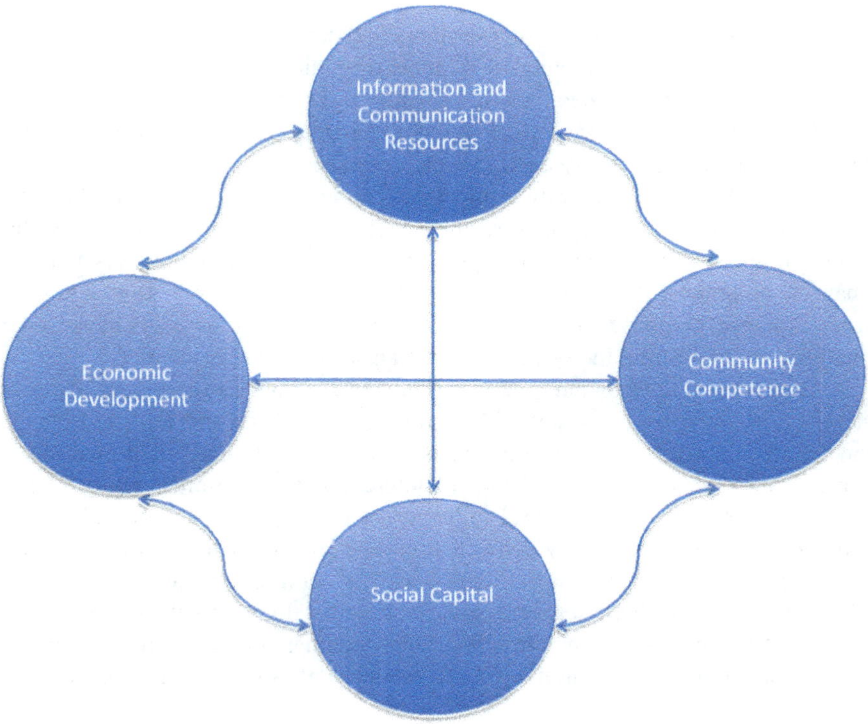

Fig. 5.1 Community Resilience as a set of networked adaptive capacities [11]

and the quality of collective decisions depends on diverse group membership [45]. Conversely (and to use an example from this study) when response diversity (the range of possible responses by Baghdad residents) was reduced, community resilience to violence was also reduced.[9]

Redundancy refers to the substitutability of resources and depends on having multiple avenues for meeting needs or dealing with specific issues. "People build in redundancy…by having large social networks or by having more than one way to solve a problem or even by having more than one lung or kidney" [46]. *Rapidity* is a related characteristic of resource robustness [46] because in crisis situations, resources that can be accessed and used quickly are more useful than those that take time to procure.

I adapted this original model by recasting community competence as being dependent on the other three sets of adaptive capacities.[10] According to the adapted model, community competence is *adaptation* (the actual response to stressors) rather

[9] Communities with low response diversity are less able to cope with change because they lack multiple, redundant ways to solve problems.

[10] Weine, Stevan, and Osman (2012), Ibid.

[11] [48]

than the *capacity for adaptation* (the structural indicators of resilience). It represents actions taken within the structural constraints of particular configurations of social capital, economic development, and information and communication resources. The model as adapted allows me to speak about community competence as a product of the other three sets of adaptive capacities and resilience resources.

Yet even though community competence is dependent on regime characteristics, it is also its own source of resilience because (as I wrote earlier) people's actions represent the ultimate absorptive capacity of a community. As noted in Chap. 1, outcomes of conflict resilience include low levels of casualties, intergroup violence, and physical infrastructure, but also people's actual behaviors, oriented toward preventing the spread of sectarian attitudes and behaviors.

A common critique of interpretivist frameworks, such as the model above, is that they do not specify causality. The arrows running back and forth in Figs. 5.1 and 5.2 would frustrate many positivists, who look for quantifiable cause and effect relationships between variables of interest, and find limited utility in conceptual frameworks lacking causal influence of one variable (e.g., social capital) upon another (e.g., community competence). The counter-critique offered by constructivists is that causation in the "real world" is not a linear matter of cause and effect, such that manipulation of one variable will reliably result in prespecified changes in another. The principle of causality assumes regularity in the sequence of events and their causes, but the world around us defies such predictability.

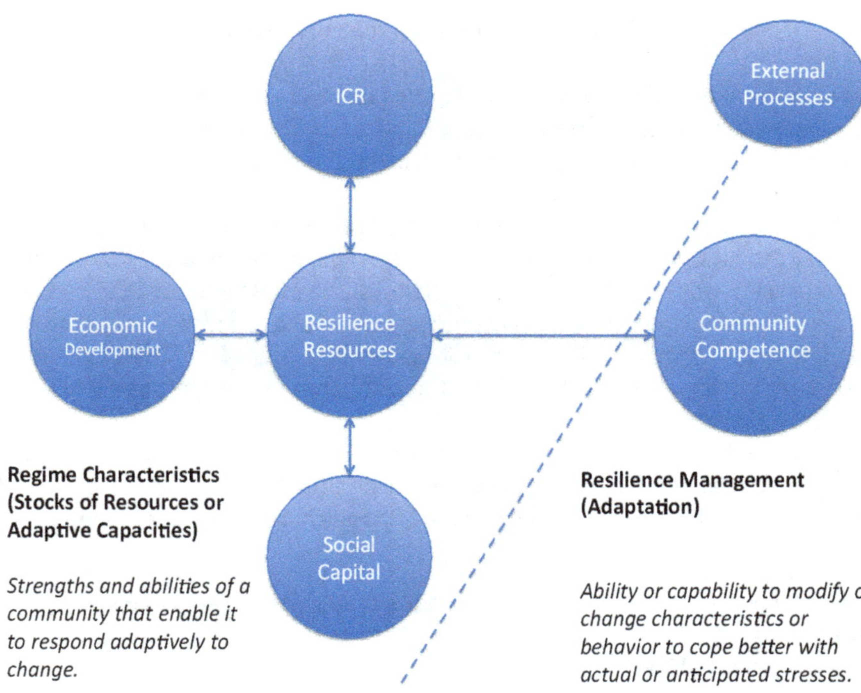

Fig. 5.2 Model of resilience to conflict

In particular, the complexity of human conflict calls for an approach that investigates conflict *as systems* of dynamic and interlocked factors and actors. The conflict system cycles through reinforcing negative feedback loops and the coils raised upon people's attitudes and patterns of behaviors. Given this complexity, our task is to ask specifically how relationships between interdependent factors and actors give rise to behaviors of the whole system, as well as how conflict systems interact with their larger environment.

However, I appreciate that a theoretical model of resilience is only useful insofar as it identifies explicit linkages between adaptive capacities and resilience outcomes. I will introduce these linkages in Chap. 7, after exploring the influences of each regime characteristic—social capital, economic resources, information and communication—on systemic adaptation.

Conclusion

Resilience is a complex concept. We need an analytical framework that places complex data within a conceptual system of definitions and classifications that makes it easier to understand what we are looking at, how we should look at it, and why it is relevant. This Chapter has laid a conceptual foundation for the rest of the book, and introduced an analytical framework for making sense of resilience. Community resilience to sectarian violence uses the lens of systems resilience—the ability of social systems to cope, adapt, and reorganize in response to dramatic challenges [2]. The component parts of the social system—its regime—are crucial to the capacity to absorb large shocks and prevent a regime shift. Specifically, the capacity to cope is dependent on four sets of adaptive capacities: social capital, economic development, community competence, and information and communication.

Each of the following chapters teases out the causal influence of a specific resilience resource—social capital, economic development, and information and communication resources—on conflict resilience. As you recall, I define conflict resilience as the ability of a social system to absorb disturbance while retaining its basic identity, structure, and function, in this case, its ethnic composition, preexisting relations, and basic functions. Each of the four adaptive capacities: social capital, economic development, community competence, and information and communication is really a complex set of variables, and the reader is invited to consider each in turn. Chapter 7 offers an integrative analysis linking each adaptive capacity with specific aspects of community competence.

References

1. Davis, D. 2012. Urban resilience in situations of chronic violence. Final report of the urban resilience in chronic violence project, USAID GRANT no. AID-OAA-G-10-00002: 9.
2. Menkhaus, K. 2013. Making sense of resilience in peacebuilding contexts: approaches, applications, implications. Geneva peacebuilding platform paper 6. Retrieved from http://www.gpplatform.

3. McAslan, A.R. 2010. *The concept of resilience: understanding its origins, meanings, and utility*. Adelaide: Torrens Resilience Institute.
4. Milliken, J. 2013. Resilience: From metaphor to an action plan for use in the peacebuilding field. Platform paper 7. Geneva peacebuilding platform. Retrieved from http://www.gpplatform (emphasis mine).
5. Nemeth, C.P. 2008. Resilience engineering: The birth of a notion. In *Resilience Engineering Perspectives, Volume I. Remaining Sensitive to the Possibility of Failure*, eds. E. Hallnegel, C. Nemeth, S. Dekker Burlington, VT: Ashgate Publishing.
6. Suraez-Ojeda, E.B., Autler, L. Community resilience: A social approach. In ed. E. Grotberg. Westport, CT: Praeger, 191.
7. Weine, S., A. Osman. 2013. Building resilience to violent extremism among Somali Americans in Minneapolis St. Paul. Final report to human factors/behavioral sciences division, science and technology directorate, U.S. Department of Homeland Security. College Park, MD: START, 2012. Retrieved from http://www.start.umd.edu/start/publications/Weine_BuildingResiliencetoViolentExtremism_SomaliAmericans.pdf.
8. Kinzig, A.P., M. Ryan, P. Etienne, H. Allison, T. Elmqvist, and B.H. Walker. 2006. Resilience and regime shifts: assessing cascading effects. *Ecology and Society* 11(1): 20.
9. Ryan, J. 2012. Infrastructures for peace as a path to resilience societies: a institutional perspective. *Journal of Peacebuilding and Development* 7(2).
10. Organisation for Economic Cooperation and Development. 2008. Concepts and dilemmas of statebuilding in fragile situations: From fragility to resilience. Retrieved from http://www.oecd.org/dac/incaf/41100930.pdf.
11. Stewart, F., Brown, G. 2010, 'Fragile states: CRISE overview 3', Centre for research on inequality, human security and ethnicity (CRISE), Oxford. Retrieved from http://www.gsdrc.org/go/display&type=Document&id=3843.
12. McAslan, A. 2010. Community resilience: Understanding the concept and its application. Adelaide: The Torrens Institute. Retrieved from http://sustainablecommunitiessa.files.wordpress.com/2011/06/community-resilience-from-torrens-institute.pdf.
13. Dalziell, E.P., McManus, S.T. 2004. Resilience, vulnerability and adaptive capacity implications for systems performance. Presented at the international forum for engineering decision making (IFED); Stoos, Switzerland. December 6–8, 2004. Retreived from http://ir.canterbury.ac.nz/bitstream/10092/2809/1/12593870_ResOrgs_IFED_dec04_EDSM.pdf.
14. Weiss, J. 2002. Tuzla, the third side, and the Bosnian war. In *When spider webs unite: Five case studies of the third side in action*, ed. J. Weiss. Cambridge: Program on Negotiation Books.
15. Tuzla, City of Hope in War-Torn Bosnia. European Platform for Conflict Prevention and Transformation. Retrieved from http://www.gppac.net/documents/pbp/1/7_tuzla.htm.
16. Norris, F.H., S.P. Stevens, B. Pfefferbaum, K.F. Wyce, and R. Pfefferbaum. 2008. Community resilience as a metaphor, theory, set of capacities and strategy for disaster readiness. *American Journal of Community Psychology* 41: 127–150.
17. Adapted from previous thinkers including Walker, B., Carpenter, S., Anderies, J., Abel, N., Cumming, G., Janssen, M., Lebel, L., Norberg, J., Peterson, G.D., Pritchard. R. 2002. Resilience management in social-ecological systems: a working hypothesis for a participatory approach. Ecology and Society 6(1):14.
18. Cumming, G.S., and J. Collier. 2005. Change and identity in complex systems. *Ecology and Society* 10(1): 29.
19. Adger, W. 2000. Social and ecological resilience: Are they related? *Progress in Human Geography* 24: 347–364.
20. Jutersonke, O., Kartas, M. (2012) Resilience: Conceptual reflections geneva peacebuilding platform, 2. Retrieved from http://www.gpplatform.
21. Nugent, T. 1949. *The spirit of the laws*. New York: MacMillan.
22. Keslan, H. 1945. Trans by A. Wedberg. 20th century legal philosophy series: Volume I. Cambridge: Harvard University Press, xxxiii, 516.

23. Antic, M. 2004. *Democracy versus dictatorship: The influence of democratic regime on GDP growth*. Hungary: Central European University.
24. Krasner, S.D. 1983. Structural causes and regime consequences: regimes as intervening variables. In *International regimes*, ed. S.D. Krasner. Ithaca: Cornell University Press.
25. Young, O.R. 1989. *International cooperation: building regimes for natural resources and the environment*, 13. Ithaca: Cornell University Press.
26. Gunderson, L.H., and C.S. Holling. 2002. *Panarchy: Understanding transformations in human and natural systems*. Washington, D.C.: Island Press.
27. Norris, F.H., Stevens, S.P., Pfefferbaum, B., Wyce, K.F., Pfefferbaum, R. 2008. Community resilience as a metaphor, Theory, set of capacities and strategy for disaster readiness. *American Journal of Community Psychology* 41.
28. Bah, M.D. 2012. State resilience in Guinea: Mitigating the 'bad neighbourhood effect'of civil war next door. *Australasian Review of African Studies* 33(1): 13–33.
29. Verner, D. 2005. Social resilience and state Fragility in Haiti. The World Bank. Retrived from https://openknowledge.worldbank.org/handle/10986/6836.
30. Jabri, V. 1996. Discourses on violence: Conflict analysis reconsidered. England: Manchester University Press 7.
31. Rose, A., and S. Liao. 2005. Modeling regional economic resilience to disasters: A computable general equilibrium analysis of water service disruptions. *Journal of Regional Science* 45(1): 75–112.
32. Bruneau, M., Chang, S.E., Eguchi, R.T., Lee, G.C., O'Rourke, T.D., Reinhorn, A.M., Shinozuka, M.,Tierney, K., Wallace, W.A., von Winterfeldt, D. 2003. A framework to quantitatively assess and enhance the seismic resilience of communities. Earthquake Spectra 19(4):733–752. (emphasis mine).
33. Pfefferbaum, B., D. Reissman, R. Pfefferbaum, R. Klomp, and R. Gurwitch. 2005. Building resilience to mass trauma events. In *Handbook on injury and violence prevention interventions*, ed. L. Doll, S. Bonzo, J. Mercy, and D. Sleet. New York: Kluwer Academic Publishers.
34. Davis, D. 2012. Urban resilience in situations of chronic violence. Final report of the urban resilience in chronic violence project, USAID GRANT no. AID-OAA-G-10-00002:9.
35. Alker, H.R., Gurr, T.R., Rupesinghe, K. 2001. Journeys through conflict: Narratives and lessons. Lanham: Rowman and Littlefield.
36. Rodriguez-Garcia, R., Macinko, J., Solorzano, X., and Schlesser, M. 2001. How can health serve as a bridge for peace? The George Washington University School of Public Health and Health Services. Retrieved from http://www.certi.org/publications/policy/gwc-12a-brief.PDF.
37. Davis, J.L., and T.R. Gurr. 1998. *Preventive measures: Building risk assessment and crisis early warning systems*, 97. Lanham: Rowman and Littlefield.
38. Norris, F.H., S.P. Stevens, B. Pfefferbaum, K.F. Wyche, and R.L. Pfefferbaum. 2008. Community resilience as a metaphor, theory, set of capacities, and strategy for disaster readiness. *American Journal of Psychology* 41: 128.
39. Carpenter, A. 2012. Havens in a firestorm: Perspectives from Baghdad on resilience to sectarian violence. *Civil Wars* 14(2): 182–204.
40. Maguire, B. and Cartwright, S. 2008. Assessing a community's capacity to manage change: A resilience approach to social assessment. Australian Government, Bureau of Rural Services. pp. 1–27
41. Gibbs, J.T. 1984. Black adolescents and youth: An endangered species. *The American Journal of Orthopsychiatry* 54: 6–21.
42. Lorion, R.L., A. Brodsky, and M.R. Cooley-Quille. 1999. Exposure to urban violence: A framework for conceptualizing risky settings. In *Innovations in practice and service delivery across the lifespan*, ed. D.E. Biegel and A. Blum, 124–143. Oxford: New York.
43. Myers, H.F., S. Taylor, K.T. Alvy, A. Arrington, and M.A. Richardson. 1992. Parental and family predictors of behavior problems in inner-city Black children. *American Journal of Community Psychology* 20: 557–576.
44. Osofsky, J.D., S. Werers, D.M. Hann, and A.C. Fick. 1993. Chronic community violence: What is happening to our children? *Psychiatry* 56: 36–45.

45. Singer, M., T. Anglin, L. Song, and L. Lunghofer. 1995. Adolescents' exposure to violence and associated symptoms of psychological trauma. *Journal of the American Medical Association* 2(73): 477–482.
46. Longtaff, citing Surowiecki, J. 2004. The wisdom of crowds: Why the many are smarter than the few and how collective wisdom shapes business, Economies, Socieites and Nations. New York: Doubleday.
47. Norris, F.H., S.P. Stevens, B. Pfefferbaum, K.F. Wyce, and R. Pfefferbaum. 2008. Community Resilience as a Metaphor, Theory, Set of Capacities and Strategy for Disaster readiness. *American Journal of Community Psychology*. 41: 134.
48. Norris, F.H., S.P. Stevens, B. Pfefferbaum, K.F. Wyce, and R. Pfefferbaum. 2008. Community Resilience as a Metaphor, Theory, Set of Capacities and Strategy for Disaster readiness. *American Journal of Community Psychology*. 41: 136.

Chapter 6
Social Capital

Abstract What was the relationship of social capital to escalation dynamics in Baghdad neighborhoods? This chapter explores social capital and conflict resilience in Baghdad neighborhoods in two broad categories: relationships between people, and relationships between people and the neighborhood. Concerning the former, this chapter explores the difference between crosscutting and overlapping ties for conflict resilience; concerning the latter, it discusses the importance of three sociopsychological concepts: sense of community, citizen participation, and place attachment. Preexisting community connectedness and infrastructure are critical components of adaptation during crisis, but are fragile connections that easily fray during crisis without intentional, reinforcing actions.

Keywords Social capital • Conflict escalation • Trust • Resilience • Conflict prevention • Interethnic • Sectarian • Place attachment • Sense of community • Citizen participation • Tribal • Identity • Crosscutting bonds • Overlapping bonds

> *If you get sick, the people who bring you chicken soup are likely to represent your bonding social capital. On the other hand, a society that has only bonding social capital will look like Belfast or Bosnia—segregated into mutually hostile camps.*
>
> Robert Putnam

John Paul Lederach, a leading scholar and practitioner of peacebuilding, once described resilience as "the capacity to forge solidarity, to sustain hope and purpose, and to adapt and negotiate creatively with the challenges presented" [1]. Solidarity, hope, adaptation, creativity—none of these would be possible without social capital. Social capital exists in the relations among people. It is characterized by attributes such as trust, reciprocity, collective action, and participation. Social capital is therefore key to resilience.

This chapter focuses on the relationship of social capital to conflict escalation in Baghdad neighborhoods. Some areas experienced regime shifts consisting of large-scale displacement and a deep deterioration in Sunni–Shia relations, while

A. C. Carpenter, *Community Resilience to Sectarian Violence in Baghdad*, Peace Psychology Book Series, DOI: 10.1007/978-1-4614-8812-5_6,

others did not. All areas engaged in early intersect cooperation to protect neighborhood boundaries from "outside" groups. What was the role of social capital in why some communities ultimately succeeded, while others did not?

Defining Social Capital

Definitions of social capital abound. For some, social capital refers to collective action and cooperation: "the ability of people to work together for common purposes in groups" [2] or the "web of cooperative relationships between citizens that facilitate resolution of collective action problems" [3]. In other words, social capital is defined by its *function* of facilitating action [4].

For other theorists, social capital is not synonymous with collective action, but rather *those things that are required to bring about* collective action. Some of those things include "a culture of trust and tolerance" [5], "sense of social solidarity" [6], and "information, trust, and norms of reciprocity" [7]. For Fukuyama, the specific norms that lead to cooperation in groups are those "related to traditional virtues like honesty, the keeping of commitments, reliable performance of duties, reciprocity and the like" [8]. For Putnam, "cooperation, trust, reciprocity, civic engagement, and collective wellbeing" are required [9]. Social capital can also be defined in quantitative terms; for example, as "the number of people who can be expected to provide support and the resources those people have at their disposal" [10] or as the aggregate of the actual or potential resources that are linked to possession of a durable network of relationships [11].

The most fundamental determinant of social capital is trust. Trust is a critical factor in solving what political scientists and economists call collective action problems faced by people in any social context; namely, how can people coordinate and solve problems without knowing the true intentions of others? Three theoretical frameworks exist for studying the role of trust in collective action. They all share the common understanding of trust "as expectations about whether or not a trustee, in the context of a risky exchange relationship, will behave in a manner beneficial or at least not detrimental to the truster [12]". Rotter's Generalized Trust Framework [13, 14] theorizes that trust is a general predisposition on the part of individuals regardless of the context. Levi's Transaction Cost Theory maintains that trust is built over time through repeated interactions where the truster verifies that the trustee is able to keep promises and shares similar interests [15]. Sabatier and Jenkins-Smith's Advocacy Coalition Framework (1993) theorizes that people trust those who share similar belief systems and interests [16].

Whatever the definition, social capital is about the value of people's relationships that link them together. Social capital and conflict resilience in Baghdad neighborhoods consisted in two broad categories: (1) the nature of relationships between people and (2) the nature of relationships between people and the neighborhood. The former refers to relationships between neighborhood residents and also between neighborhood residents and external (tribal) networks. The latter refers to three sociopsychological dimensions: sense of community, place attachment, and citizen participation [17].

The two categories are confoundingly interdependent, but so are most elements of complex systems. I decided to draw the analytical distinction for the simple sake of sense-making. There is, after all, some level of difference between people's relationships to a particular place—a soccer field, a university, or a family home—and people's relationship to the other people with whom they share that space. Though they cannot be separated, they can be analyzed somewhat independently. The reason for doing so is simply to shed additional light on complicated relationships.

Relations Between People

In Chap. 2, I wrote that the history of relations between groups and their perceptions of each other (vis-à-vis cultural, political and economic discrimination) influences the likelihood of violent conflict [18]. On the one hand, all of the communities save one (Zafaraniyya) reported strong internal social support mechanisms. Social support "refers to social interactions that provide individuals with actual assistance and embed them into a web of social relationships perceived to be loving, caring and readily available in times of need [17]." For the reasons discussed earlier, the nature of social support was largely informal. For conflict resolution, including simple and complex disputes, respondents reported relying on interfamily dialog, tribal dialog, respected individuals, wise old men, respected families, and the "street" intervention of friends and passersby. To avoid paying bribes, tribes and families were the primary loan-makers. Neighborhood services, specifically trash collection, street cleaning, and aid to the poor, were organized through spontaneous cooperation between neighbors. Humanitarian assistance to the needy was organized by community members and executed by wealthy families, individuals, and Imams through collections at mosques. However, preexisting community structure is a determinant of whether communities "hold together or polarize in the face of conflict between subgroups." The primary issue is whether these social support networks are *crosscutting* or *overlapping*.[1]

Crosscutting Bonds

Crosscutting bonds (also referred to as "bridging ties" or "bridging capital") span social networks, connecting their capital and opportunities. Crosscutting ties contribute greatly to the potential for intergroup cooperation. Pruitt and Kim explain, "In a community with a heavy *crosscutting* structure, almost everybody is linked with almost everybody else by at least one kind of bond [19]". Effective crosscutting networks are characterized by "reciprocal links, frequent supportive interactions, overlap with other networks, the ability to form new associations, and cooperative decision-making

[1] Handbook of Conflict Resolution, Deustch, 857.

processes [17]." A well-known study by Ashutosh Varshney, which compared riot-prone cities in India with their peaceful counterparts, demonstrated that people with crosscutting ties were more likely to take action to prevent conflict escalation [20].

Researchers who study social networks contrast bonding ties, which are trusted relations between smaller networks of families, friends, and neighbors, with bridging ties that link those small networks together.

> Research suggests that...networks composed of "bridging" links to a diverse web of resources strengthen a community's ability to adapt to change, but networks composed only of local "bonding" links, which impose constraining social norms and foster group homophily, can reduce resilience. Diversity, we believe, is critical to a community's ability to move beyond adaptive management to proactively maintain and enhance resiliency [21].

One of my original assumptions was that crosscutting ties between Sunni and Shia residents did not exist to the same extent in conflict-vulnerable areas compared to those resilient to violence. However, all ten neighborhoods had crosscutting clubs and organizations, including sports teams and schools. Most also had markets, which were places of socialization as much as commerce. Below are respondents' descriptions of previous opportunities for crosscutting interactions.

> *Dura*: The shopkeepers in that market were mixed; Sunnis and Shiites. Young people used to meet with their friends there. As for my friends and I, we used to go to a shop in the centre of this market, because of its position; many young people would hang out there... Before 2005, this market was the best place for meeting new people because people from Bab Al-Mu'adham, Bayaa and Ur.

> *Amiriyya*: People in my neighborhood used to hang out in Karradah [a Shiite-dominant area] since only the bridge separates us from it. So we see many people from other neighborhoods in Karradah.

> *Adhamiyya*: Sports matches were held every two months. People from Al-Jihad neighborhood and Ghazaliya neighborhoods came to Amiriyya for football matches, including Shiite neighborhood Al-Kasra once a month.

With all the caveats previously mentioned in Chap. 1, all respondents (except Sadr City and Zafaraniyya stated that intergroup relations were strong before the war. "Amiriyya was a normal neighborhood," recalled our Sunni respondent, "a commercial area that...was safe and no one was asked about their sects or origins." He believed that sectarian differences were not deeply felt.

> I used to hang out with my friends, who were two Sunnis and three Shiites, in Arasat till 2 a.m, then go back to Amiriyya which would still be open at that time. We never thought that Sunnis represented the majority while Shiites did not.

As discussed in the Chap. 1, self-reports of good interethnic relations prior to the US invasion were subject to exaggeration. Moreover, obliviousness to sectarian tension for wealthy Sunnis under Hussein's skewed regime was a luxury of the privileged. Thus, the respondent's comment that "we never thought that Sunnis represented the majority while Shiites did not" can be interpreted in several ways. It might mean other social identities—one's profession, for instance—were more salient. Alternately, it might represent a sort of blindness to the un-expressed feelings of Shia neighbors as it was forbidden under Hussein's regime to speak of sectarian politics.

Still, this individual believed that intersect relations were strong. "We used to help the Shiites in their cooking rituals at the 10th of Muharram," he explained, referring to Ashura celebrations in which Sunni Iraqis have traditionally taken part. A Bayaa resident reiterated, "We didn't care about Shiites or Sunnis. We didn't know about those things. I prayed with Sunnis many times as well as with Shiites. Sunnis did the same thing; many of them prayed in Husseiniyas when they were nearby at the time of prayer."

Echoing the interviews above, the Sunni respondent from Adhamiyya reported, "I think the relations were healthy [before 2003]. We didn't think about the sectarian issues back then." With the same caveats, it is worth noting that this Sunni respondent described Shiites in Iraq as coming from "noble generous Arab tribes that would stand by you in case you need something." He also seemed to express genuine surprise at the sectarian turn of events, remarking,

> We never imagined that this could happen someday because in the same tribe there are Sunnis and Shiites. We're mixed as you see.

Anecdotally, intersect solidarity in Adhamiyya was on full display during the tragic Baghdad bridge stampede in 2005[2] as an example of frequent post-critical incident response of amplified solidarity, the temporary disappearance of community conflicts, and a sense of altruism (Fritz 1961: 692). However, the overwhelming Sunni majority in Adhamiyya may have made it hard to see whatever discomfort Shiite residents felt as sectarian violence escalated elsewhere in the country and city. In the following statement, the respondent seems to shrug off the sectarian tension mounting in other parts of Baghdad.

> Whenever something happens to the other sect, it didn't make any difference in my neighborhood since the majority are Sunni. I remember whenever I left my neighborhood, I was able to see the anger and annoyance on the Shiite's faces… I didn't see this in my neighborhood because most of the people there were Sunnis.

"Everything went nice and easy in my neighborhood" corroborated the respondent from Dura. "People used to come and go freely. You would be able to see people of all religions and sects—Sunni, Shiite, Arabs, Kurds….There is a

---

[2] As described earlier, the al Aimmah bridge connecting Adhamiyya and Shiite-dominant Kazimiyya had been closed in 2005. In September of the same year, Shia pilgrims on their way to the sacred shrine of the Imam Musa al-Kazim in Kazimiyya became panicked as rumors of an impending suicide bomb attack spread throughout the gathering. People crowded onto the bridge, overcoming the gate which had sealed the entrance. Tragically, gates on both sides of the bridge opened inward, making the exit on the opposite side of the bridge impossible. The bridge collapsed under the weight of so many people, and hundreds dropped into the Tigris below. People from both sides dove into the water to help those drowning; "on the Sunni side, calls went out from the loudspeakers of local Mosques to help those in trouble." Teenager Othman Abdul Hafez, "a Sunni Arab from the other side of the bridge, drowned as he tried to pull yet another Shia pilgrim from the River Tigris, having saved up to seven others." By accounts on Wikipedia, Adhamiyya residents pulled hundreds of Shia from the water, "where their fellow residents transported them to hospitals and mosques, in some cases using the mattresses from their own beds as makeshift stretchers." See http://news.bbc.co.uk/2/hi/middle_east/4214926.stm and http://en.wikipedia.org/wiki/Adhamiyya.

whole section in my neighborhood populated by Christians. Everyone was free to practice their rituals." Over time, as in the previous two cases, alienation increased gradually between Sunni and Shia sects.

> I remember one day I was praising the resistance in Fallujah; one of the Shiites was upset and left the group because of this very ordinary talk. We used to speak up and talk about these things before without any misunderstanding or sensitivity.

Many respondents mentioned conversations like the one described above. They were flashpoints for conflict over religious and political differences and must not be minimized. Studies of group dynamics have demonstrated that when people participate in group discussions like the one described above, they are more likely to express extreme positions and advocate riskier actions than they did before [22]. Moreover, discussions about identity politics between high-prejudice individuals have been shown to increase and intensify preexisting attitudes, worsening group polarization [23].

The Iraqi research team I worked with had experienced this phenomenon many times (which is one of the reasons we chose not to conduct our interviews in focus groups).

> After 2003 when people from different sects, even friends, were trying to lead any discussion about any political issue, it immediately turned out very personal, sensitive and hot and accusation for each other erupts and you literally can't lead a civil conversation. We used to conduct Sunni groups and Shia groups separately and when we were doing mixed groups because, we could see the stress, tension and hard feelings and even quarrels some times.
>
> And this just shows how different the opinions were and how much there is lack of real understanding of each other, each one was starting the discussion by preoccupied ideas about the other and he builds all the conversation depending on these preoccupied ideas and it is hard to find a place of agreement especially on political issues.
>
> Religious and more specifically sectarian attitudes determine to a big extent the course of such conversation, there is a clear and wide difference in opinion nearly in every political matter between Sunni and Shia. That's why many friends from different sects were unable to have any friendly discussion about any related topic, some times very bad hard feelings and quarrels erupt after such conversation and it may lead to walking away from each other.

A particularly memorable event for one respondent took place in 2005. "One day, Shiites in my neighborhood wanted to change the name of the neighborhood to Fatima Al-Zahra'a." (Fatima Al-Zahra'a was Muhammad's only surviving child and wife to Ali, the first Imam in the Shia tradition.) "We Sunnis refused because we didn't want any sectarian names since the neighborhood used to be a mixed one." The Shiite's opinions on the matter were presented in a meeting by an ironsmith, respected by Sunni residents because he was *Sayyid* (descendent from Muhammad) from the holy city of Najaf. The issue was not resolved, however, and resentment appears to have widened the rift as described below.

> There was neither rejection nor acceptance [no resolution]. I remember that they invited us for one of their rituals; we went there but we didn't like the ritual at all, so we left and never shared their rituals again.

Transcripts do not reveal what ritual this may have been, and it is not clear what this individual meant when he said "we didn't like the ritual at all." So far, we have seen that cooking rituals during Ashura were sometimes shared. Perhaps the dislike for what was once a shared ritual indicates the formation of hostile attitudes. Or, perhaps the ritual was a Nikah wedding (a fixed-term contractual marriage) or a short-term Mutah wedding, both deeply frowned upon in the Sunni tradition. Whatever the case "from that time on, the separation between the two sects started and the rift became wider and wider."

In other cases, the rift did not grow wider and crosscutting ties endured. I will explore the endurance of crosscutting ties further in Chap. 8 as a function of people's active engagement with the risks of sectarian violence. The bottom line for now is that preexisting crosscutting bonds can deteriorate rapidly in high-risk environments without concerted efforts to nurture, protect, and strengthen them.

Overlapping Ties

Overlapping ties bond members of a subgroup to other members of the same subgroup. Tribal affiliation falls into this category of social capital, but its relationship to conflict resilience is complicated. Tribal affiliation implies a cultural identity (discussed Chap. 1) that differs from the culture and values of urban Iraqis. One of my Iraqi colleagues explained the difference. His use of the word "civilized" refers literally to his sense that urbanites have modern values, including moral and intellectual advancement. As mentioned in the Chap. 10, the word is more akin to "urbanized."

> Baghdad is very mixed in terms of rural and urban: there's civilized areas and tribal areas. But when Baghdad was exposed to immigration from rural areas, Sadr City was established and brought tribal traditions with them. The culture in Sadr City is based on tribal values; they still perform honor killings. If a woman is suspected, she will be killed and that tradition is traced back to the desert. Actually in the desert it's not common practice, because they are living in a closed tribe protected by brothers and fathers and cousins. It's more cruel and common in the cities because females there work and shop, so the possibility that she'll be suspected is much higher.

Sociologist Ali Wardi theorized that Iraqi society was deeply split between culture and values of nomadism (masculinity, honor, revenge, loyalty to tribe and kinship networks) and of urbanism (individualism, less religiosity, progressive ideas of class, gender, sexuality, and welfare, loyalty to smaller friendships or professional networks). The respondent from Adhamiyya said much the same during his interview. When the moderator asked about local configurations of governance, he reported a combination of tribes which "dealt mostly with municipal issues" and "Old Baghdadis" including the Shakkuka and Hasan Kafir families. He commented,

> People lived there for generations so they are kind of one big family. I remember an old lady, who used to come to the playground where we used to play football and she used to call us by our mothers' names. She was amazing, she knew every single one of us although we were not from the same street. You know how Adhamiyya is big!

AQI could enter neighborhoods more easily where strong overlapping tribal ties existed. "Tribes play a big, very important role in Anbar," a respondent told us. "It's a tribal based society, there's no way you can operate there without the approval of the tribes." The exogenous change in the behavior of Sunni tribes in Anbar to support AQI therefore had profound effects for tribally affiliated neighborhoods. The Baathist elites and former government officials who lived in Amariya were situated within a complex tribal network that connected members of Hussein's al-Bu Nasir tribe to the Dulaimi tribes in Al Anbar[3] where AQI had been operating with tribal support since 2004.

The border between Anbar Province, Syria and Jordan was "theoretical," the Iraqi team director explained. "Smuggling of terrorists and black market products was huge across the border. The tribes used to make their living doing this, they were smuggling petrol from inside Iraq and sell it Jordan and Syria, also sheep and beef raised in Iraq, and guns." AQI operatives leveraged this social network to enter Baghdad neighborhoods, cultivating relationships with local leaders and residents.

Entry is not the same as support, as told by residents of Adhamiyya, Amiriyya, and Dura. But once inside, the overwhelming threat of violence reduced response diversity (discussed in Chap. 4 as the range of possible responses) to active or tacit cooperation. In Amiriyya, "[independent] community leaders stood away just watching". In Dura, "the Imam in the mosque would never been able to protect his neighborhood [without cooperating with AQI] because if he criticized them or objected to their acts, they might have killed him." In Adhamiyya, local leader Haj A'ayid, head of the city council in the period 2003–2004, who had "negotiated with the American troops to improve the services in the neighborhood, made efforts to improve the services and…paved half of the streets in the neighborhood," was assassinated upon AQI's arrival.

Relations with "the Community"

Social capital is not just about relationships between people, but also the attachment of individual people to the larger neighborhood. The sociopsychological aspects of these relationships include trust in others, or the willingness to take risks; expectations of reciprocity in behavior and attitudes; and personal and collective efficacy, meaning the willing engagement of citizens to participate in their community. Norris et al. have clustered these qualities into three dimensions: sense of community, citizen participation, and place attachment.

[3] Long, Austin (2008) "The Anbar Awakening," Survival, 50:2, 74. Al Anbar is the largest province in Iraq, and its residents entirely Sunni from the Dulaim tribe whose membership extends into Syria, Saudi Arabia and Jordan (Al Zarqawi's birthplace). These linkages dated back to the Iran–Iraq war. As more and more party members (especially members of the Baath militia known as the Popular Army) were sent to the front, thinning out the presence of loyal Baathists in tribal areas. This forced increasing reliance on tribal loyalty and Saddam widened the circle of tribes he relied on, drawing heavily on the large Dulaimi confederation of Anbar.

Sense of Community

Sense of community is defined as "an attitude of bonding (trust and belonging with members of one's...locale, including mutual concerns and shared values." According to Goodman, "both the frequency and intensity of interactions (social embeddedness) and the benefits members receive from their social ties (received and perceived support)" are components of community resilience [16, 139]. Resilience to sectarian violence requires that sense of community consists of bridging social capital. Characteristics like "high concern for community issues, respect for and service to others, sense of connection, and needs fulfillment" [24] count toward conflict resilience *only* when they transcend the boundaries of communal identity groups. Stories from conflict resilient neighborhoods highlighted *close relationships* between Sunni, Shia, and Christian residents.

> *Karada*: The good relationship between the people that was built in the previous years was sufficient to face those tensions.... People knew each other. Young people and old men cooperated among themselves to help the others.
>
> *Palestine Street*: People in small neighborhoods knew each other well.
>
> *Kuraiaat*: Sunnis and Shiites had good relations with each other and they worked and cooperated to main security in the neighborhood. The people respect and value the old relationship.
>
> *Al-Dhubat:* Relations were excellent; I considered my neighbors as family; people we used to play at certain play grounds in the neighborhood; the young people used to play as teams that consisted of Shia, Sunnis, and Christian guys; this is still happening; still meet at cafes; in neighborhood; mixed elementary schools and high schools.

The felt commitment to the people with whom one lives provides the motivation to actively participate in the life of the community. It is therefore interesting to contrast the accounts above with what residents from Zafaraniyya, where the Mahdi Army was allowed to operate, had to say:

> People in my neighborhood didn't have ties with each other. Every person minded their own business. We used to go the funeral ceremonies to participate by reciting a Verse of Qur'an and that is it. The same thing occurs in marriages. I personally faced a problem; I needed money for an operation to my son; I wasn't comfortable about asking for help from the others; I sold something I have and I paid for the expenses of the operations.
>
> People of the neighborhood don't know each other [they are anonymous]. Sometimes a man in the mosque says that a person is in need of money because they needed an operation, they don't mention his name. The man says that they will accept donations for a particular period of time. Many people received help this way.

Sense of community was certainly not enough to predict a community's capacity to regulate militia activity. But at the least, it is the psychological equivalent and prerequisite for citizen participation. As William Ury wrote, "the single biggest obstacle to [conflict] prevention remains the fatalistic belief that fighting, violence and war are inevitable [25]". Perhaps the opposite dynamic is at work in communities with a history of acceptance, good relationships, and cooperation. Perhaps such histories constitute belief in the practicality and possibility of peace [17, 123].

The schism between so-called tribal and civilian identity affects sense of community and social cohesion. Most areas of Baghdad contain mixtures of residents who define themselves by one or the other identity. My colleague S.S. Motlak explained one day, over tea and a map of Baghdad.

> Baghdad is very mixed, not homogenous in terms of rural and urban, there's civilized and tribal areas. But when Baghdad was exposed to immigration from rural areas to it, Sadr City was established and brought tribal traditions with them.

Sadr City has the largest population in Baghdad. Motlak drew a line separating Sadr City in two parts. "The upper part is Sadr City proper" he explained, "and the front part is not like the back part—for one thing, it is a [college district] inhabited by students from Al Mustansiriya, Baghdad's largest university. It has a different demography than the rest of Sadr City—and [a civilian culture]." Salaam was careful to point out that tribal identity coexists with civilian (urbanized) identity in many places. "People from Samarra and Mosul will describe themselves as being from this tribe or that tribe. But the community *as a whole* is not a tribal community, so when you think about the big head of the region it's not a tribal head—the head is from a family."

Citizen Participation

Citizen participation refers to involvement and engagement of community members in local organizations. It is about people's self-organized involvement and engagement.[4] Citizen participation is closely related to social cohesion, which is the act of cohering, uniting, or sticking together.[5] Harvard researcher Richard Sampson found that levels of social cohesion, measured by how regularly people work together to achieve common goals, determined resilience to conflict escalation immediately following a violent incident [26]. By accounts, Baghdad neighborhoods differed on the variability of social cohesion. As previously noted, people coordinated efforts in some neighborhoods to solve community problems including organizing trash collection and collections for poor families, collecting signatures from all residents on a petition, and cooperating to settle disputes. Conversely, the respondent from Sadr City told us "there was no coordinated neighborhood action to help 'the needy'; a neighbor might hear about the problem and go to the hospital, but it's not people making a joint decision together." His counterpart from Zafaraniyya reported that "people don't meet or gather" to solve community problems.

---

[4] While discussions about this set of capacities often include *leadership* as a variable, I have chosen to cover leadership in *Chapter Five Community Competence*.

[5] Adapted from the Oxford Dictionary's definition as "the action or fact of forming a united whole [including for physics] the sticking together of particles of the same substance."

Preexisting community connectedness and infrastructure are critical components of adaptation during crisis, and these joint activities indicate a level of contact, communication, and coordination between residents that predated the formation of self-defense groups (covered in Chap. 7). In Zafaraniyya where (according to our respondent), "people didn't know each other," residents organized in a different way. "How did you protect your neighborhood?" one of our facilitators asked.

> I didn't have to; my neighborhood didn't accept people from the other side. Shiites didn't welcome Sunnis and Sunnis didn't welcome Shiites in the neighborhood. People working in the Husseiniyas wanted to arrange checkpoint at night in return for collecting 10 thousand Iraqi Dinars from each family, but most people didn't pay. Most people said that they didn't need any protection. They said that they would protect themselves.

Place Attachment

Place attachment is closely related to one's sense of community [27]. It implies an emotional connection to one's neighborhood or city, somewhat apart from connections to the specific people who live there [28]. Place attachment consists of positive bonds to physical and social settings. These bonds build and reinforce group identity, feelings of pride, and positive affiliations with neighbors. Place attachment is "nourished by daily encounters with the environment and neighbors, seasonal celebrations, continued physical personalization and upkeep, and affective feelings toward and beliefs about the home and neighborhood [29]". Neighborhoods do not have to be wealthy or even reasonably safe for place attachments to be strong. Research by Fried suggests that place attachment may be particularly resilient in lower income neighborhoods because they are isolated from society and self-reliant on their own support mechanisms.

My interviews indicated that place attachment was an important element of positive resilience. Respondents echoed a 2003 study of place attachment, which found that long-term residents reported more positive overall place attachments. Long-term residency was one of the answers Pinkston received during his visit to Al Nil:

> The question is: Why is Al Nil seemingly immune to the poisonous attitudes that fuel the violence here? One possible answer from Abdul Abdullah Muzban, a Shiite who runs a security service: "We're close to each other and we like each other," he says. "Most of us have lived here 40 years, so we know each other."

Individuals from Karada and Al-Dhubat made similar statements about old, trusted relationships:

> *Karada*: My neighborhood didn't witness sectarian violence because the people of neighborhood are old and we didn't have new residents.

> *Al-Dhubat:* We have long-time residents and not a lot of newcomers; most of the people in my area inhabited it since the 1960s; they are the original residents of Zayouna.

Place attachment may be a necessary component of conflict resilience, but it certainly is not sufficient. As we read above, Adhamiyya was also described as having a core of residents "who lived there for generations

[and] are kind of one big family." In fact, it may turn out that place *detachment* had an equally important effect. People driven out of their own communities sometimes become disruptive in the places where they settled. For different reasons, respondents from Al Doura, Al-Dhubat, and Al Bayaa believed that early internal displacement also influenced community polarization. First, wealthy residents who could afford to leave did so as tensions mounted, leaving behind poor residents who were more easily preyed on. The respondent from Al Bayaa described this as a mechanism whereby both AQI and Mahdi Army gained a presence in the neighborhood:

> Many Sunnis and rich people left their houses to Syria and Jordan. Only poor people remained and they suffered from terrorism. Many of them were forced to serve the terrorists; the people had to cook for them and harbor them in their houses.

Secondly, new arrivals might support militias in the areas to which they moved:

> *Al-Dhubat*: The violent areas of Zayouna are… places in which displaced people settled, who spread sectarian attitudes (Al-Dhubat).

> *Dura*: The displaced Sunnis from other neighborhoods who lived in my neighborhood supported the foreigners at that time and caused the chaos in my neighborhood. I think they wanted to revenge from anyone by displacing the others and making them suffer as they suffered when they were displaced. Cars filled with men from Amiriyya used to come to our neighborhood every now and then and cause more chaos.

Ultimately, both AQI and Mahdi Army came to operate in Dura resulting in terrible intercommunal violence. It was the first neighborhood where the US Army erected barriers between Sunni and Shia enclaves to try to stem the killing.

Conclusion

This chapter has focused on the influence of social capital on conflict escalation trajectories over time, and contrasted crosscutting with overlapping bonds. Overlapping bonds may have negatively impacted conflict resilience, in the sense that sectarian actors could leverage the tribal social network to enter Baghdad neighborhoods. On the other hand, there is evidence to suggest that people in most of the neighborhoods we studied had varying degrees of crosscutting bonds and frequent supportive interactions.

These crosscutting bonds were fragile. "The relationship between Sunni and Shia was a based on mutual ignorance of each other and certain degree of distrust…the law prohibited any discussions in political or religious issues, so even the good relationships between many Sunnis and Shia were mainly based upon ignoring, overlooking or hiding differences rather than really addressing, accepting and living with them as what happened in the more tolerant communities [29]."

Suggested in these accounts is that crosscutting social structure—one of the most important regime characteristics in resilience to violence—can dissolve quickly when the intent to nurture and protect those linkages is sufficiently lacking. Cross-cutting ties have dissolved in several of the neighborhoods under study, as the accounts below describe.

Amiriyya: The neighborhood is closed. No stranger can enter and so we are safe from the car bombs. However, customers from other neighborhoods …have to get badges to enter the neighborhood. Amiriyya looks like a state that you can't enter without a passport.

Adhamiyya: The people are all Sunnis. This is so relieving…because all people in my neighborhood have the same attitudes and beliefs. We won't have to argue over essential issues. I can't listen to or understand the other's beliefs.

Dura: 99 % of people are Sunni, and there is preference for this… No one from the mosque made an effort to improve our relationships with the Shiites in the neighborhood.

Respondents from both Al-Dhubat and Kuraiaat claimed that their neighborhoods did not experience a decline in social capital. The respondent from Al-Dhubat indicated that "the young people used to play as [sports] teams that consisted of Shiite, Sunnis and Christian guys; this is still happening" and that a new park was opened in 2008 that draws people of all faiths from nearby areas. A respondent from Kuraiaat also emphasized that Sunni and Shiite residents still rely on their strong intercommunal relationship to resolve conflicts and manage day-to-day problems. Anecdotal accounts are insufficient to the task of assessing the decline or strength of social capital and we can go far beyond sports teams and intercommunal problem-solving as indicators. More likely is that social capital has eroded even in the neighborhoods successful in preventing sectarian violence and forced displacement.

Karada: While in the past people of all neighborhoods used to welcome any stranger coming in the neighborhood asking about a particular person and they helped them, this has changed…the people lost trust in the others and this is a very big problem.

Palestine Street: Nobody was forcibly displaced from Palestine Street [but] seventy percent of the neighborhood has changed now. People used to know each other very well, unlike now. The people had a stronger relationship with each other.

If accurate (a significant "if," given the lack of census data), the level of reported displacement from Palestine Street indicates a decline in place attachment, sense of community, and social cohesion. Perhaps having the choice to leave rather than being forced to flee overnight counts for some level of difference from areas like Dura; however, the end result in both cases is social trust lost.

References

1. Lederach, J.P. 2005. *The moral imagination: The art and soul of building peace*, 14. New York: Oxford University Press.
2. Fukuyama, Francis. 1995. *Trust : the social virtues and the creation of prosperity*, 10. London: Hamish Hamilton.
3. Brehm, John, and W. Rahn. 1997. Individual-level evidence for the causes and consequences of social capital. *American Journal of Political Science* 41: 999–1023.
4. Coleman, James S. 1990. *Foundations of social theory*, 203. Cambridge: Harvard University Press. Emphasis mine.
5. Inglehart, R. 1997. *Modernization and post-modernization: Cultural, economic and political change in 43 societies*, 188. Princeton: Princeton University Press.

6. Richards, P., Bah, K. and Vincent, J. (2004). Social capital and survival: Prospects for community driven development in post-conflict Sierra Leone. World Bank, Social Development Papers, p 1.
7. Woolcock, Michael. 1998. Social capital and economic development: Towards a theoretical synthesis and policy framework. *Theory and Society* 27: 151–208. 153.
8. Fukuyama, Francis. 1999. Social capital and civil society. The Institute of Public Policy at George Mason University. Prepared for delivery at the IMF conference on second generation reforms.
9. Putnam, R.D. 1993. *Making democracy work: Civic traditions in modern Italy*, 177–181. Princeton New Jersey: Princeton University Press.
10. Boxman, E.A.W., P.M. De Grant, and H.D. Flap. 1991. The impact of social and human capital on the income attainment of Dutch managers. *Social Networks* 13(51–73): 52.
11. Bourdieu, P. 1986. The forms of capital. In *Handbook of theory and research for the sociology of education*, ed. John G. Richardson, 241–258. New York: Greenwood Press.
12. Lubell, Mark. 2007. Familiarity breeds trust: Collective action in a policy domain. *The Journal of Politics* 69(1): 237–250.
13. Rotter, J.B. 1971. Generalized expectancies for interpersonal trust. *American Psychologist* 26(5): 443–452.
14. Rotter, J.B. 1980. Interpersonal trust, trustworthiness, and gullibility. *American Psychologist* 35(1): 1–7.
15. Levi, Margaret. 2000. When good defenses make good neighbors. In *Institutions, contracts, and organizations: Perspectives from new institutional economics*, ed. Claude Menard, 137–157. Chichester, England: Edward Elgar.
16. Sabatier, Paul, and Hank Jenkins-Smith. 1993. *Policy change and learning: An advocacy coalition approach*. Boulder, CO: Westview Press.
17. Norris, Fran H., Susan P. Stevens, Betty Pfefferbaum, Karen F. Wyce, and Rose Pfefferbaum. 2008. Community resilience as a Metaphor, theory, set of capacities and strategy for disaster readiness. *American Journal of Community Psychology* 41: 139.
18. Brown, Michael E. 2001. Ethnic and internal conflicts. In *Turbulent peace: The challenges of managing international conflict*, ed. C. Crocker, F. Hampson, and P. Aall. Washington, DC: United States Institute of Peace Press.
19. Pruitt, Dean, and Sung Hee Kim. 2004. *Social conflict: Escalation, stalemate and settlement*, vol. 3, 138. Boston, MA: McGraw Hill.
20. Varshney, Ashutosh. 2001. Ethnic conflict and civil society: India and beyond. *World Politics* 53(3): 366.
21. Newman and Dale. 2005. http://www.ecologyandsociety.org/vol10/iss1/resp2/.
22. Isenberg, D.J. 1986. Group polarization: A critical review and meta-analysis. *Journal of Personality and Social Psychology* 50(6): 1141–1151.
23. Myers, David G., and G.D. Bishop. 1970. Discussion effects on racial attitude. *Science* 169(3947): 778–779.
24. Goodman, R., M. Speers, K. McLeroy, S. Fawcett, M. Kegler, E. Parker, et al. 1998. Identifying and defining the dimensions of community capacity to provide a basis for measurement. *Health Education and Behavior* 25: 261.
25. Ury, William. 2000. *The third side: Why we fight and how we can stop*, 2000. New York: Penguin Group.
26. Carey, Benedict. 2013. Diagnosis: Battered but vibrant. New York Times, Jan 7. http://www.nytimes.com/2013/01/08/science/lessons-in-community-from-chicagos-southside.html?pagewanted=all&_r=0.
27. Tartaglia, S. 2006. A preliminary study for a new model of sense of community. *Journal of Community Psychology* 34: 25–36.
28. Manzo, L., and D. Perkins. 2006. Finding common ground: The importance of place attachment to community participation and planning. *Journal of Planning Literature* 20: 3.
29. Brown, Barbara, Douglas Perkins, and Graham Brown. 2003. Place attachment in a revitalizing neighborhood: Individual and block levels of analysis. *Journal of Environmental Psychology* 23(2003): 259–271.

Chapter 7
Information and Communication

Abstract This chapter explores three enablers of adaptation related to information and communication: sources, spaces, and narratives. Trusted sources of information enable people to respond flexibly and quickly during times of change. Collective adaptation in crisis is particularly affected by the sense-making and communicative activities of leaders. Just as important are spaces for sharing information, which reinforce trust and communication during crisis and self-organize as new events unfolded. Spaces for sharing information helped people keep in touch with each other during crisis, quash divise rumors, self-organize as new events unfolded, and build trust. Finally, group narratives reinforce group solidarity and set the boundaries for "appropriate" responses to events in general, including large disturbances, crises, and conflicts. How groups of people interpret events that happen determines how they cope with them.

Keywords Information • Communication • Adaptation • Sources • Spaces • Narratives • Sense-making • Leadership • Self-organization • Media • Trust • Conflict resilience • Media bias • Cultural narratives • Social capital • Communication systems • Markets • Facilitators • Social support • Enclave •Images • Self-esteem • Coping ability

> *"…communication is a central or the mediating factor facilitating and contributing to collective change process."*
>
> Mary Olufunke Adedokun et al. [1]

Some say that information and communication are the most essential elements of resilience and adaptive capacity [2]. For one thing, fast and accurate access to information enables individuals and groups to adapt fast during crises [3, 4]. According to Longstaff, individuals need three types of information in order to cope in the face of adversity: information about "freedom of movement (Can I get away from the danger?), the nature of the danger (How bad? How local? How

A. C. Carpenter, *Community Resilience to Sectarian Violence in Baghdad*,
Peace Psychology Book Series, DOI: 10.1007/978-1-4614-8812-5_7,

soon?), and options for survival and recovery (What is working for other people like me? What is not working? Should I be cooperating with neighbors?)" [5].

Not only individuals, but groups need these three types of information as well. Additionally, they need mechanisms for communicating among group members, and in the case of coalitions ("groups of groups"), they need boundary-spanning communication mechanisms. This chapter explores three enablers of adaptation related to information and communication: sources, spaces, and narratives. Sources included clerics, neighbors, word of mouth from families and friends living elsewhere, all major forms of media—newspaper, radio, and television—domestic telephone lines and (starting in summer 2003) cellular service. Spaces for communication included mosques, local councils, neighborhood committees, and tribal councils. Narratives, introduced in Chap. 1 as stories about a group's origins, history, and relationship with other groups, can either bolster or undermine conflict resilience. Specifically, narratives emphasizing empowerment, agency, and solidarity are positively associated with community resilience after disaster [6], while those emphasizing loss, abandonment, and hopelessness are associated with lower levels of resilience [7].

Sources: Leaders, Media and Working Trust

Generally, people believe information that comes from a trusted source and/or is consistent with the facts as known. Word of mouth is a trusted sources of information if coming from "someone who people do not perceive to have a reason to lie to them and who they believe has access to accurate information" [3]. In addition, people tend to rely more on messages about what is happening from those around them, those within close proximity [3]. For example, when we asked people how they organized to keep their neighborhood safe, nobody mentioned television reports, social media, or phone calls with distant relatives. People trust messages from other people more than they trust information from more distant organizations or institutions. "In the last analysis, only people can move other people" [8].

By sharing information between neighbors, people can respond flexibly to changes in their immediate environment, protecting the integrity of the whole system through self-organized adaptation. Trusted sources are key because "the likelihood of information moving from one person to another is proportional to the strength of their relationship" [9]. Again, those sources "are often likely to be local sources who can deal with local variability (what is trustworthy for you may not be for me). Those sources also need to have…reliable scanning capabilities (what's really happening here?) and who don't have an interest in misleading anyone" [5, p. 6].

One source for trusted information was community leaders. While not the determinant factor in conflict resilience [10], leadership is a key component of adaptive capacity. Mary Anderson and Marshall Wallace [10] observed that leadership in "non-war" communities displayed two key characteristics. First, individual leaders are already in place. Based on the unique history and identity of local communities, [10: 50] leaders in Baghdad neighborhoods included religious leaders, prominent families, tribal sheikhs, and respected community members. Akin to Anderson and Wallace's observations of other conflict-resilient communities, local leaders negotiated on behalf of the community with external authorities.

> *Respondent* (*Amiriyya*): There were some unofficial respectful men in my neighborhood and they were the leaders of my neighborhood at that time. They were well known in the neighborhood because their families have been in Amiriyya for a very long time ago; Kbeisat, Dlaim and other well-known families.
>
> *Interviewer*: "*What was the main duty of the wise men in your neighborhood*?"
>
> *Respondent*: They were the bridge between the lawmakers and us; they used to speak on our behalf and we chose them to represent us…[After 2003] they usually negotiated with the Americans and the police station in the neighborhood since they have the guts to do so. They used to ask the US army to release any arrested young man. We also used to ask for their help in case we needed any.

Collective adaptation in crisis is critically supported (or stymied) by the sense-making and communicative activities of leaders. The behavior of religious leaders in Baghdad neighborhoods was extremely important. They interpreted the post-2003 Iraqi world in sermons and conversations, using religious–historical frames to argue for sectarian violence or sectarian peace. Frames are explanatory narratives, or cognitive short cuts for making sense of complex information—"collections of perceptions and thoughts that people use to define a situation, organize information, and determine what is important and what is not."[1] People develop frames for labeling situations, identifying and interpreting courses of action, and communicating that interpretation to others.[2] Importantly, because frames are developed on the foundation of underlying norms and values, they can exist (and affect individual decision-making) unconsciously.

Like their counterparts in South African and Nigerian conflict zones, clerics and imams in Baghdad "could challenge and transform religious narratives compelling violence and mobilize communities to support peace" [13]. In other words,

> religious actors build peace when they act religiously, that is, when they draw on the deep wells of their traditions, and extract from those depths the spiritual instincts and moral imperatives for recognizing and embracing the humanity of the other; and, when they employ the distinctive ritual and symbolic and psychological resources of religion for transforming the dream of a common humanity into a tangible, felt reality. They exhibit greater capacity for peace when they form alliances and spend the social capital they have gained through years and decades of confidence-building service to the local community.[3]

Secondly, leadership *as an institution* was embedded in local traditions and norms that were larger than any one individual. Thus, in areas where traditions and norms emphasized acceptance and social solidarity, people at least tried to reject

[1] Lewicki, Saunders and Minton [11].

[2] Buechler [12].

[3] Comments by Appleby [14], Cited in [15].

leaders with narratives that did not fit with the community norms. Respondents from to violence-torn areas, Adhamiyya and Amiriyya, did not hide their disillusionment with the inflammatory role played by local clerics.

> *Adhamiyya*: The clerics in Abu Hanifa mosque were so respected at that time and their advices were heard in my neighborhood whether in the Friday sermons or on a personal level. People in my neighborhood depended on them to add credibility to their stories.

> *Amiriyya*: "The religious people distorted the image of Islam"; "the biggest mistake of the clerics of a particular sect (I don't like using the words Sunni or Shiite) did was advising the people not to join Iraqi Army and Police. Sunni clerics would refuse cooperating with the USA and according to them, if you did, *you are not Muslim anymore* (emphasis mine).

Consistent with previous studies, leaders in conflict-resilient neighborhoods also played several key roles, the most important of which was *articulating core values and tradition* in order to mobilize conflict prevention strategies. Leaders in conflict-resilient communities tended to communicate their vision through cultural narratives that linked collective identity to non-violent, non-retributive strategies [16, 17]. I will elaborate on cultural narratives as enablers of adaptation in the final section of this chapter.

Media was another source of information and communication. Prior to the US invasion of 2003, the Baath Party was in complete control of Iraq's media sector which consisted of two television channels, four radio stations, and five daily newspapers [18]. The private media sector has expanded hugely since then, but with a considerable negative impact.

> This new life and the tons of new media and the tons of different attitudes and opinions and debate on TV stations was really a new task for Iraqis. Under Saddam's dictator regime there was no debate, no media and no discussions, there was one way of doing things "the leader (Saddam) orders and everyone else should silently and without raising his eyebrows execute what the president wants" those who argue, discuss or even ask will be sent to jail if not to hell.

To further complicate the "new task" of free speech and open debate, the private media sector has had a considerable negative impact on sectarian relationships in the new Iraq. According to the United States Institute of Peace,

> the private sector media in Iraq have developed rapidly and dramatically since 2003, with the Iraqi public increasingly able to access a vast array of news and information. This is one of the most positive outcomes of recent institutional developments in Iraq, yet the speed of the media transformation also brings negative side effects that are often hallmarks of media environments in transition… Given their ownership structures and scarce advertising revenues, the channels rely on political patronage for financial support. This becomes particularly problematic during election periods, when political parties and their candidates turn to television stations to carry their campaign messages…As the private media sector has grown, so has the number of untrained, unprofessional journalists [who] may fall back on divisive clichés, tell stories in simplistic ways, and lack the capacity to report in a conflict-sensitive manner. They also may not know how to confront interviewees who make inflammatory statements.

In one of the few empirical studies of Iraqi news media, Ibrahim Al-Marashi concluded that television and newspapers are primarily ethno-sectarian in nature, and "are providing the psychological groundwork for bitter divisiveness and conflict, with one channel [al-Zawra] already making direct exhortations for violence against other Iraqi communities" [19].

> [Al-Zawra] produces its own announcements that directly incite violence by calling on Iraqis to join the "jihad" against "US and Iranian occupation." It also attacks Iran reflecting a pro-Iraqi Arab Sunni sentiment that alleges Iran is aiding its coreligionists in Iraq. Announcements on the channel denounce the "crimes of Muqtada and of the gangs 'Aziz al-Hakim," a reference to Muqtada al-Sadr, leader of the primarily Shi'a Sadr Trend, and 'Abd al-'Aziz al-Hakim, leader of the SCIRI group. The station calls upon the "free youth of Iraq" to join the groups that are "defending" the nation to keep "Baghdad free from the Safawis," referring to the sixteenth to eighteenth century Safavid Empire of Iran, but meant as a derogatory term against Iraq's Shi'a. The channel also features footage of what it alleges are "Sunni civilians" attacked by Shi'a militias.

According to Al-Marashi, almost every news channel had (and has) an implicit bias toward one or another sect or ethnic group; all Shi'a and Sunni political parties operate their own radio stations, newspapers, and satellite channels, as do Iraqi Kurds, Turkmen, and Christian Assyrians. Al-Iraqiya, the state-owned TV channel, may be the most benign in that its content stresses progress, reconstruction, and security and more importantly, "attempts to minimize the differences between Iraq's Sunni and Shi'a by broadcasting live coverage of Friday sermons where religious leaders from both communities preach against the nation's sectarian divide and stress "Iraqi unity" [19: 9].

But Al-Iraqiya has its own pro-government bias which, given the current predominance of the United Iraqi Alliance of Shi'a Islamist groups and the Kurdish coalition, manifests as "an inherent Shi'a-Kurdish bias." Al-Marashi quotes an Iraqi journalist Muhammad Sahi (one of the few who allowed their name to be used in his study), who blamed the fragmentation of Iraqi media along ethno-sectarian lines for increasing social tensions.

> Accordingly, the Iraqi street and viewers are being divided with regard to their favored channels and news coverage based on their political loyalties and inclinations. Hence, it is inevitable for them to adopt the political discourse of their favored television channels and to act in accordance with the statements made by political leaders. The Iraqis have found themselves to be indirectly involved and supporting some political leaders or perhaps even among their followers [20].[4]

A final source (broadly conceptualized) of information and communication is working trust. Longstaff and Un undertook a study to measure the effects of trust on crisis management outcomes. They differentiated between internal trust (the level of trust that group members display toward their own group) and external trust (the level of trust displayed toward parties other than their own). They found that when trust within groups (internal trust) was high, those groups coordinated crisis communications to a significantly higher degree—communication was ongoing and coordinated between multiple actors. We can think about internal trust as trust existing between residents in Baghdad's neighborhoods. In

[4] Cited in [19].

conflict-resilient areas, trust was the social capital required for cooperation and organization to prevent the entry of sectarian militias.

> *Karada*: The good relationship between the people that was built in the previous years was sufficient to face those tensions.
>
> *Palestine Street*: People in small neighborhoods knew each other well.
>
> *Kuraiaat*: Sunnis and Shiites had good relations with each other and they worked and cooperated to main security in the neighborhood. The people respect and value the old relationship.
>
> *Al-Dhubat*: We kept Al Qaida out because the people were supportive to each other.

All these accounts really tell us that is that working trust necessary for collective action. That is to say, trust and solidarity was not lacking in other areas in Adhamiyya where, according to a resident, "my whole neighborhood loved AQI and supported them in the beginning."[5] To count toward conflict resilience however, trust and solidarity must *span* sectarian boundaries. When it does, working trust facilitates boundary-spanning behaviors that serve an entire community (covered in Chap. 8).

Spaces for Information-Sharing and Communication

Spaces for sharing information helped people keep in touch with each other during crisis, quash divise rumors, self-organize as new events unfolded, and build trust. By sharing information between neighbors, people responded flexibly to changes in their immediate environment. The structure of communication systems varied from neighborhood to neighborhood and ranged from pre-existing structures to new ones that emerged in response to the crisis. I focus below on four in particular: tribal councils, neighborhood committees, Friday prayers, and public gathering spaces.

Indigenous tribal councils enabled the Ghaydat tribe to defend Salaam-Fajr, the Sunni neighborhood in Kazimiyya District, against Mahdi Army militias in 2006 and 2007. Through consultations with each other and residents, tribal leaders coordinated roof-top defense squads that repelled fierce attacks by Mahdi fighters determined to clear Kazimiyya district of all Sunni residents.[6]

Neighborhood committees, which, like tribal councils, oversaw security groups, tended to be headed by "wise old men." They were spaces where men gathered to discuss and strategize the protection of a particular area. The committees consisted of trusted community members, and it appears that part of their role was to make sure that residents were informed about the rules and strategies that defined a neighborhood response to escalating sectarian tensions and violence.

Friday prayer meetings served as another venue for meetings between Muslims with their leaders although, as discussed above, leaders used that venue either to

---

5 Interview Adhamiyya, July 2010.

6 Residents of Salaam-Fajr were not interviewed as part of this study. This story was documented by Wesley Morgan in 2008, in interviews with tribal leaders in the presence of Task Force 1-502 Infantry. Morgan, Wesley (2008). "In Shia Baghdad, a Sunni tribe recalls weathering the storm." *The Long War Journal.*

spread messages urging violence or non-violence. In cases above, leaders facing the threat of violence (rioting, invasion, violent crime) tied the group's motivation to act to a collectively held and valued identity—"who we are and what we believe"—so that the norms and structures of the existing community regime became the interpretive lens for choosing courses of action.

Finally, the availability of public spaces where people come together to socialize and connect affects the quality and availability of information and communication. Throughout the book so far, Zafaraniyya has stood out as a neighborhood seemingly lacking the level of interpersonal interaction, community cooperation, and overall solidarity expressed in the narratives by residents of other areas. One explanation, with strong support from research on geospatial dimensions of resilience, is its physical layout

> *Zafaraniyya (respondent)*: My neighborhood is isolated; it doesn't have nearby neighborhoods; we don't have large markets. I used to go to Baghdad Al Jadida or Saydiya when I wanted to shop. We don't have big markets so young people gather locally in their regions.
>
> *Interviewer:* Where do the people, old people, meet in your neighborhood?
>
> *Respondent:* They don't meet or gather.
>
> *Interviewer:* Why?
>
> *Respondent:* This is the nature of the neighborhood; we didn't have football playgrounds.

As this resident described, the lack of public places to gather, like football stadiums and markets, reduced contact between residents putting Zafaraniyya at what Peter St. Jean might call an "ecological disadvantage" in that it limits opportunities for building social capital [21]. Most respondents described markets as places of social interaction. Markets were less important (pre-2003 anyway) as places of commerce as they were for meeting or reconnecting friends and acquaintances and having conversations. "It's very common for people to meet at markets," one respondent commented. "One might see friends there that you hadn't seen for years." In this sense, we might conceptualize markets as facilitators of social capital, not indicators of economic development as I had previously assumed.

If markets are facilitators of social capital, community enclaves serve the opposite function. For example, Bayaa neighborhood had an enclave structure before 2003, such that most Sunni and Shiite residents lived in separate areas, with some intermixing. As we read in Chap. 4, trust (social capital) is a function of the frequency and intensity of contact between people. Enclave structure affected the frequency of interaction and communication (and therefore the density of cross-cutting relationships) between Sunni and Shia residents in Bayaa. When asked about social support, the respondent told us that residents pulled together in smaller groups, not neighborhood-wide ones.

> The self-organized help groups weren't centrally organized, but "by street"—families close to the individual in need. There is an active person in every street in the neighborhood.

As AQI began to target the Shi'a enclaves with car bombs, the self-defense groups that formed armed checkpoints around different neighborhoods of Bayaa had a de facto sectarian character. These groups later coalesced under the Mahdi Army's banner.

It remains an open question for me whether enclave structure *in mixed areas* like Bayaa limited the cross-cutting relationships that helped people organize in broad coalitions. In areas where one sect was dominant, enclave structure may have *facilitated* resilience. Carlos Forment observed that "the responsiveness of enclave institutions to the needs of their local residents produces a level of self-reliance and public trust seldom found among other…communities" [22]. As a consequence of spatial concentration and stability, residents of ethnic enclaves tend to have strong bonding ties that reinforce ethnic identity and social cohesion. A resident of Shia-dominant Karada reported: "We didn't have to arrange for meetings; our houses were close to each other we used to talk to each other like neighbors."[7]

Narratives

A different type of structure that affects the social system of human interaction consists of narratives.[8] As discussed previously, narratives are dynamic "frameworks for action" through which people make sense of the world. Group narratives—"stories that members of social and political groups tell about themselves and their relations with selected 'others'"[9]—reinforce group solidarity and set the boundaries for "appropriate" responses to events in general, including large disturbances, crises, and conflicts. How groups of people interpret events that happen determines how they cope with them, and narratives structure or guide the behavior of groups by ruling particular options "in" or "out." Thus, religious leaders in particular played important roles in the rejection or adoption of violence.

The ability to vision the future in situations of crisis is both extremely important and quite challenging in settings "characterized by high levels of violence [and] driven by multiple day-to-day crises" [25]. Narratives are enablers for adaptation when they convey five key elements: sense of safety, calm, efficacy, connectedness, and hope [26]. Scholarship shows that hopefulness, a positive communal identity, and collective narratives that give tragedy meaning and purpose bolster community resilience. The Committee on Increasing National Resilience to Hazards and Disasters concluded that "the extent which communities frame themselves as capable, adaptable, and self sufficient—rather than victimized or helpless—will affect their decision-making, actions, and ability to cope in the face of adversity [27]."

The importance of narratives to resilience derives in great part from the field of clinical psychology. "A lot of psychotherapy is about telling the story of the past

---

[7] Interview, Karada Baghdad, June 2010.

[8] "A fundamental principle of systems dynamics states that the structure of the system gives rise to its behavior [and in] complex systems, different people placed in the same structure tend to behave in similar ways." See [23].

[9] Funk and Said [24].

and reinterpreting that story so that instead a story that locks the individual into a set of problems or a sense of failure or inadequacy, it becomes a story that frees up energies and potential to act differently" [28]. The powerful images narratives contain and the judgments they make about the motivations and actions of their own group, and others, are emotionally significant for groups and individuals. Self-esteem, mental health, and coping ability are closely connected to whether events are self-explained in empowering or disempowering terms.[10] From the psychological subfield of trauma research, a volume of evidence indicates that optimism about the future predicts individual resilience; "to the extent that people are encouraged to view their posttraumatic situation as one in which growth can occur, growth is more likely to take place."[11]

Such narratives must be widely shared to serve as sources of collective resilience [32]. Shared narratives are sometimes called "resilience narratives," stories that unite potentially adversarial individuals and groups within a shared, coherent interpretation of "what is happening" and "what to do." Following the 2013 World Economic Forum in Davos, devoted to the theme of "resilient dynamism," Amy Zalman blogged, "It should be an indispensable part of the resiliency toolkit to align stakeholders' idioms and understandings at the earliest possible stage by building relationships and communications that support collaborative work" [33]. Other authors have pointed to the high degree of intra-community consensus required for conflict resilience. The variable of leadership is critically important to developing and *maintaining* consensus. We have read how residents of Adhamiyya, Amiriyya, and Bayaa mounted armed resistance against outside militias, but still these communities fell prey to AQI's agenda of sectarian civil war. Blocking streets and defending borders did not work in Adhamiyya and Amiriyya. Sectarian militias overwhelmed these communities, and their leaders (and residents) became divided into active supports and "independents." In both places, important community leaders were not on board with the agenda of preventing violence, giving AQI a crucial threshold.

Conclusions

The contribution of information and communication to conflict resilience is complex. The flow of information between neighbors is one variable, influenced by pre-existing levels of social capital and cohesion. In turn, both are affected by the physical structure of neighborhoods (among a host of other potential variables). Information only contributes to resilience if it is correct and correctly transmitted. The media shapes how events are framed in ways that influence how people interpret and understand. Arguably, the "media effect" is even more pronounced and

[10] (Buchanan and Sligman [29]; Seligman [30]).

[11] Carver [31]: 256.

potentially damaging during situations of crisis [34–36]. Unfortunately, the prevalence of inflammatory language and images in Iraqi media did (and continues to) contribute to conflict escalation. The role played by the media was often inflammatory, but we do not know how people in each area regarded the reports and images or were affected by them. We also do not know how many residents of each area had televisions and radios, or the extent to which they relied on media reports when deciding what to believe and how to act. However, we *do* know from a D3 Systems survey that the majority of all Iraqis owned a television, 75 % were concerned with current events, and 95 % of respondents watched television at least once a day.[12]

We know more about the influence of group narratives on collective behavior. Communities that viewed themselves as agents of their own destiny are inherently more resilient, but we cannot know whether the self-perceptions of efficacy pre-existed successful resistance of sectarian militias or emerged as a result of it. Also, when communities frame themselves as empowered and capable, their resilience to adversity is enhanced [27] through greater organization and preparation. (This topic will be further explored in Chap. 8.)

At the same time, "more crisis preparedness can lead to significantly less attribution of blame onto other parties [3: 14]." Blame attribution is an important feature of resilience. Numerous psychological studies have demonstrated that when people blame adverse outcomes on others, they experience poor psychological outcomes. At the community level, attributing responsibility for adversity to the community itself is more likely to spur preparedness, facilitate learning through experimentation, and promote positive adaptation. A positive feedback loop exists here: When a community frames itself as adaptive and empowered, it is more resilient because it is more likely to prepare. That preparedness in turn reduces the attribution of blame for negative events onto other parties, thereby strengthening collective efficacy.

We also know that the behaviors of religious leaders in Baghdad were extremely important, because they interpreted the post-2003 Iraqi world in sermons and conversations, using religious–historical frames to argue for sectarian violence or sectarian peace. But how can we disentangle the influence of tradition and local norms on how leaders behaved versus how leader behavior (primarily through speech acts [38][13]) influenced and/or reinforced those very norms? Complexity science, the theoretical foundation upon which resilience rests, discourages an either/or approach to such questions. According to this theoretical perspective, communities are *complex adaptive systems* (*CAS*) involving a large number of agents that act interdependently with each other to generate emergent, system-wide patterns of behavior for the whole. Our analysis is therefore oriented to the mutual influence of structures and agents on each other, in line with

[12] D3 Systems "Iraq Media Study-National Audience Analysis, executive summary, IREX, Washington DC, April 21, 2010, 3. Cited in [37].

[13] According to Searle, speech is a form of action—particularly statements because they communicate meaning and intent.

constructivism (discussed in Chap. 1). Chapter 9 offers this integrated analysis, summarizing the structures and outcomes of conflict resilience, and their relationship to each other through causal mechanisms.

References

1. Adedokun, M.O., Adeyemo, C.W., and Olorunsola, E.O. 2010. The Impact of Communication on Community Development. *Journal of Communication* 1(2): 101–105.
2. Comfort, L. 2005. Risk, security, and disaster management. *Annual Review of Political Science* 8: 335–356.
3. Longstaff, P.H., and Yang, S. 2008. Communication management and trust: Their role in building resilience to surprises such as natural disasters, Pandemic Flu, and Terrorism. *Ecology and Society* 13(1): 3, http://www.ecologyandsociety.org/vol13/iss1/art3/.
4. Pfefferbaum, B., Reissman, D., Klomp, R., and Gurwitch, R. 2005. Building resilience to mass trauma events. In *Handbook on injury and violence prevention interventions,* eds. Doll, L, Nonzo, S. Mercy, J., and Sleet, D. New York: Kluwer Academic Publishers.
5. Longstaff, P.H. 2005. *Communication policy for resilience to natural disasters and terrorist attacks*. Cambridge: Center for Information Policy Research, Harvard University.
6. Landau, J., and Saul, J. 2004. Facilitating family and community resilience in response to major disaster. In *Living beyond loss: Death in the family*, eds. Walsh, F., and McGoldrick, M, 285–309. New York: Norton.
7. Abramowitz, S. 2005. The poor have become rich, and the rich have become poor: Collective trauma in the Guinean Languette. *Social Science and Medicine* 61: 2106–2118.
8. Lazarsfeld, P. F., Bernard, B., and Gaudet, H. 1944. *How the voter makes up his mind in a presidential campaign*. New York. Duell, Sloan and Pearce, 158.
9. Burt, R.S. 2002. Structural holes. In *Contemporary Sociological Theory, eds*. Calhoun, C., Gerteis, J., Moody, J., Pfaff, S., and Virk, I, 208. Oxford, UK: Blackwell.
10. Anderson, M., and Wallance, M. 2013. *Opting out of war: strategies to prevent violent conflict*. Boulder, CO: Lynne Reinee:, 48.
11. Lewicki, R. J., Saunders, D. M., and Minton, J.W. 1999. Negotiation 3rd ed. Boston: Irwin McGraw Hill
12. Buechler, S. 2000. *Social movements in advanced capitalism*. New York: Oxford University Press. pp 1–240
13. Hayward, S. 2012. *Religion and peacebuilding: Reflections on current challenges and future prospects*. Washington DC: United States Institute of Peace, 5.
14. Appleby, R.S. 2011. *Religion and peacemaking: Reflections on current challenges and future prospects*. Washington, DC: USIP public event.
15. Susan Hayward. 2012. *Special Report: Religion and peacebuilding: Reflections on current challenges and future prospects*. Washington DC: United States Institute of Peace, 5,6.
16. Folke, C.T., Hahn, P. Olsson, P., and Norberg J. 2005. Adaptive Governance of social-ecological knowledge. *Annual Review of Environment and Resources* 30: 441–73.
17. Folke, C., Carpenter, S., Elmqvist, T., Gunderson, L., Holling, C.S., Walker, B., Bengtsson, J., Berkes, J.F., Colding, J., Danell, K., Alkenmark, M.A., Gordon, L., Kasperson, R., Kautsky, N., Kinzig, A., Levin, S., Ma''ler, K., Moberg, F., Ohlsson, L., Olsson, P., Ostrom, E., Reid, W., Rockstro,''M, J., Savenije, H., and Svedin, U. 2002. *Resilience and sustainable development: building adaptive capacity in a world of transformations*, Ambio 31/5 (August 2002), Royal Swedish Academy of Sciences.
18. Amos, D. 2010. Confusion, contradiction, and irony: The Iraqi media in 2010, discussion paper series no. D-58, *Joan Shorenstein Center on the Press, Politics and Public Policy*, Harvard University. Cambridge, MA, June 2010, 10. dash.harvard.edu/handle/1/4421401.

19. Al-Marashi, I. 2007. The dynamics of Iraq's media: Ethno-sectarian violence, political Islam, Public Advocacy, and Globalization. *Cardozo Arts and Entertainment Law Journal* 25(1): 95.
20. Sahi, M. 2006. Television map in Iraq; Iraqi satellite television channels between politics and promotion of sectarianism. *Al-Zawra* newspaper, (No relation to the Al-Zawra satellite channel) March 27, 2006, p 2.
21. St.Jean, P.K.B. 2007. *Pockets of crime: Broken windows, collective efficacy, and the criminal point of view*. Chicago: University of Chicago Press.
22. Carlos F.A. 1989. Political practice and the rise of an ethnic enclave: The Cuban American case 1959–1979. *Theory and Society* 18: 47.
23. Sterman, J. 2000. *Business dynamics: Systems thinking and modeling for a complex world.* New York City: McGraw Hill, 28–29.
24. Funk, N.C. and Said, A.A. 2004. Islam and the West. Narratives of Conflict and Conflict Transformation. *International Journal of Peace Studies* 9(1): 1–28
25. Lederach, J.P. 1997. *Building peace: Sustainable reconciliation in divided societies.* Washington, DC: United States Institute of Peace.
26. Hobfall, S.E. et al. 2007. Five Essential Elements of Immediate and Mid-Term Mass Trauma Intervention: *Empirical Evidence*. Psychiatry 70(4).
27. *Committee on increasing national resilience to hazards and disasters. Disaster resilience: A national imperative*. Washington DC: The National Academics Press, 2012.
28. Bateson, M.C. 2007. *Interchange: A quarterly review of education*, 38(3): 213–222.
29. Buchanan, G. M., and Seligman, M. E. P. eds. 1995. Explanatory style. Hillsdale, NJ: Erlbaum.
30. Seligman, M. E. P. 1991. *Learned optimism*. New York: Knopf.
31. Carver, C.S. 1998. Resilience and Thriving: Issues, Models and Linkages. *Journal of Social Issues* 54(2): 245–266.
32. Menkhaus, K. 2013. *Making sense of resilience in peacebuilding contexts: Approaches, applications, implications*. Geneva Peacebuilding Platform, Working Paper 6.
33. Zalman, A. 2013. *Resilience narratives key to a resilient system*. URL: http://strategic-narrative.net/blog/2013/01/resilience-narratives-key-to-resilient-systems/.
34. Schlesinger, P., Murdock, G., and Elliott, P., 1983. *Televising terrorism: Political violence in popular culture*. London: Commedia Publishers.
35. Alali, O.A., and Eke, K.K.,. eds. 1991. *Media coverage of terrorism: Methods of diffusion*. Thousand Oaks, CA: Sage Publications.
36. Alexander Y., and Picard, R., 1991. *In the camera's eye: News coverage of terrorist events*. Washington, DC: Brasseys.
37. Maureen, T., and Dolan, T. 2013. *Mitigating media incitement to violence in Iraq: A locally driven approach*. Washington DC: United States Institute for Peace.
38. Searle, J.R. 1969. *Speech acts*: An essay in the philosophy of language. Cambridge: University Press.

Chapter 8
Economic Resources

Abstract This chapter draws on a range of research relating to the relationship between economic resources, group mobilization and civil war. Economic aspects of resilience varied across Baghdad neighborhoods, contributing to the overall resilience or vulnerability of particular places to extremist violence. This chapter discusses socioeconomic status (SES) as a composite of education, occupation, and income. While the links between poverty and community resilience are obscure, high SES may have positive effect on people's capacity to act in innovative ways, on ability to access and attract resources, and on individual resilience to sectarian recruitment.

Keywords Economic resources • Economic development • SES • Resilience • Vulnerability • Civil war • Poverty • Social class • Access to resources • Well-being • Human development • Freedom • Psychological changes • Psychosocial vulnerability • De'Baathification • Protection narrative • Rule of relative advantage • Tribal networks • Trade networks • Criminal networks

> *On a grander scale, when a society segregates itself, the consequences affect the economy, the emotions, and the ecology.*
>
> Joel Salatin 2007

A contemporary definition of economic development is *an increase in living standards, improvement in self-esteem needs and freedom from oppression, as well as a greater choice* [1]. This definition incorporates the famous insights of Amartya Sen, Professor of Economics and Philosophy at Harvard University, who recast economic development as human development wherein freedom of choice is the ultimate goal. For Sen, "unfreedoms" include poverty, famine, and lack of political rights [2].

What is the relationship between the level of economic development and resilience to sectarian violence? To date, no single study has interrogated this particular question, and neither does this one. Instead, this chapter draws on a range of research relating to group mobilization and civil war, as well as individual

A. C. Carpenter, *Community Resilience to Sectarian Violence in Baghdad*, Peace Psychology Book Series, DOI: 10.1007/978-1-4614-8812-5_8,

propensity for violence. Economic aspects of resilience vary across Baghdad neighborhoods, contributing to the overall resilience or vulnerability of particular places to extremist violence. Conclusions are somewhat wanting, but that can only encourage further investigation of this important question. Insights shared by the people we interviewed are illustrative and insightful, but not conclusive.

According to Neil Adger, economic structure is a key parameter for observing social resilience. It encompasses economic growth, stability of livelihoods, income stability, and equitable distribution of resources. These variables tend to vary by community in cities around the world, often correlating with racial, ethnic, religious, or sectarian composition. In Baghdad, Hussein purposefully marginalized Sadr City because its residents were Shiite (and eventually to punish the elder al-Sadr for speaking out against Hussein's regime). Since the diversity and volume of resources is an important source of resilience, it holds that poorer communities are inherently more vulnerable. The literature on disaster resilience has confirmed that poor communities are at greater risk for death and damage [3], and post-disaster trauma [4].

In addition, armed non-state actors are more likely to emerge in places suffering from state neglect, including extreme poverty and institutional weakness of the type already described by residents: social, political, and economic benefits skewed toward a specific margin of society, intentional policies of repression targeted toward others, and overall state weakness exacerbated by international sanctions. Many different types of non-state armed actors exist, by a recent typology by Ulrich Schneckener cast them into six categories: *rebels or guerilla* fighters (groups fighting for regime change), *militias or paramilitaries* (irregular combat units who fight rebels), *clan chiefs or big men* (traditional, local authorities who head particular communities), *warlords* (local rulers who control territory through private armies and resource exploitation), *terrorists* (groups who use terror tactics to achieve political goals), *criminals* (gangs, mafias, smugglers), *mercenaries and private security companies* (soldiers for hire), and *marauders* (former combatants who loot and pillage) [5].

Lack of opportunity, lack of voice, and lack of spaces of economic and political participation go hand in hand with risk factors for factional violence. Armed non-state actors occupy power voids, whether those are political, spiritual, or economic. Iraq's economic void has been well documented and fits with typical indicators of welfare deficits associated with fragile states: "the systematic exclusion of particular groups from access to economic resources; several financial and economic crises; the unequal distribution of wealth; decreasing state revenues; high rates of unemployment; a significant decline in human development; poor public infrastructure; degradation of the educational and/or health system; and environmental degradation (e.g., shortage of water)" [5, p. 32].

The major prewar armed groups in Iraq consisted of tribal leaders (who would fall into Schneckener's *big men* category) and Kurdish militia members in Northern Iraq. Shi'a tribes Bani Lam and Albu Muhammed had the major influence in southern Iraq; Sunni tribes in Anbar Province who smuggled across the border of Syria. As described in the previous chapter, socioeconomic status (SES) and tribal affiliation are associated, in that tribal identity was stronger in poor Sunni neighborhoods and in poor Shia neighborhoods, but not in neighborhoods where social identity was built around old families and/or where the business class made up a large component of an areas residents. As one member of the research team explained,

> The demography and history of Sadr City and Karada, both Shia dominant areas, is VERY different. Shia areas like Karada with high education and employment levels are not tribal based communities; no one describes themselves by tribe, they are instead known by their families. But when Baghdad was exposed to immigration from rural areas, Sadr City was established and brought tribal traditions with them.

I have chosen to use the economic concept of *SES* to explore the economic structure of the ten neighborhoods. Unfortunately, I do not have data sufficient to get as specific as measuring income inequality between residents, or equitable distribution of resources. But by using SES indicators to code interview data, and triangulating those accounts with other reports, we can establish a very general relationship of local economic structure to conflict resilience.

Socioeconomic Status

SES is not just about money or standing. The United States measures SES based on occupation, monthly household income, education, and overall "well-being." Braveman et al. measure SES in terms of maternal and infant health [6]. The MacArthur Foundation defines traditional indicators of SES as measures of education, occupation and wealth, individual and family income[1]; other scholars have used expenditure patterns instead of income. Recognizing that income is not the most reliable indicator of SES in some countries, the World Bank uses a household wealth index that includes indicators like type of flooring, water supply, type of vehicle, sanitation facilities, and persons per sleeping room.[2]

As with most of the concepts introduced so far, there is no agreed upon definition for SES. This is because "choosing the best variable or approach for measuring SES is dependent in part on its relevance to the population and outcomes under study."[3] The literature on SES covers important and grand debates regarding its origin, and its comparability to social class and social grade, but most authors tend to agree that, "all terms lack a clear consensus on their conceptual meaning,

---

[1] According to the MacArthur Scale of Subjective Social Status.

[2] Rutstein, S.O. Retrieved from http://www.childinfo.org/files/DHS_Wealth_Index_(DHS_Comparative_Reports).pdf.

[3] Shavers, V.L. Retrieved from http://www.ncbi.nlm.nih.gov/pubmed/17913111.

let alone their measurement" [7]. It is not my purpose to engage in this debate, and thus, I have chosen to focus on three variables traditionally used to assess social standing: education, occupation, and income.

One assumption of this study was that high SES would correlate with resilience to sectarian violence. This assumption was based on two grounds: First, high SES indicates access to resources—connections, material goods, money, power—and access to such critical resources underpinned social resilience [8]. This argument emphasizes the ability to gain, control, and maintain access to valuable resources "defined broadly as the ability of a community to actually benefit from [resources which] are embedded in the social and environmental histories of a region" [8]. Second, high SES correlates with economic and psychological well-being, and therefore, I hypothesized that people would not be vulnerable to the adoption of sectarian attitudes and behaviors. I was primarily interested on whether and how SES had affected a neighborhood's resilience to conflict escalation.

Based on a rather large literature, I assumed a significant effect. Poverty is associated—albeit in complex ways—with greater vulnerability to violence. To begin with, previous studies have demonstrated strong correlations between poverty, underdevelopment and conflict. According to Elbadawi, civil wars reduce stocks of human and physical capital affecting both short- and long-run levels of economic output and the rate at which it grows. Displaced populations and increased insecurity as an outgrowth of internal conflict lead to lower overall growth [9]. Henderson and Singer's study *Civil War in the Post-Colonial World* 1946–1992 found that greater economic development reduced the probability of civil war [10]. Hegre et al. [11] along with Collier and Hoeffler [12] reported the same finding.

In addition, a series of prominent studies on war economies argued that conflicts in the developing world are fueled by economic factors ("greed"), including David Keen's *The Economic Functions of Violence in Civil Wars*, Paul Collier *Doing Well out of War*, Paul Collier and Hoeffler *Greed and Grievance in Civil War*, William Easterly and Gatti *What Causes Political Violence*, and Berdal and Malone *Economic Agendas in Civil Wars*. These studies argue that violent conflict is rational when it provides a means of employment, identity, and survival. Written by economists (and largely commissioned by the World Bank), these studies focus extensively on economic explanations of civil wars.

For example, Paul Collier's accounting of civil wars held that rebel movements tended to follow an economic agenda (greed), rather than advancing a coherent political agenda (grievance) [13]. David Keen attributed the outbreak of civil war not to "irrational" sources of social grievance or the breakdown of social order but economic exploitation by disgruntled elites [14]. The political economy of conflict included "rational decisions" by the poor themselves—for example, Humphreys and Weinstein's interviews with ex-combatants in Sierra Leone suggest that persistent levels of poverty may make soldiering a more attractive means of earning a living when nonviolent livelihoods are in limited supply [15].

SES and Resilience to Violence

We asked respondents, and the YouGov research team, to hazard a guess at about average income and levels of education in their neighborhood. Their perceptions are as follows:

Income	"Good," "High" Amriyya, Adhamiyya, Dura, Palestine Street, Al-Dhubat	"Moderate to Good" Karada, Kuraait, Bayaa, Zafaraniyya	"Poor" Sadr City
Education	"Good," "High" Amriyya, Adhamiyya, Karada, Al-Dhubat	"Moderate" Bayaa, Palestine Street	"Poor" Sadr City, Zafaraniyya

If these self-reports are in any way accurate, then high SES does not correlate with conflict resilience. Of the five "high income" areas, two are classified as conflict resilient (Palestine Street and al-Dhubat), while three (Adhamiyya, Amriyya, and Dura) suffered some of the worst sectarian violence. Of the four "high education" areas, two areas (Karada and al-Dhubat) are conflict resilient. If we combine the both measures, three neighborhoods—all Sunni dominant—qualify as having high income *and* education: Amriyya, Adhamiyya, and al-Dhubat. Of course, this relationship makes some sense. Under Saddam Hussein, Sunni-dominant areas were more likely to receive government services and educational opportunities, and handpicked supporters (often from Saddam's home town of Tikrit) were settled in Adhamiyya including high-ranking government and security officials.

So even if high SES does not necessarily buffer against the adoption of sectarian attitudes and behaviors, does low SES heighten individual vulnerability? My original thinking was that "the poorer an area, the more vulnerable its residents to recruitment by sectarian militias." Respondents also believed this to be the case, arguing that lack of income and education rendered young people psychologically vulnerable to recruitment:

> *Bayaa* Unemployed, desperate and less educated people can be recruited easier to those militias that were paying well…

> *YouGov Facilitator* I do agree with the role of unemployment as a co-factor in the spread of violence in general, and sectarian militias especially. We have seen that in our studies a lot: unemployed, desperate and less educated people can be recruited easier to those militias that were paying well to their followers, and it also gave them kind of "social position" as those young men became powerful and people became afraid of them. This was very appealing for young men who can't get such social position by any merit they have other than being part of that militia.

> *Palestine Street* Sectarian violence occurred in very big neighborhoods with regard to area like Hurriya and Sadr city. Most of those neighborhoods were harmed by the previous regime. The people in those neighborhoods lived under very bad and poor conditions. Those circumstances made some individuals think that it was their chance. Sectarian violence didn't take place in small neighborhoods with better standards of living. People in small neighborhoods knew each other well…Sectarian violence spread easily in poor neighborhood. Most members of Mahdi Army and other militias were uneducated.

As noted, resilience to violence begins with the ability to withstand certain psychological changes that commonly accompany the conflict escalation. Studies have shown that young people growing up in urban environments with high levels of poverty, overcrowding, and violence internalize symptoms such as anxiety, post-traumatic stress symptoms, and depression [16–20]. Both Sadr City and Zafaraniyya shared these characteristics and reported ease of recruitment and permissive attitudes toward Mahdi Army. We might conclude that insofar as Mahdi Army provided two basic functions—physical security and social identity—its relevance to peoples' lives was not strong in places where residents were middle-class, professional, and felt relatively safe from their neighbors.

In point of fact, Mahdi Army's membership was primarily made up of the young, poor, and disenfranchised residents of Sadr City. "The middle class viewed Mahdi Army as a challenge," the resident of Karada explained. "In wealthy areas, Mahdi Army was not able to get established. I saw them try to come to Karada and essentially they couldn't get supporters there. They could get people from other regions and bring them in, but they were rejected by the people."

Lack of empathy for Mahdi Army in wealthier areas has an alternative (yet complementary) explanation. Discussed earlier, Sadr City residents are predominantly from Southern Iraq. Many are Marsh Arabs who "suffered terrible prejudice against them in the form of the mistaken notion—encouraged by the Saddam Hussein regime—that they were an unsophisticated and insignificant section of the population."[4] The Sadr City we spoke to told us that many Baghdadis "thought that the people of our neighborhood were evil." It is certainly plausible that Mahdi Army was associated with a *class* identity that trumped sectarian affiliation for middle-class and wealthy Shia Baghdadis.

The relationship between low SES and vulnerability to the adoption of sectarian attitudes and behaviors is not cut and dry. All three Sunni neighborhoods (Amriyya, Adhamiyya, and Dura) were reported to have high SES, and AQI still found ample recruits. As one respondent put it, "in both rich and poor Sunni neighborhoods, men joined al-Qaʿida and were eager to embrace violence."[5] This perception is likely exaggerated; however, it is true that the bulk of AQIs support derived from internal sources. According to Department of Defense Report to Congress, "AQI has remained viable by evolving into a more indigenous organization, increasingly recruiting Iraqis for funding and manpower."[6] It evolved in 2006 and 2007 from an organization populated primarily by foreign fighters, to an overwhelmingly Iraqi organization. "It managed to convince a lot of large, influential Sunni groups to work together under its banner," said terrorism consultant Evan Kohlmann in an interview with the Washington Post in 2007 [21].

---

[4] Remarks by Baroness *Nicholson of* Winterbourne of the Marsh Arab Heritage Project. Retrieved from http://www.amarfoundation.org/heritage/chapters/050.php.

[5] Field interview, Bayaa, August 2010.

[6] Department of Defense (2009). Measuring Stability and Security in Iraq. December 2009 Report to Congress: 27.

Research by social psychologists offers a few clues as to the apparently differential effect of SES on vulnerability to sectarian attitudes and behavior between Shia and Sunni communities (although this line of inquiry needs more rigorous empirical investigation). According to Franke Wilmer, under conditions of economic and political instability, psychic stress is more likely to induce cognitive and emotional changes that make scapegoating, projection, and ultimately violent behavior more likely. Although the US invasion produced psychic stress for all Iraqis, Sunni Iraqis may have suffered disproportionality greater psychic vulnerability as overnight power relations in Iraq shifted, and previous monopolies on political and economic power (social status) were suddenly reversed. De'Baathification reinforced the perception that the group was under threat, and Sunnis saw the timing of Hussein's execution on the eve of Eid al-Adha as a deliberate insult.

> In such a climate, that in 2003, Sunni Arabs had neither a significant sense of themselves as a differentiated group nor a myth of unique communal victimhood made their feelings of fear and encirclement all but inevitable particularly given that the newly empowered ethnic and sectarian elites did little to assuage those fears [22].

Sunnis felt victimized and significantly mistrustful of the American forces and the new government. When people interpret experiences from the perspective of actual or potential victimhood, they are more likely to succumb to appeals by ethnic entrepreneurs aimed at arousing toxic emotions toward "the other." In fact, one of the primary features of conflict-vulnerable communities was acceptance of the narrative by sectarian militias that "we are here to protect you." This *protection narrative*, as I have dubbed it, was rejected in other communities that resisted AQI and Mahdi Army. Acceptance of the *protection narrative* indicated a threat felt in Sunni area communities so considerable, that—against cultural norms—people and leaders accepted an armed group that they did not know, aside from the simple similarity that "we are all Sunnis." Psychosocial vulnerability coupled with the appeals from leaders who emerged who were willing and able to exploit the emotional vulnerabilities of ordinary people whose psychological life was unsettled by crisis: the invasion, deposition of Hussein, and restructuring power relations between the majority and minority.

Mechanisms of Influence

However, in a study like this one, going back to the interviews provides a deeper layer of nuance about the specific effects of SES on resilience to violence. High SES indicates that people have access to critical resources—connections, material goods, money, power—which underpins social resilience [23]. It is therefore unlikely that resources did not in some way factor into the ability of particular areas to keep extremist groups out. Al-Dhubat is a perfect case in point, which is probably why it popped up as the only conflict-resilient neighborhood where SES mattered the most.

According to the resident with whom we spoke, the wealthy Tabra family had played a traditional governing role in the neighborhood, not dissimilar to the role played by wealthy earls, dukes, and other landed elites in the eighteenth and nineteenth centuries Europe. They provided the neighborhood with local electricity generators and were the main providers of service provision in Dhubat. "At first it was a charity," the resident explained, "then it became a commercial business." During the peak of sectarian violence in 2006, the Tabra family provided the neighborhood with cameras and civilian checkpoints. "They are not affiliated to the military checkpoints outside the neighborhood," the resident clarified. "They belong to the Tabra family."

A few months prior to completing this manuscript, the Boston Marathon bombings occurred. As my sister, my nephew, and I were glued to live news feeds on the last day of the manhunt before Dzhokhar Tsarnaev was captured, my sister asked, "Is the trade-off worth it? All these cameras—are they an invasion of privacy or a necessary feature of post 9–11 US society?" My answer then, by which I still stand, is that electronic eyes and ears have replaced the function performed by neighbors and busybodies in close-knit communities. Where warnings of danger cannot be transmitted person to person, by word of mouth, surveillance technology enables neighborhoods of people to monitor the comings and goings of potential harm-doers.

This general line of discussion is very controversial, but the resident of Al-Dhubat with whom we spoke with credited electronic surveillance with the community's ability to protect itself. On the same day of the Boston Marathon bombings, coordinated bomb attacks killed 55 people across Iraq. One bomb went off inside a café in Adhamiyya. I found myself wondering whether residents of these communities wished for the high-tech monitoring capabilities of wealthier cities and neighborhoods.

Still, high SES is not necessary for good surveillance. The study out of Minneapolis (discussed in Chap. 6) concluded that community resilience to violent extremism involves reducing the perceived social legitimacy of violent extremism, and reducing the potential for contacts with terrorist recruiters or associates.[7] Broadway Heights is an example of a minority community in San Diego that enhanced its resilience to violence by tackling these factors head on. Separated by one street from a notoriously crime ridden area dominated by a large and well-organized street gang, Broadway Heights has the lowest crime rate in the southeastern division of the city (traditionally a low-income area) and has reduced its murder rate to 0 %. Leaders in the neighborhood from long-standing families launched a community organizing campaign, aimed at breaking down the racial barriers between Hispanic and African American residents and building social solidarity. They constructed a highly organized community council, an autonomous youth council, forced drug houses to close, and built intentional bridges with the police department, culminating the establishment of their own personal police beat.

---

[7] http://www.start.umd.edu/start/publications/Weine_BuildingResiliencetoViolentExtremism_SomaliAmericans.pdf

Although Broadway Heights exemplifies the efficacy of community organizing to prevent violence, it is the exception to most surrounding neighborhoods. SES *does* matter in terms of accessing resources; and not only that but access to resources attracts more resources. Kaniasty and Norris call this the "rule of relative advantage" where political connections and social class determine the availability and accessibility of resource [24]. It is a positive feedback loop for the well connected, while poorer communities who need resources the most are continually marginalized. Karada, for example, had many resources before 2003. It was a center of commerce that had attracted "many companies, non-governmental organizations, big restaurants, hotels, whole sale stores for home supplies and [hosted] many other economic activities."[8] Its *human* resources consisted of people with good income and educational attainment; other physical resources included close proximity to Baghdad University, and spacious homes. Thus, it is not surprising that after the regime fell in 2003, new officials and visitors set up residence there. According to our respondent, the added security played a big role in neighborhood resilience.

> *Respondent*: My neighborhood didn't witness sectarian violence because the people of neighborhood are old and we didn't have new residents. Karrada also became a center for the residence of the officials.
>
> *Interviewer: Was that important?*
>
> Respondent: Yes surely. They were protecting themselves and the people.
>
> *Interviewer: To clarify, the presence of a large number of security forces in the neighborhood maintained its security?*
>
> Respondent: Yes

Without security, would Karrada have been able to prevent sectarian attitudes and behaviors from taking hold? Would it have been able to prevent large numbers of its residents from fleeing, thereby feeding the effects of dislocation? It is impossible to say with certainty. In other wealthy regions, high SES actually increased the odds that violent attacks would be attempted; for example kidnapping gangs targeted areas with high concentration of wealthy residents. In Kuraait, this was perceived to be a problem.

> There was fear from gunmen coming from other neighborhoods, Allasa, they mostly came for the money; the neighborhood economical condition was good. Those were our main fears. The state grew stronger and the army began to deploy checkpoints and this saved the people from kidnapping.

Trade Networks

Tribal affiliation affected local conflict resilience for two reasons. For one thing, neighborhoods in West Baghdad were connected to rural tribes to a higher degree than neighborhoods in South Baghdad, and this proved significant for how

---

[8] Interview, Karada Baghdad, July 2010.

sectarian violence spread. In general, militants can gain entry to an area more easily if there already exists a trade network between their point of origin and the area they want to enter. As noted in Chap. 2, both Sunni and Shia neighborhoods had deep connections with organized criminal activities run by tribes. According to Phil Williams, tribal groups were initially involved in smuggling commodities—tea, alcohol, electronics, and animals—but graduated to drug trafficking so that by 2002, "the entire route along the Euphrates River in Al Anbar had essentially developed into a sanctuary for illicit traffickers and criminal entrepreneurs" [25]. In an email conversation about black market networks, one of my Iraqi colleagues wrote,

> That's absolutely true and well known about smuggling on the west border of Iraq, and many tribes worked on this business (including the Awakening leader Abu Risha's tribe, which also worked on highway robbery during Saddam's time) and it's amazing that these communities are very conservative and religious, still they find these kind of illegal activities are kind of ok! I had a friend from Ramadi and he told me that smuggling across the borders was the job for so many people and he said that they justify it by saying that this is the only way they got to make their living and support their families and even Saddam's regime couldn't stop it.

Williams' research indicated that Sunni tribes defected from AQI because of conflicts over these smuggling routes. Mahdi Army also profited from organized crime in Iraq, though it is not clear the extent of activities carried out by Mahdi Army proper or splinter groups. According to Williams, four revenue streams benefited Mahdi Army members: "extortion and protection; black market sales of petroleum; seizures of cars and houses inextricably linked with, if not done completely under the guise of sectarian cleansing; and involvement in oil smuggling in Basra." Members recruited to both AQI and Mahdi Army were unwitting (at first) participants in a fight that had less to do with nationalism or sectarian ideology than with profit.

> At first those militias gave them what they claim to be "support" for Mujahedeen, but it turns out as a big business and those militias were dominated by criminals who have strong criminal background who had both the experience and the intention to do criminal operations to get money and this is true for all militias.

However, the influence of smuggling routes in generating local support for sectarian militias must not be overstated. Smuggling was more extensive and active on the Kurdistan region of Iraq, across the borders with Iran and Turkey, but—as my colleague pointed out "this didn't cause or help in making it easier for terrorist groups to enter and operate there. I guess the reason is obvious; Kurdish Iraqis don't feel a loss of power in the new Iraq."[9]

Conclusions

The links between poverty and community resilience are "elusive, variable, and strongly conditioned by a wide range of non-economic factors" [26]. The pattern emerging in the above accounts is that high SES appears to operate through

[9] Email correspondence, YouGov Iraq research director, March 2011.

specific mechanisms and, like social capital, its effect on conflict resilience is not directly causal. Sociopsychological mechanisms include *human agency*, as in the decisions made by Dhubat's wealthy family to provide security services for their community, and (potentially) reduced *individual vulnerability* to the adoption of sectarian attitudes and behaviors. As one person said, commenting on the difficulties Mahdi Army encountered when attempting to recruit supporters in Kuraiaat and Karada—areas with high concentrations of commercial centers and working professionals—"businessmen know full well that violence is bad for profit."

Another mechanism is the positive feedback loop between existing and future political and social connections (the "rule of relative advantage"). Clearly, the diversity and volume of resources is an important source of resilience, and communities with preexisting economic capitals are more resilient in the face of disaster than poor ones. However, the case of Broadway Heights and others neighborhoods like it, highlight that the *willingness of a community to organize* is just as important in opening access to necessary resources.

This point brings us to community competence, the topic of the following chapter. Community competence is about the organized action of people, communities, and institutions to prevent, manage, and learn from crisis. The capacity to act collectively in ways described earlier as positive resilience are greatly influenced by the ways in which communities are set up, including cultural differences in regimes and roles. The following chapter casts community competence as comprising *factors and processes that link regime characteristics to people's actual behaviors*, linking key elements of social capital, information and communication, and economic development to the organized action of people, communities, and institutions to prevent, manage, and learn from crisis.

References

1. Todaro, Michael. 2011. *Economic Development*. Pearson Education.
2. Tejesen, S.A. 2004. Amartya Sen's development as freedom. *Graduate Journal of Social Science* 1(2): 344–347.
3. Norris, F.H., S.P. Stevens, B. Pfefferbaum, K.F. Wyce, and R. Pfefferbaum. 2008. Community resilience as a metaphor, theory, set of capacities and strategy for disaster readiness. *American Journal of Community Psychology* 41: 137.
4. Ahern, J., and S. Galea. 2006 Social context and depression after a disaster: The role of income inequality. *Journal of Epidemiology and Community Health* 60: 766–770.
5. Schneckener, U. 2006. Fragile statehood, armed non-state actors and security governance. In *Private actors and security governance*, ed. A. Bryden, and M. Caparini. Zurich: Transaction Publishers.
6. Braveman, P., Cubbin. C., Marchi, K., Egerter, S., and Chavez, G. 2001. Measuring socio-economic status/position in studies of Racial/Ethnic disparities: Maternal and infant health. Public Health Reports 116. Retrieved from http://www.ncbi.nlm.nih.gov/pmc/articles/PMC1497365/pdf/12042609.pdf.
7. Higgs, N. 2002. *Measuring Socio-Economic Status: A Discussion—Letting the Gini out of the Bottle—plus Some Thoughts on Well-Being*.
8. Langridge, R., Christian-Smith, J, and Lohse, K.A. 2006. Access and resilience: A nalyzing the construction of social resilience to the threat of water scarcity. *Ecology and Society* 11(2): 18. Retrieved from http://www.ecologyandsociety.org/vol11/iss2/art18/.

9. Elbadawi, I. 1999. *Civil wars and poverty: the role of external interventions, political rights and economic growth*. Mimeo.
10. Henderson, E., and Singer, J.D. 2000. Civil War in the Post-Colonial World 1946-1992. *Journal of Peace Research* 37(3): 275–299 (International Peace Research Institute, Oslo).
11. Hegre, H., Ellingsen, T., Gates, S, and Gleditsch, N.P. (2001) Toward a democratic civil peace? Democracy, political change and civil war, *American Political Science Review* 95 (1):33–48.
12. Collier, P., and A. Hoeffler. 1998. On economic causes of civil war. *Oxford Economic Papers* 50(4): 563–573.
13. Collier, P. (2000). Doing well out of war: An economic perspective. In *Greed and Grievance: Economic agendas in Civil Wars*, eds. Berdal, M., and Malone, D.M, 91–112.
14. Keen, D. 1998. The economic functions of violence in Civil Wars. New York: Oxford University Press (Adelphi Paper 320).
15. Humphreys, M., and Weinstein, J. 2004. *What the Fighters Say: A Survey of Ex-Combatants in Sierra Leone*. CGSD Working Paper no. 20, Center on Globalization and Sustainable Development. New York: The Earth Institute at Columbia University.
16. Gibbs, J.T. (1984). Black adolescents and youth: An endangered species. *The American Journal of Orthopsychiatry* 54: 6–21.
17. Lorion, R.L., Brodsky, A., and Cooley-Quille, M.R. (1999). Exposure to urban violence: A framework for conceptualizing risky settings. In *Innovations in practice and service delivery across the lifespan*, eds. Biegel, D.E., and Blum, A., 124–143. New York: Oxford.
18. Myers, H.F., S. Taylor, K.T. Alvy, A. Arrington, and M.A. Richardson. 1992. Parental and family predictors of behavior problems in inner-city Black children. *American Journal of Community Psychology* 20: 557–576.
19. Osofsky, J.D., S. Werers, D.M. Hann, and A.C. Fick. 1993. Chronic community violence: What is happening to our children? *Psychiatry* 56: 36–45.
20. Singer, M., T. Anglin, L. Song, and L. Lunghofer. 1995. Adolescents' exposure to violence and associated symptoms of psychological trauma. *Journal of the American Medical Association* 273: 477–482.
21. DeYoung, K., and Pincus, W. 2007. *Al-Qaeda in Iraq May Not Be the Threat Here*. Washington Post, Sunday March 18, 2007.
22. Haddad, F. 2013. Iraq's Sectarian Inheritance. Foreign Policy: Middle East Channel.
23. Langridge, R., Christian-Smith, J., and Lohse, K.A. 2006. Access and resilience: analyzing the construction of social resilience to the threat of water scarcity. *Ecology and Society* 11(2): 18. Retrieved from http://www.ecologyandsociety.org/vol11/iss2/art18/.
24. Kaniasty, K., and Norris, F. 2004. Social support in the aftermath of disasters, catastrophes, acts of terrorism: Altruistic, overwhelmed, uncertain, antagonistic, and patriotic communities. In *Bioterrorism: Psychological and public health interventions*, eds. Ursano, R., Norwood, A., and Fullerton, C., 200–229. New York: Cambridge University Press.
25. Williams, Philip. 2009. *Criminals, militias and insurgents: Organized crime in Iraq*. Strategic Studies Institute.
26. Nelson, J.M. 1998. Poverty, inequality, and conflict in developing countries. *Rockefeller Brothers Fund Project on World Security*.

Chapter 9
Community Competence

Abstract Community competence is about organized action of people, communities, and institutions to prevent, manage, and learn from crisis. Chapter 8 explores the influence of psychological and behavioral components of community competence in Baghdad neighborhoods. Social cohesion, working trust, and place attachment were all decisive elements in the capacity of communities to self-organize in protective ways. Four strategies were predominant: self-defense groups, advocacy for violence prevention, countering extremist attitudes, and community mediation. Non-sectarian leaders also critically supported collective adaptation.

Keywords Community competence • Efficacy • Collective action • Governance • Decision-making communication management • Community empowerment • Collective efficacy • Inward orientation • Group narratives • Place attachment • Social agency • Activated social networks • Social capital • Place attachment • Social cohesion • Social control • Place detachment • Self-defense groups • Third side • Community mediation • Advocacy • Leadership • Leaders • Socioeconomic status • SES • Protection narrative

Although the world is full of suffering, it is also full of overcoming it.

Helen Keller

Several years ago, I was studying how communities in Guatemala coped with the threats posed by armed gangs. As in Baghdad's neighborhoods, some communities formed local defense groups to prevent violence. They worked with parents to engage with their children and actively encourage young people not to join armed groups. Communities applied Mayan law and order against offenders, and their

A. C. Carpenter, *Community Resilience to Sectarian Violence in Baghdad*, Peace Psychology Book Series, DOI: 10.1007/978-1-4614-8812-5_9,

methods range from *restorative* approaches through which an offender repairs harm in order to be accepted back into the community to *retributive* approaches through which punishment was used as a deterrent [1]. One of my students studied similar coping mechanisms in Cherán Mexico, a community that has self-organized to protect residents from kidnappings, rapes, and murder by drug-trafficking organizations. Cherán organized a self-defense group called the Communitarian Police and reinstated an indigenous non-punitive judicial system and other governance structures.

Whether Mayan law and order in Guatemala's highlands, self-defense groups in Cherán, Mexico or third-party conflict resolution in Baghdad neighborhoods, *community competence* is about organized action of people, communities, and institutions to prevent, manage, and learn from crisis. Resilience to violence takes conscious planning, preparation, foresight, insight, communication management, and coordination. "The capacity [of communities] to manage resilience with intent", wrote Walker et al., "determines whether they can successfully avoid crossing into an undesirable system regime" [2]. Collective action, governance, decision-making, and leadership are at the heart of contemporary definitions of community competence [3].

The idea of *competence* as something that could be studied apart from a community dates back to the 1970s.[1] In 1976, Cottrell proposed that competent communities are able to prioritize community problems through consensus and work together effectively to solve them [4]. Community competence is related to other similar concepts including *community readiness* or "residents' willingness to engage in collective problem-solving" [5], *community empowerment* or "the ability of people to gain understanding and control over personal, social, economic, and political forces in order to take action to improve their life situations", and *collective efficacy* which is "people's shared belief in their collective power to produce desired results" [6].

But where do agency, action, and belief in success come from? The literatures on community efficacy, empowerment, and competence highlight quite a long list of properties related to effective community action including everything from "participation; leadership; skills; resources; social and interorganizational networks; sense of community; understanding of community history; community power; community values; and critical reflection" [7, 8]. In my opinion, these literatures tend to conflate behavioral and psychological aspects of community competence. I have made this distinction clear by breaking community competence into two *psychological processes* and four *behavioral processes* associated with resilience to violence. Below, I describe each in turn and then explain their relationship to one another.

[1] According to a literature review undertaken by Johns Hopkins University Women's and Children's Health Policy Center (WCHPC). Retrieved from http://www.jhsph.edu/research/centers-and-institutes/womens-and-childrens-health-policy-center/publications/resrcgd.PDF.

Psychological Components of Community Competence

The psychological components of community competency include *collective efficacy* (belief in success) and *inward orientation* (motivation to protect local regimes). Collective Efficacy refers to a shared belief in collective power to produce desired results. Inward orientation refers to a shared motivation to protect a particular neighborhood instead of a particular sect or tribal alliance. We might write this relationship as community competency = *f*(Collective Efficacy + Inward Orientation). Where collective efficacy was lacking in cases of inward orientation (motivation to protect); communities were more likely to rely on militias for protective services. Where inward orientation was lacking in cases where collective efficacy (belief in success) was high, communities fragmented into factions, some of which supported sectarian militias.

Collective Efficacy

Efficacy is defined as social cohesion among neighbors combined with their willingness to intervene on behalf of the common good [9]. Efficacy is about agency, "a belief that a situation is not immutable and that 'we' can change it". How well people adapt to adversity thus depends in large degree on the extent to which they perceive personal and collective control over situations requiring rectification and opportunities to "engage in activities that are consistent with one's values and life priorities that reflect a stake in the future" [10].

Therefore efficacy is precisely defined as a combination of social cohesion and social control. Social cohesion can be measured by looking at things like people's frequency of contact, familiarity with other residents (e.g., how many neighbors they could name by sight), and how much people felt they had in common with their neighbor. Social control can be evaluated as a measure of involvement in neighborhood activities, feeling of control over events in the neighborhood, willingness to join a neighborhood association of organization, belief that neighbors would keep an eye on one's children, and level of interaction with local or city officials [11].

Efficacy is an extremely convincing determinant of community competence. Collective efficacy is strongly associated with reduced violence.[2] Research by social psychologists has demonstrated that when people perceive the efficacy of their group to be high, they display higher resistance, solidarity, and performance in the face of impediments and setbacks.[3] Social networks become *activated* or turned on so that people actively engage with changes in their circumstances. Activated social networks "during times of crises can mitigate, suppress or coun-

---

[2] Sampson et al. [12], Ibid.

[3] Ibid.

teract the deleterious effects of stressors by providing needed tangible and emotional resources and promoting effective coping strategies" [13].

People's willingness to act and intervene requires a sense of agency and control and/or belief in the possibility of success. In the words of Albert Bandura,

> Unless people *believe* that they can produce desired effects and forestall undesired ones by their actions, they have little incentive to act. The growing interdependence of human functioning is placing a premium on the exercise of collective agency through shared beliefs in the power to produce effects by collective action.[4]

It is therefore worth reiterating that the language used by Baghdadi residents to describe positive resilience reflects just that sense of agency. Recall from Chap. 5 how respondents from Karada, Kuraiaat, and Al-Dhubat used language reporting that JAM "never caught the land"; that "people didn't allow them to get dominant there", and that "no one gave the armed groups the chance to become in control".

We cannot know that these attitudes *predated* the US invasion, as opposed to being a *result* of the successful resistance to sectarian forces. Still, it is worth noting these same respondents self-described their communities as (1) close-knit places where people valued "civilian identity" and multiethnic relationships between Sunni and Shia residents and (2) having a pre-existing history of working together on community projects. These elements of social capital described in Chap. 3 (sense of place, citizen participation, and social support) inform people's psychocultural interpretations—their "shared, deeply rooted worldviews which… provide psychologically meaningful accounts of a group's relationships with other groups" [14]. As described in Chap. 1, these shared interpretations are represented as group narratives that play a causal role in conflict dynamics "by ruling certain political options either 'in' or 'out' for communal groups" [15].

Why do some communities believe they can "produce desired effects" more than others? Collective efficacy is generated through emotional attachment—not just to other people, but also to the larger community as a whole. Sense of community and place attachment, the emotional connection to one's neighborhood, provides the motivation to actively participate in the life of the community. By accounts, Baghdad neighborhoods differed on the variable of social cohesion. But where residents felt social solidarity—a sense of unity or oneness—they were more likely to band together in defense of the whole community. This held true both for neighborhoods that won out against militias and those that eventually succumbed.

According to Goeppinger and Baglioni [16], different definitions of community competence have in common "the notion that parts of a community develop congruent perceptions of each other through social interaction and that congruent perceptions are necessary for the identification and resolution of community issues" [16]. Congruency means that people know enough about each other to

---

[4] Retrieved from, http://148.216.10.92/archivos%20PDF%20de%20trabajo%20UMSNH/Aphilosofia/2007/NEUROPSICOLOGIA/BanExercise.pdf.

spontaneously organize in times of crisis, as did residents of Al-Dhubat to protect the Yaqin mosque, or residents in Kuraiaat where more coordinated efforts were undertaken to form an "official" neighborhood security group.

> [People] self organized to protect Yaqin mosque that was inside of the neighborhood and no one was able to reach it. They were not organized; they just wanted to protect the mosque from any enemy; no one could have attacked the mosque despite the armed men's attempts to do so. They remained organized to guard the mosque because it is the house of Allah. There was no leader (Al Dhubat).

Harking back to Chap. 5, the actual capacity of residents to self-organize in these ways is a result of bridging capital that has been accumulated over many years. Ashutosh Varshney studied conflict-resilient cities in India and concluded that intercommunal civic traditions are the principal determinant of ethnic conflict or peace. He wrote:

> In peaceful cities…what might be called an institutionalized peace system exists. When organizations, such as trade unions; associations of businessmen, traders, teachers, doctors, lawyers; and at least some political parties—different from the ones that have an interest in polarizing—are integrated, when Hindus and Muslims are integrated, countervailing forces are created…Local police and civil administrations are far more effective in such circumstances. Civic organizations, for all practical purposes, become the ears and arms of the administration [17].

Varshney's key finding was that "prior and sustained contact between members of different communities allows communication between them to moderate tensions and pre-empt violence". In the peaceful cities, people activated their social networks, meaning they came together and organized in times of tension. They pro-actively formed peace committees consisting of members of both Hindu and Muslim communities and brought pressure to bear on the police and other authorities to exercise their powers to maintain law and order.

Inward Orientation

The second psychological aspect of community competence is what I call *inward orientation*. Inward orientation is not about competing with an adversary, but instead focuses collective attention on community security. Conflict-resilient communities in Baghdad engaged in activities designed to protect resident's security and community institutions or way of life. Armed defense groups were motivated to protect neighborhood boundaries rather than drive out residents or carry out attacks in other places. The opposite of inward orientation consists of other-focused and competitive strategies against perceived adversaries, attacks, and counter-attacks that generate destructive conflict spirals and self-perpetuating conflict systems.

We might think of inward orientation as a type of "simple rule", discussed in Chap. 4, which directs collective behavior toward community needs and wellbeing. As we also read in Chap. 4, good and complex solutions come from simple rules if they serve as a dominant organizing framework for people's actions and are widely shared to be effective in fostering self-organized actions. Importantly, the simple rule of inward orientation made groups in Palestine Street and Kuraiaat resistant to aspire for greater power, manipulation by political elites, or co-option by sectarian and criminal actors.

Inward-looking communities or leaders are sometimes maligned in other literatures as being narrowly focused on the needs and problems of a particular subgroup to the exclusion of a wider community. In point of fact, the same could be said of Baghdad neighborhoods where residents were more concerned with protecting their own borders than becoming involved in the insurgency in larger Baghdad or Iraq. Level of analysis obviously matters very much! But at least when it comes to preventing *community-level* escalation, inward-oriented actions appear to be highly functional.

Critics would be correct to point out that inward orientation applies as much to warring communities as peaceful ones. Place attachment can be understood as territoriality; social cohesion can lead to antisocial as much as pro-social behavior; and sense of community can refer to an ingroup, rather than a larger heterogeneous community. For those reasons, inward orientation only counts toward conflict resilience when its gaze encompasses a whole community, not parts of one. Efforts to protect people reinforce unity when directed towards the larger whole (a community, a nation), but cause division when directed towards subgroups like a particular sect, ethnic group, or tribal alliance.

Behavioral Components of Community Competence

This study identified four behavioral processes of community competence. First, conflict-resilient neighborhoods reported the *organization of non-sectarian security groups* to protect neighborhood borders and ward off outside groups. Jutersonke and Kartas have pointed out that "the neighborhood watch initiatives that typically emerge as a response to violence and insecurity are a systematic attribute worth supporting" only if they eschew arbitrary and exclusionary practices, resist political manipulation and co-option by criminal networks, and do not aspire for the level of autonomy that challenges state authority [17]. Indeed, the security groups that operated in Kuraiaat, Karada, Palestine Street, and Al-Dhubat met these characteristics.

> *Palestine Street*: Some alleys formed self-protection groups, only for a limited period of time, played a role only at the beginning, when they faced the extremists. They were all our friends. The people had good relationships with them. They didn't make problems with the people. They prevented the entry of extremists to the neighborhood and they didn't misuse their power.

> *Kuraiaat*: Some good people in the neighborhood donated their rifles and trusted the young people of the neighborhood to protect… Nobody paid them. They didn't misuse their authorities and had a good relationship with the people. They didn't belong to any party.

Speaking of rifles, while access to weapons was necessary for the self-protection groups to operate successfully, respondents from some several conflict-resilient areas reported that civilians did not carry arms publicly. In Kuraiaat, this was an explicit rule; in Palestine Street, it was an informal norm because "people trusted the self protection group". These findings reinforce Anderson and Wallace's assertion that the possession and use of firearms are an important code of conduct in communities that reject war and violence. In their study of non-war communities, weapons were often prohibited within a community's borders to prevent tensions from turning violent.

Secondly, people reportedly played the role of "third-siders" in order to counter extremist attitudes. Taking the third side—the side of non-violence and conflict resolution—is extremely effective in reducing conflict escalation in small communities [18]. *Third party interventions* (and non-sectarian leadership, discussed below) helped to keep the local defense groups from taking on a sectarian identity as they coalesced and helped to prevent psychological changes that might have motivated area residents to join outside groups with a sectarian character [19].

Taking the third side was also extremely important in reducing conflict potential in post-2003, because of the social disruption caused by the introduction of "open discussions and debate" over previously taboo subjects. Third-party interventions consisted of people's inserting themselves as mediators into street conversations, earlier described as flashpoints for conflict over religious and political differences. The intervention strategy was reported in all conflict-resilient areas: Shiite-dominant, Sunni-dominant, and mixed[5]:

> *Kuraiaat*: There were heated arguments between Sunnis and Shiites; they started calling each other names and accuse each other of being sectarian but no killing; people from both communities would intervene to settle those arguments.

> *Al-Dhubat*: I don't mean they never talked about such things; I meant that they don't talk about Sunnis or Shiites in a degrading way; when arguments started people tried to calm things down while other guys [in other areas] make things worse.

Advocacy for violence prevention was a third critical variable in the collective ability to resist undesirable influences.[6] On the one hand, some leaders advocated for violence prevention. A local Imam in Karada explicitly forbade young people from attacking Sunni Mosques.[7] In Kuraiaat, Karada and Palestine Street religious leaders spoke out against sectarianism. On the other hand, Harith al-Dari, a prominent cleric in Anbar, welcomed AQI and convinced people and tribes to cooperate with them. "Al-Qaʿida from us and from us Al-Qaʿida" was a frequent message in one of his many public statements encouraging resistance against US and ISAF forces. Many of these stories were covered in Chap. 4. The cleric of the famous al-Askari mosque in Adhamiyya admonished that anyone working with the US or the new

[5] Although respondents from SMP areas did not report this strategy, it is probable that individuals from those areas attempted the same sorts of intervention, especially during early stages of escalation.

[6] Norris et al. [3], Ibid: 141.

[7] Interview, Karada, May 2010.

Iraqi government were *kafir*, or "unbelievers". The Sunni mosques of Adhamiyya were already becoming openly hostile and fearful of the Shia before the invasion. Allawi wrote that Sunni clerics fanned the fires: "Some of the preachers were careful to maintain a public posture of sectarian accommodation, but others began to use code words behind which they could hide their true inclinations and fears" [20].

The fourth behavioral component of community competence was *border monitoring*. For example, clerics in Kuraiaat chose individuals trusted by everyone in the community arranged in shifts to protect the neighborhood from outside militias.[8] In Al-Dhubat, a wealthy family set up sophisticated surveillance equipment. In other neighborhoods, border monitoring was self-organized and somewhat ad hoc. On a larger scale, the tribal networks that have formed over the past ten years to counter sectarianism technically engage in a form of border monitoring as well. Perhaps, these lessons have purchase for communities beyond Iraq as well. The well-known Sunni Awakening movement was nurtured and supported by ISAF forces. Less well known are the similar efforts of the predominant Shiite tribe, Bani Assad, to control Shiite militias, and a joint initiative between Sunni and Shia tribes in the Taji region (brokered by US forces in 2007) to fight AQI and other militias. More recently, seven tribes in Baghdad agreed in 2011 to join forces in order to protect Bagdad International Airport. The Baghdad Operations Command of the Iraqi Army facilitated an agreement between the al-Jubor, al-Amuri, al-Magasi, al-Janabi, Zawbaa, al-Hamdani, and al-Hawashimm tribes to "assist Iraqi security forces in preventing terrorist groups from setting up bases from which they could launch mortar shells or rockets, or plant improvised explosive devices" [21].

Linkages Between Regime Characteristics and Community Competency

A theoretical model of resilience is useful to the extent that it identifies explicit linkages between adaptive capacities and resilience outcomes. The truth is that in all the neighborhoods we studied, aspects of all these variables existed. Still, community regimes in Baghdad conflict-resilient neighborhoods, which had seemingly robust capacities for adaptation, were characterized by five particular configurations of social and economic capitals.

One of most important social determinants of conflict resilience was working trust between community subgroups. Findings support the social learning or transaction cost theories of trust introduced in Chap. 5, where working trust between Sunni and Shia neighbors was history-based and domain-specific, built through local experiences and past encounters with other people. Unsurprisingly, then, working trust is derivative of citizen participation, also introduced in Chap. 5 as a history of interaction in joint activities and organizations. Histories of promise keeping, similarity of interests, and competence all contribute to the thickening of working trust [22].

[8] Interview, Kuraiaat, June 2010.

A second determinant was the combination of people springing into action (collective efficacy) in order to prevent intracommunity violence (inward orientation). Place attachment involves positive bonds between people and feelings of pride and emotional connection to a physical area. Findings indicate that place attachment *in particular* is linked with the self-organized actions of Baghdad residents, which supports the findings of an earlier 2002 study which documented a positive relationship between place attachment and collective efficacy at the block level in a US city [23]. However, place attachment is not enough for community resilience to violence; place attachment *plus* working trust between Sunni and Shia residents laid the relational foundation for self-organized and spontaneous adaptation that spanned identity groups, as opposed to being limited to one or another.

By contrast, place *detachment* implies a low emotional connection to a particular community, with associated negative effects for collective efficacy. The "ecological disadvantage" posed by enclave housing and a neighborhood's physical layout was one factor leading to less-intense social interactions, less-dense social networks, and by extension, lack of working trust. Dense overlapping ties (bonds between members of a subgroup) such as tribal ties potentially have the same effect of reducing collective efficacy of a particular neighborhood. For one thing, certain tribes played an explicit role in the formation of sectarian militias. In addition, strong ties to any subgroup reduce boundary-spanning place attachments, thus during crisis, people may be more likely to seek protection from community subgroups which spurs community fragmentation.[9]

Third, non-sectarian leaders influenced inward orientation and by extension the motivation of defense groups. Information and communication are essential elements of resilience, and Chap. 5 emphasized the critical role played by non-sectarian leaders who used religious–historical narratives that "ruled out" violence and communicated a motivation to protect entire communities—diverse people, their relationships with each other, and ways of life.

The fourth and fifth linkages between regime characteristics and community competence are related to economic resources. Very few definitive connections exist between socioeconomic status (SES) and resilience to violence; however, high SES was associated with the rejection of the "Protection Narrative" (discussed in Chap. 6) and was instead associated with the opposite motivation to protect local regimes by keeping sectarian militias *out*. In other words, socioeconomic status (SES) was *sometimes* a proxy variable for people's vulnerability to recruitment by extremist groups, even though the true underlying motivators are security and identity concerns.

The fifth linkage is that high SES enabled some neighborhoods to benefit from sophisticated border-monitoring mechanisms. Greater access to economic resources provided the technological capacities to monitor neighborhoods more efficiently (in some cases) than eyes and ears alone. In Al-Dhubat, surveillance

---

[9] Much additional research is needed on this topic. Loyalty to tribal leadership can also be a source of positive adaptation, as when tribal leaders have decided to cooperate with each other for the sake of protecting people and communities.

Table 9.1 Resilience resources (adaptive capacities)

Social capital	Economic development (SES)	Information and communication resources	Community competence	
			Psychological aspects	*Behavioral aspects*
Working (interpersonal) trust	Income	Sources of information	Inward orientation	Third-party interventions
Civilian identity	Education occupation	Spaces for communication	Collective efficacy	Self-defense groups
Crosscutting ties		Narratives		Countering extremist attitudes
Sense of community				Monitoring borders
Place attachment				Advocacy for violence prevention
Citizen participation				

equipment was installed and operated by the Tabra family, and Kuraiaat benefitted from a variety of security mechanisms put in place by ISAF to protect expatriates and centers of commerce (Table 9.1).

The fifth linkage in particular has to do with the rule of relative advantage that accrued resources to already wealthy neighborhoods and its Jekyll counterpart where negative effects were further amplified. The behavior of Baath Party officials provides another example of the accrual of positive or negative effects. As discussed earlier, Baath officials were perhaps more likely to target poor neighborhoods with repressive actions, not the wealthier neighborhoods in which they themselves lived.

Conclusions

"Sectarian violence has changed the shape and nature of Iraqi society," said BBC World Service reporter and Baghdad resident Subhy Haddad during a 2013 interview on NPR.

> Before 2003 I had many friends that I never knew where they belonged to, you know whether they were Sunnis or Shia you know? We were friends you know, we were Iraqis, you know we were from the same neighborhood we went to the same school, we never asked who was Sunni and Shia; after 2003 we started to paying more attention to that, is he Sunni or is he Shia?
> Interviewer: *Did that divide you from some of your friends?*
> It didn't actually but I changed the way I look at them because when you sit and you talk, you can feel this is not the friend that I knew, he is adopting the government point of view.

I have placed a great deal of emphasis on the constructed nature of sectarian identity in post-2003 Iraq; however, I have not denied the historical core of prejudice and grievance embedded in the relationship between Sunni and Shia Iraqis. As one of my early professors wrote a decade ago, "identity can be constructed, expressed and otherwise experienced in terms of other criteria…such as gender, religion, class and nationality [but] the felt expression, satisfaction, and violation of ones needs for identity through ethnicity can border on primordial intensity" [24]. Indeed, the atrocity of violence that erupted in Baghdad in 2006 challenges the human capacity for understanding. One step forward is acknowledging that the dynamics characterizing social conflict are social–psychological in nature, rooted in perception of enmity, and deep-rooted fear "coupled with the immediacy of having the enemy living virtually next door".[10]

But I cannot emphasize enough that structural crises like the one caused when the United States invaded Iraq do not in and of themselves cause ordinary people to go to war. As Franke Wilmer put it so well,

> It is not rational for ordinary people to go to war, it is irrational. People do not think: 'Oh, well, there is much to be gained by putting my life and property at risk, even if my children, parents, husband, wife or neighbor are very likely to be killed; but my life will be better afterwards…' War both requires and provokes fear, anger, and a willingness to do harm to others that is very often rationalized on the basis of the others inferiority, guilt or both. The ordinary Others of our daily lives must be transformed into despicable Others. They must be transformed into threatening enemies…"

The process of transformation from others to despicable others is a gradual process involving changes in people's psychological states, changes in the way groups function, and changes in a larger heterogeneous community (conflict escalation). Resilience to conflict escalation involves the capacity to adapt to a series of episodic, cascading stressors. As we have read, these stressors have began with the US invasion and the toppling of the reigning political regime; the disbanding of the Baath Party; the ascent to power of the majority Shia population and disenfranchisement of the Sunni minority; the entrance of Al-Qa'ida in Iraq whose explicit intent was to start a civil–sectarian war; the rise of the Mahdi Army and other militias bent on a combination of defense and revenge and the subsequent series of bloody, terrifying attacks on places of worship, of commerce, or study, and of residence.

Against this backdrop, I introduced the notion of adaptation as the ability to manage change so that systemic resilience is not lost, a function of how individuals and groups manage communities [26]. Though it sounded simple, in practice, it meant managing the dynamics of conflict escalation so as to limit competition against perceived adversaries in favor of protective strategies aimed at bolstering one's own community. The ultimate capacity for violence or non-violence—whether in neighborhoods, villages, or whole cities—is situated in local institutions and leaders that urge cooperation, resolve conflicts, and promote community participation. Above all, conflict resilience required communities to pull together in order to manage conflict escalation, chiefly by interrupting psychological changes that lead to group polarization.

---

[10] Lederach [25], Ibid: 14.

Finally, resilience to violence also relied on a healthy dose of luck. Baghdad neighborhoods could not change their physical layout; they could not overcome the influence or connection of clerics sympathetic to sectarian ideologies; they could not choose their pre-existing socioeconomic status. Both physical and social composition made some neighborhoods more vulnerable to violence than others. And yet, the story of Broadway Heights in San Diego, of Jaghori District in Afghanistan, of Tuzla in Bosnia, and of Cherán in Mexico remind me that solidarity, agency, trust, hope, and action are extremely important determinants of resilience.

According to John Paul Lederach, they are *the most* powerful determinants of resilience. "Resiliency is not so much about comparative quantitative advantages like employment, poverty rates, access to education, housing and healthcare", he wrote of Columbia's displaced people. People's capacity to transcend violence "came from their willingness to risk an innovative capacity…from how they sought engagement through dialogue within and outside their communities, from how they mobilized around a deep sense of belonging, and how they creatively brought into existence spontaneous nonviolent processes of change". The following chapter explore what this means, exactly, for the project of enhancing conflict resilience in Iraq and beyond.

References

1. Carpenter, A.C. 2013. Contested authorities: Alternatives to state law and order in post-conflict Guatemala. *Journal of Law and Conflict* 12(5).
2. Walker, B.H., Gunderson, L.H., Kinzig, A.P., Folke, C., Carpenter, S.R., and Schultz, L. 2006. A handful of heuristics and some propositions for understanding resilience in social-ecological systems. *Ecology and Society* 11(1): 13. Retrieved from http://www.ecologyandsociety.org/vol11/iss1/art13/.
3. Norris, F.H., S.P. Stevens, B. Pfefferbaum, K.F. Wyce, and R. Pfefferbaum. 2008. Community resilience as a metaphor, theory, set of capacities and strategy for disaster readiness. *American Journal of Community Psychology* 41: 127–150.
4. Cottrell, L.S. 1976. The competent community. In *Further explorations in social psychiatry*, ed. B.J. Kaplan, R.N. Wilson, and A.H. Leighton, 195–209. New York: Basic Books.
5. Peyrot, M., and H.L. Smith. 1998. Community readiness for substance abuse prevention: Toward a model of collective action. *Research in Community Sociology* 8: 65–91.
6. Raudenbush, R.J., Stephen, W., and F.E. Sampson. 1997. Neighborhoods and violent crime: A multilevel study of collective efficacy. *Science*, 277, 918–924. Cited in Norris, et al (2007), Ibid: 142.
7. Goodman, R.M., A. Wandersman, M. Chinman, P. Imm, and E. Morrissey. 1996. An ecological assessment of community based interventions for prevention and health promotion: Approaches to measuring community coalitions. *American Journal of Community Psychology* 24: 33–61.
8. Goodman, R., M. Speers, K. McLeroy, S. Fawcett, M. Kegler, E. Parker, et al. 1998. Identifying and defining the dimensions of community capacity to provide a basis for measurement. *Health Education & Behavior* 25: 258–278.
9. Raudenbush, R.J., Stephen, W., and F.E. Sampson. 1997. Neighborhoods and violent crime: A multilevel study of collective efficacy. *Science* 277(5328): 918–924.

10. Meichenbaum, D. 2007. *Important facts about resilience: A consideration of research findings about resilience and implications for assessment and treatment.* The Melissa Foundation.
11. Brown, B., D. Perkins, and G. Brown. 2002. Place attachment in a revitalizing neighborhood: Individual and block levels of analysis. *Journal of Environmental Psychology* 23(2003): 259–271.
12. Sampson, R.J., S.W. Raudenbush, and F. Earls. 1997. *Neighborhoods and violent crime: A multilevel study of collective efficacy*. Science. 277: 918–924
13. Cohen, S. 2004. Social relationships and health. American Psychologist 59: 680.
14. Ross, M.H. 2007. *Cultural contestation in ethnic conflict*, 32. Cambridge: Cambridge University Press.
15. Funk, N. and A, Said. 2004. Islam and the West: Narratives of conflict and conflict transformation. International Journal of Peace Studies 9(1).
16. Geoppinger, J., and A.J. Baglioni. 1985. Community competence: A positive approach to needs assessment. *American Journal of Community Psychology* 13: 507–523.
17. Jütersonke, O. and M, Kartas. 2012. Resilience: Conceptual reflections (Platform Brief 6): 4.
18. Ury, B. 2003. *The third side: Why we fight and how we can stop*. London: Penguin Books.
19. Carpenter, A. 2012. Havens in a firestorm: Perspectives from Baghdad on resilience to sectarian violence. *Civil Wars* 14(2): 182–204.
20. Allawi, A. 2008. The occupation of Iraq: Winning the war, losing the peace: 236.
21. al-Qaisi, M. 2011. Tribal leaders pledge to protect Baghdad airport against terrorist attacks. Retrieved from, http://al-shorfa.com/en_GB/articles/meii/features/main/2011/04/04/feature-02.
22. Bacharach, M. and G. Diego. 2003. Trust in signs. In *Trust in society*, ed. Cook, K, 148–184. New York: The Russell Sage Foundation.
23. Perkins, D.D.and Long, D.A. 2002. Neighborhood sense of community and social capital: A multi-level analysis. In *Psychological sense of community: Research, applications, and implications. The Plenum series in social/clinical psychology* ,ed. Fisher, A.T., Sonn, C.and B.J. Bishop, 291–318. New York, NY, USA: Kluwer Academic/Plenum Publishers.
24. Sandole, D. 2002. Virulent ethnocentrism: A major challenge for transformational resolution and peacebuilding in the post-cold war era. *The Global Review of Ethnopolitics* 1(4): 10.
25. Lederach, J.P. 1997. *Building peace: Sustainable reconciliation in divided societies.* Washington, DC: United States Institute of Peace.
26. Holling, C.S. and Walker, B. 2003. Resilience defined. Entry prepared for the internet encyclopedia of ecological economics. Retrieved from http://www.ecoeco.org/publica/encyc_entries/Resilience.pdf.

Chapter 10
Looking Ahead

Abstract Nation and state building in Iraq remains a fragile and fraught enterprise, but mechanisms for strengthening community resilience and conflict prevention exist. This chapter argues for a "middle-ground" approach to peacebuilding that integrates structural with relational approaches, in order to address social reconciliation through institutional restructuring. Ultimately, enhancing resilience means looking for sources of adaptive capacity and finding ways to support locally driven initiatives whose outcomes support strengthening of the institutional context giving rise to them.

Keywords Sectarian violence • Collective efficacy • Insecurity • Conflict escalation • Conflict prevention • Violence • State building • Nation building • Social capital • Economic resources • Information • Communication • Community competence • Urban resilience • Peacebuilding • Resilience mechanisms • Structural peacebuilding • Relational peacebuilding • Reconstruction • Structural interventions • Intergroup relations • Social trust • Trauma care • Narrative therapy • Visualization • Positive imaging • Narratives • Development aid • USAID • Transactional capacity • Infrastructures for peace • I4P • Peace leaders • Syria • Group trauma • Local

If you look beyond the short term violence and instability, you do see significant activities on the part of the Iraqi people that indicate they understand the commitment necessary to govern themselves. It's not clear how they will do it, but it never is.

Bob Kerrey

A. C. Carpenter, *Community Resilience to Sectarian Violence in Baghdad*,
Peace Psychology Book Series, DOI: 10.1007/978-1-4614-8812-5_10,

In 2010, the International Republican Institute released an insightful poll regarding the political mood in Iraq. Over 60 % of Iraqis said that they approved of the national government and parliament. Views on the particulars of governance were mixed, but across-the-board Iraqis agreed that it was important for Ayad Allawi, a secular Shiite whose cross-sectarian Iraqiyya bloc is widely popular with Sunnis, to have a role in the new government. Even in the Shia south, which does not support Iraqiyya, people seemed to understand that the legitimacy of the new government depended on Sunni representation and participation.

Unfortunately as I write, sectarian violence is re-escalating in Iraq. Conflict between Allawi and Prime Minister Nouri al-Maliki has resulted in a largely ineffective central Iraqi government. The previous Vice-President charges that that the Iraqi government has failed. "We all have become hostages", Adel Abdul Mahdi wrote in April 2013. "The Sunnis are hostages; they cannot support the policies of authorities that weaken them in their regions and threaten them in other regions. The Shias are also hostages. They stand helpless before daily killings and menacing threats while they find themselves unable to discuss failing policies related to their security, politics and services" [1].

Since December 2012, Sunni Iraqis have been protesting by the tens of thousands against discriminatory policies of the Shiite-led government including mass detentions believed to be random and arbitrary and governmental neglect of Sunni-dominant areas. The collective efficacy of the protestors may be bolstered by the Syrian civil war, which lends credence to the possibility of a regional shift in the Sunni–Shiite balance of power in the Middle East. Meanwhile, insecurity in Baghdad is worsening; bombers have targeted mosques, markets, street corners, and bus stops in Shiite and Sunni neighborhoods, in assaults reminiscent of the sectarian bloodletting five years ago. The recent escalation of violence is motivated by perceived repression and fears generated among Sunnis about their political and economic future. And as it was a decade ago, particular groups and leaders are driving the violence instrumentally.

Some scholars trace the failure of state building in Iraq to the lack of cohesive relationships between tribes, sects, and the variety of organized groups that have formed since 2003. Lemay-Hébert argues that without cohesive sociopolitical relationships, efforts to construct state institutions cannot work. In his words, "it is impossible to conceive of state-building as a process separate from nation-building" [2]. Hawzhin Azeez concurs Iraq is a case that "may require an emphasis on rebuilding the nation rather than the state".

> …on one level there needs to be horizontal reconstruction of communities that in some instances had suffered decades of internal strife; while on the other hand there needs to be a simultaneous vertical line of institution and capacity building within the state. Therefore the question is not so much that of defining such activities as either state-building or nation-building but that in fact such practices involves *both* [3].

But "the world is not just nation-states", said Richard Stren at a conference in 2012 on Community Resilience at the Woodrow Wilson Center. "The world is very rich at the local level and there are many different things going on." Over the past nine chapters, I have situated the "things going on" within the theoretical contributions and broad categories of social capital, economic resources, and information and communication and also identified specific linkages between these categories of things and the organized action of people, communities, and institutions to prevent, manage, and learn from crisis (community competence).

This chapter builds on those linkages in discussing strategies for strengthening urban resilience. After all, as I wrote back in the Introduction, resilience thinking directs us to value prevention, to work on peacebuilding at local levels by harnessing strengths instead of fixing weaknesses. "A resilience based approach," said Helen Clark in a speech at Cambridge University, "builds on the innate strength of individuals, their communities and institutions to prevent, mitigate the impacts of, and learn from the experience of shocks of an type" [4]. The agenda for this chapter is to focus on resilience mechanisms and how they can be promoted. Since I wrote in Chap. 1 that "this book is not about the war in Iraq", this chapter is therefore not about peacebuilding, state building, or nation building in Iraq writ large. Instead, it pulls together lessons for *local* peacebuilding that integrate structural with relational approaches.

Structural Versus Relational Approaches to Resilience

The structural approach to peacebuilding and reconstruction emphasizes economic and political reform as tools of peacebuilding, economic and political stabilization strategies such as democracy building, restoration of infrastructure, and provision of financial aid to promote economic growth. Structural interventions target the reconstruction of economic systems that have been devastated by internal conflict, promote political reforms that offer a voice to citizenry, introduce measures to curb corruption, and seek to enhance rule of law. Development discourse and practice focuses on institutional capacity building—building up the ability of national organizations to do their jobs well. Particularly important since the late 1990s has been an emphasis on capacity-building institutions of good governance in vulnerable states.

Relational approaches address intergroup relations explicitly. Social conflicts are lodged in long-standing relationships, often characterized by enduring intergroup animosity, perception of enmity, and deep-rooted fear. This is coupled with the immediacy of having the enemy living virtually next door. These social–psychological perceptions, emotions, and subjective experiences drive social conflicts, and they can be wholly independent of the substantive or originating issues.

The emphasis on strengthening national institutions fits with the general idea of resilient, strong states. Structuralists are therefore right to argue that peaceful societies require laws and institutions that uphold equality of economic opportunity and political representation. At the same time, "the immediacy of hatred and prejudice, of racism and xenophobia, as primary factors and motivators of conflict means that its transformation must be rooted in social–psychological and spiritual dimensions that traditionally have been seen as either irrelevant, or outside the competency of international diplomacy" [5]. I witnessed these both in Northern Ireland and Cyprus during visits to study these divided societies. While I heard much about the political peace process and negotiations being hashed out by political elites; very few people knew of anything being done to help heal divided communal relationships. Structural approaches to violent conflict typically do not engage the relational component that is important for sustainable peace.

Resilience research offers the insight that in addition to long-term, slow-moving institutional change, it is important to look for short-term variables of more dynamic change. A middle-ground approach between structural and relational approaches derives from my earlier analysis of the conflict's underlying conditions (discussed in Chaps. 1 and 2). Social inequity and aspects of intergroup relations (such as trust and civility) can only be addressed through social reconciliation *and* concomitant domestic restructuring.

Strengthening Community Resilience

Conflict-resilient communities have certain regime characteristics: community organizations, resources, and community processes are set up in ways that build and increase collective capacity for learning, conflict prevention, adaptation, and self-organization. They are built on the social–psychological foundations of place attachment, bridging capital (or working trust between identity groups), collective efficacy, and collective narratives, emphasizing positive futures, agency, and hopefulness. However, these social resources are usually lacking in post-conflict environments. At minimum, enhancing community resilience requires (1) spaces where people can begin envisioning positive futures and images of "the other", (2) projects to address local needs that are designed to require collaboration by members of different identity groups, and (3) support for neighborhood-level "peace leaders" who are interested in rebuilding social trust.

Spaces for Visioning

The desperate and critical need for psychological care is an often overlooked dimension of post-conflict rebuilding, though it makes perfect sense in the context of a study that has placed so much emphasis on the social infrastructure of conflict-resilient communities. "All mass violence is made up of single acts", wrote Roberto Culbertson and Beatrice Pouligny [6].

> In the most intimate sites of any instance of mass violence—the street, the household, the public square, the prison cell—individuals make choices and take action, and remain haunted by them. Victims may turn in their neighbors and so become indirect perpetrators. Many witness atrocities without defending the victims or even speaking out.

Culbertson and Pouligny argue persuasively, "all of these subtleties must come out in the stories of mass crime if those involved are to see themselves as human actors rather than monsters or saints". Where are the forums for telling stories of mass violence in Baghdad? Our respondent from Al Doura pointed out that to date "most people from mosques have not attempted reconciliation or talked about relationships" adding that only one Imam in his neighborhood had made an effort on the subject.

Although it seems counter-intuitive to recommend the establishment of spaces where people can begin envisioning positive futures where violence still plagues daily life, conflict practitioners like John Paul Lederach have argued that this is precisely the time where it is most needed because the occurrence of day-to-day crisis limits people's ability to envision different futures. Visualization is a powerful tool. It can stimulate the growth of new cells in the body, it can trigger the release of certain endorphins and hormones, it can improve performance, increase self-confidence, ease many physical symptoms including different types of pain, and can affect our emotions. More to the point of this study, human systems exhibit an observable tendency to evolve in the direction of positive anticipatory images of the future just as plants exhibit a tendency to grow in the direction of sunlight.

People need spaces to begin envisioning positive futures, even when violence still plagues daily life. In Acapulco a group of schoolteachers, church officials, business people, university professors, ex-guerillas, and NGO representatives have been gathering to figure out ways to address cartel violence. This group has the conviction that cities can and must organize in order to open "non-violent roads to build change and social cohesion" [7]. They purposefully built a space through which they aimed to fortify people's abilities to analyze and understand violent conflict, theories of peace and justice, and work on peacebuilding projects together.

Baghdad is not free of sectarian violence and may not be for some time yet to come. But traumatized populations cannot move toward new and better futures without a capacity for vision. In particular, groups of people that can cultivate and strengthen positive images of "the other" are more conflict-resilient than those who do not. Positive images of others trigger an increased capacity to access from memory positive rather than negative aspects of others and perceive ambiguous situations for the positive rather than their negative possibilities. Whereas preventing violence would not have been possible without trust between neighborhood residents; violence *could* be mobilized in places where "damn Sunnis", "Kafiri", or "Saddam lovers" were not recognized as legitimate members of a community or a society.

But perhaps the most important consequence of positive imaging of "the other" is that it supports new kinds of behavior. To understand the self as a social creation is to understand that human beings are essentially modifiable, open to new development, and—at the risk of becoming too esoteric—products of the human imagination and mind. We are each made and imagined in the eyes of one another. There is an utter inseparability of the individual from the social context and history of the projective process. And positive interpersonal imagery, the research now shows, accomplishes its work very concretely.

One way of encouraging personal efficacy, the precursor to collective efficacy, is to help individuals break free of the politicized, manipulated, and emotionally charged narratives that mobilized groups of people to act on sectarian symbols, stories, and histories.

> It may be interesting for you to know that once my Sunni friend in college before 2003, thought that Shia don't worship God, that we worship our Imam (Ali) who we consider God and so we are not "true Muslims". He was shocked and I guess he didn't totally believe me when I told him this is not true!! This is written in their books, despite the fact that there are thousands of Shia mosques and books that mention otherwise and Shia openly worship God every day. I was really laughing at that time, but now I feel it was really sad rather than funny…

Recall that conflict can be defined as competing stories that tend to be simple constructions that built on negative assumptions about the intent and character of "the other" [8, 9]. Marc Howard Ross has written extensively on how people make sense of emotionally powerful events and come up with different, even contradictory, accounts of what has happened. I discussed narratives in Chaps. 3 and 5, describing them as "explanations for events (large and small) in the form of short, common sense accounts (stories) that often seem simple" [10]. Narratives are especially significant when the world seems uncertain, dangerous, and stressful.

In these times, people try to make sense of their experiences by talking about things and telling stories to each other. "September 11", as it is known in the United States, took place 10 days into my doctoral program at George Mason University. The most immediate academic conversations focused on theories of violence and globalization. But the most immediate *personal* conversations I had revolved around "where we were" when the event occurred. Some of us watched it live on TV that morning; some of us were in other countries and heard about it after the fact. One of my new colleagues at George Mason lost his best friend who, having flown all the way over from China to visit, connected through Boston on United Airlines Flight 175. "Where we were" conversations gave conversational space to each person's lived experience of a nationally traumatic event. Next, these conversations transitioned to "who?", "why?", "why now?", and "how?"—stories about causation, attribution, and what should happen next. This is what Ross meant when he wrote that we make sense of stressful events through storytelling.

Baghdad residents are living through terrible times, far more traumatic than the World Trade Tower attacks that triggered the US invasion of Iraq.[1] They were living through terrible times before, too. People find reassurance and cope with highly stressful situations through shared narratives about "what is happening and

[1] This is my personal opinion, however the 'depth of trauma' can be assessed by looking at various indicators: to name only a few, the duration of traumatic incidents (bombings, assassinations, military incursions); the number of people killed and injured; effects on families of the killed and injured; and the effects of violence on overall economic and human development.

why".[2] Unfortunately, Iraqis are divided on the narrative of what the last decade of US occupation has meant. In line with the theory that groups with different experiences and worldviews construct different narratives of the same events, Sunni and Shia Iraqis differ in their understanding of self and other. Important misconceptions include the following, described to me by the Iraqi research team in debriefing.

> From the Shia point of view, Sunnis like Saddam until now, accepted and approved of what he did to Shia Iraqis—the killing and displacement. They don't think Sunnis admit that Shias were oppressed during Saddam's time and were killed in thousands. They see Sunnis as being the main generals of the army and intelligence forces that killed Shias. They observe that Sunnis kind of supported, or liked, or at least overlooked the terrorist groups operated in their region. Shia believe Sunnis look upon Shias with a sense of superiority even though Shia are the majority, and don't accept the political process.
>
> From the Sunni point of view, they look to Shia with great suspicion and distrust. They associate Iraqi Shia with Iran, and refer to them as *Farisi* or *Safawis*; both words are kind of ugly terms in the Sunni Arabic culture. Sunnis also think that Shia and Iran are trying to displace them from Iraq and exile them. The majority believes that the government is a pro-Iranian government and that most of its members are actually not Iraqis at all. They believe the Shia-led government allowed the Shia militias to operate in the name of Iraqi security forces and kill Sunnis. Sunnis usually refer to Shia politicians as having "come over the tanks of the occupier".

Opposing narratives get in the way of conflict resolution. Narrative interventions—sometimes called narrative mediations—are designed to generate new information, "news of difference" that decreases the coherence of conflict stories, opening up psychological space for new understandings. Narrative is also therapeutic for traumatized groups and individuals in that it highlights the significance of historical events as stories around which violence is/was sanctioned. Self-esteem, mental health, and coping ability are closely connected to whether events are self-explained in empowering or disempowering terms.[3] From the psychological subfield of trauma research, a volume of evidence indicates that optimism about the future predicts individual resilience; "to the extent that people are encouraged to view their posttraumatic situation as one in which growth can occur, growth is more likely to take place."[4]

Local communities must decide when and how they are ready to undertake the task of reimagining peace. The formation of identities and realities are based in large part on narratives, the stories of our histories. More realistic than seeking an objective truth or reality are attempts to gain insight into how worlds have been constructed. The way we understand events has less to do with their occurrence than with the way they have been narrated.

---

[2] Ibid.

[3] Buchanan and Seligman [11]; Seligman [12]

[4] Carver [13]: 256.

Collaborative, Crosscutting Projects

Working on conflict does not require people to like each other. That expectation is unrealistic in highly polarized and traumatized populations. According to Arai, conflict-resolution-based approaches which seek to build "common ground" between enemies are often simply doomed from the start because of the intransigence of enemy images and deeply ingrained psychological biases that come to define people's identity in such important ways that they are highly resistant to change. Arai contends that for "functional coexistence", parties to conflict do not need to trust or even recognize each other in order to take pragmatic, self-interested steps that further their economic interests.

> Functional coexistence is an adversarial relationship that falls short of direct military confrontation, yet paves the way toward a sustained, evolving process of pragmatic interactions between conflict parties that neither trust nor recognize each other (source?).

Instead of urging parties to recognize the legitimacy of the other and their interests and goals, functional coexistence proposes that a social space for pragmatic interaction can be legitimized "if not the parties themselves as rightful political partners to deal with." For such a social space to be perceived as legitimate by diverse actors, it should be "endorsed but not controlled by state structures."[5]

Functional coexistence is not an entirely new argument. Krishna Kumar [14] has argued that development projects promote reconciliation as long as they use a participatory, community-centered strategy. The United Nations Development Program has run a variety of community-building programs based on the same principles, including the *Community Reconciliation through Poverty Reduction* project which builds community cohesion around targeted objectives like mine clearance, waste management, and income generation activities. "The project is based on the principle that a participatory and transparent approach to income generation will create a synergetic bond for municipalities to cooperate in the development of common interests and the mitigation of "hard-line" politics."[6] Other authors have explored how to use sports as political tools for post-conflict peacebuilding [15] and advocated for projects that "address practical concerns; [introduce] repeated and inter-dependent interethnic interaction; are rooted in local culture; and are difficult for people to avoid" [16].

Plenty of development aid has flowed in Iraq since 2003; over $9.1 billion at time of writing. Resilience-thinking prompts the question of how development aid can enhance self-organization. Self-organization occurs through trial and error, learning-as-you-go interactions where people experiment with various methods and figure out what works and what does not. Supporting self-organization requires creating the political space for experimentation. According to Heather

---

[5] Experts at a 2011 conference on conflict prevention reached this conclusion, among othersc. Ganson and Wennman.

[6] http://www.undp.ba/index.aspx?PID=21&RID=65

Coyne, Senior Program Officer at the U.S. Institute of Peace, a particular USAID project in Iraq took this approach of letting communities themselves determine the project designs, based on their own priorities and internal capabilities.

> The community action program (CAP)...was very successful in and of itself. We trained Iraqi mobilizers who would then go into the communities and lead them through a process of identifying needs, prioritizing them, and selecting one that they would then implement, a project with support from USAID. USAID would provide the resources from arms length, but the community itself was responsible for implementing the program... So there was a very intense process of developing community buy-in and ownership over these. And over time, leaders would emerge who had taken a major role in organizing the project, who had experience in addressing community needs, and who had earned respect of their fellow citizens.

USAID's CAP was specifically designed with conflict analysis in mind and helped boost transactional capacity in post-conflict areas. Aid that creates opportunities and lets recipients choose how to take advantage of those opportunities according to their own interests and motivations enhances collective efficacy and capacity for self-organization [17]. Ecological psychologists advocate for interventions whose design, implementation, and evaluation are informed by "local values and beliefs regarding psychological well-being and distress," and for the integration of new interventions into existing community structures and practices.[7]

One idea based on resilience thinking, proposed by a member of the research team, is to work with the families and leaders of each region to put together "reintegration support programs" for managing the negative psychological dynamics—suspicion, distrust, and grievance—that led to vulnerability to ethno-sectarian ideology in the first place.

> We have thousands of NGOs in Iraq, but it's hard to find realistic NGOs that are working for people on the ground...Families that lost loved ones are hurt, suffering psychologically and socially and financially. Are there any NGOs taking care of them? No one is providing support. People resettled suffer, and distrust their surroundings. There is no trauma healing on the local level to deal with these families and the leaders of the region, putting a program together to make those people feel at peace again. That's why any people don't want to go back to their homes, because no one is going to take care of them.

I had a similar conversation over lunch recently with a colleague who has served as legal counsel to the Office of the High Commissioner in Kosovo, following the Dayton Peace Accords that ended the armed conflict in the former Yugoslavia. He told me about a home return program in Bosnia which many view as a success story in post-conflict peacebuilding. Basically, many Serb and Croat families living in mixed areas fled their homes during the war. Either they were forced to leave, or fled ahead of feared ethnic cleansing campaigns. The program returned home titles to rightful owners, arranged property swaps, and helped rebuild damaged houses. But instead of returning home, the vast majority of displaced people stayed away. Either the houses stand vacant, or they have been rented or sold. The fear and trauma of returning "home" is still too great.

---

[7] Miller and Rasco [18]: 43.

A relatively new category of modalities has emerged in the past few years, which aim to combine relational and structural aspects of peace work. They are commonly referred to as "Infrastructures for Peace" or I4P. The commonly adopted definition of I4P is "a dynamic network of interdependent structures, mechanisms, resources, values and skills which, through dialogue and consultation, contribute to conflict prevention and peace building in a society" [19]. Common modalities include peace committees, peace secretariats, national peacebuilding platforms, conflict analysis and early warning and response systems, and insider mediators. Although such modalities can (and should) be organized at the national, regional, or local level, resilience researchers have a bias toward local capacity building *to start*—myself among them. The national peace agreement in Iraq was an elite pact that did not include broad societal participation in its design nor its implementation.

Supporting Peace Leaders

Whatever the approach, building community resilience means supporting local leaders who would advocate for democratic and participatory governance. The process of doing so, however, can either support or smother adaptive capacity. Heather Coyne described another USAID project that aimed to create local councils in all Baghdad communities to strengthen democratic participation in decision making. Unfortunately, unlike the Community Action Project described above, the Local Councils project failed to meet its objectives.

> We were under tremendous pressure to create the councils quickly, so we could establish democracy in Iraq. USAID and the Army cooperated in holding town halls so that we could select the lowest level of councilors. Then almost immediately that lowest level would select people from within the council to represent them at the next level, the district level, the higher level…and then those people selected people to represent them at the next level, the city level, up at the top. This all happened within a matter of days or weeks. So the representatives have no time to work with each other, to figure out who was be a good leader, who they would WANT to represent them at the next level, and they had no time to implement local projects that would have created a connection to their constituents.
>
> So we ended up with people on the council with very little legitimacy and no administrative experience at all. We then invested a huge amount of time and effort trying to build their capacity, but the training wasn't methodical and more importantly we didn't give them the budget or the authority to allow them to have a real impact, either in the minds of their constituents or the minds of the national ministries they were working for. So at the end of this experiment we have a bunch of organizations with no power, no ability to deliver, no constituency below, no respect from above, and no chance at all of being re-elected.

People trust the advice of leaders already embedded in local communities, not new leaders vaulted by national elites to positions of power [17, p. 51]. Embedded leaders understand the locally relevant strategies to coping and adaptation and have legitimacy in the eyes of the community. Coyne recalled the leaders who had emerged through engagement with the Community Action Project.

> Ideal candidates for the local councils, right? Unfortunately the councils had already been filled with people we picked off the streets. They'd have to wait a few years for the next election, which actually never happened...

Another reason "peace-leaders" must emerge from local communities is that leadership *as an institution* is constructed differently (e.g., tribal, civic, secular, religious) depending on the neighborhood regime. Thus, in some places, tribal leaders would be crucial allies, particularly given the challenge to communal reconciliation posed by the high social value of revenge as an equalizer in tribal society. In other places, mosques, husseiniyas, and churches are strategically positioned to embark on community advancement projects; in still others, prominent families and respected community leaders are the obvious partners for community reconciliation efforts.

Beyond Baghdad?

On December 18, 2010, a young street vendor named Mohamed Bouazizi set himself on fire after local police confiscated his street-cart, his sole means of livelihood. Bouazizi's self-immolation in the Tunisian town of Sidi Bouzid triggered the Arab Spring, a wave of civil protests and revolutions that swept dictators from power and replaced them with fledgling democratic rulers and institutions. The patterns of protest varied widely between Tunisia, Egypt, Libya, Bahrain, and most recently Syria. Yet all "shared a common call for personal dignity and responsible government [and] reflected divergent economic grievances and social dynamics" [20].

Particularly in Syria, the armed uprising that pitted the Assad regime against revolutionaries aiming to remove him from power has essentially devolved into sectarian warfare. Sectarian lines in Syria are drawn broadly between Syria's minority ruling Alawites (a Shia sect) and the majority Sunni population, many (but not all) of whom support the rebels. "Neighbor on neighbor violence between Sunni and Shiites is breaking out across Syria" reported John Hudson in March 2012, recounting stories of sectarian death squads told by human rights activists and refugees fleeing into Turkey. By December of the same year, a United Nations human rights investigation reported that fighting between government forces and rebels had become "overtly sectarian in nature". Furthermore, "feeling threatened and under attack, ethnic and religious minority groups have increasingly aligned themselves with the parties to the conflict, deepening sectarian divides" [21].

In a special issue of the Journal Peacebuilding and Development, Jordan Ryan (the Director of the Bureau for Crisis Prevention and Recovery at the United Nations Development Program) reflected, "a crucial factor in supporting the transformation from fragility to resilience is to promote dialogue so that potential conflicts can be dealt with in an inclusive and respectful manner".[8] To date, attempts to broker dialogue between elites within the Assad regime and the Free Syrian

[8] Ryan, J. 2012. Infrastructures for peace as a path to resilience societies: a institutional perspective. Journal of Peacebuilding and Development 7(2):23.

Army have failed. However, it is not too early to begin the work of dialogue with displaced Syrians, and especially with young people, as David Kirkpatrick's editorial in the New York Times made clear.

> Like all the small children in the desert refugee camp here, Ibtisam, 11, is eager to go home to the toys, bicycles, books, cartoons and classmates she left behind in Syria. But not if that means living with the Alawites and Shiites…'*I hate the Alawites and Shiites,*' Ibtisam said as a crowd of children and adults nodded in agreement. '*We are going to kill them with out knives, just like they killed us.*' If the fighters seeking to oust Mr. Assad sometimes portray their battle as a struggle for democracy, the Sunni Muslim children of the Zaatari camp tell a much uglier story of sectarian revenge. Asked for their own views of the grown-up battle that drove them from their homes, child after child brought up their hatred of the Alawites and a thirst for revenge. Children as young as 10 or 11 vowed never to play with Syrian Alawite children or even pledged to kill them…The convictions of Heza, 13, were blunt. "*We will never live together,*" he said. "*All the Alawites are security agents. After the revolution, we want to kill them.*" Even if it might mean killing a Syrian child his own age? "*I will kill him,*" Heza said. "*It doesn't matter.*"

I often encounter resistance when suggesting that there is room to challenge and transform the predictable psychological changes that accompany the experience of violence and fear. What evidence, I am asked, is there that brutalized individuals are capable of entering into these exercises of imagery and creativity when their existence is threatened daily? Yet there *is* evidence that people can envision positive futures in situations of crisis, and en masse. The field of thriving, a new approach in psychology that extends beyond previous inquiries into resilience, studies the ability of individuals not only to cope with stress, but also to experience significant mental growth following traumatic experiences.[9]

> It is widely accepted that trauma is transformative and than in the aftermath of a traumatic event nothing is again the same. We are most familiar with negative aspects of this change…but trauma also leads to other transformations, including the reconstruction of meaning; the renewal of faith, trust, hope, and connection; and the redefinition of self, self-in-relation, and sense of community. Those who physically survive trauma begin to recover *even as its full horror is still registering*…Adaptation stems from our attempts to survive and *to heal in the midst of our suffering.*[10]

Group trauma, of the type experienced by Baghdad residents and Syrian refugees, is a more politically significant phenomenon than individual trauma because it represents collective social damage on a large scale. It is a marker of social instability and requires a different type of infrastructure. Individual forms of intervention are not appropriate for "post-traumatic destruction".[11] "Now", wrote Sandra Bloom, "we see whole populations traumatized by war, famine, plague, disaster, and political oppression…We must find larger scale, group forms of intervention to escalate the rate of transformation or the balance may very well shift further in the direction of global self-destruction."[12]

---

[9] Calhoun and Tedeschi [22], Saakvitne et al. (1998);

[10] Saakvitne et al. 282.

[11] Bloom, Sandra [23]: 208.

[12] ibid.

None of this casts doubt on the actuality of conflict environments in the sense that extensive bloodshed, human rights violations, and other humanitarian emergencies are immediate and vital realities. However, the underlying issues driving the continuation of conflict and the relationships between conflicted parties are in many ways constructions of politicized, manipulated, emotionally charged narratives that mobilize groups of people around emotionally and historically pregnant symbols, acts, or stories. Working now with Syrian refugees may have lasting benefits when the war ends.

Concluding Thoughts

Studying resilience is a contrasting approach to studying fragility, communities, and/or states with weak or ineffective governing, economic, and social institutions. Studying subnational resilience in fragile states gives an accounting of the ability to rebound, maintain, or strengthen functioning during and after a disturbance or to cope successfully in the face of extreme adversity or risk. Key factors in strengthening resilience are strong institutions, cross-scale communications, social justice, and political space for experimentation. In developing states, this amounts to a combination of long-term, slow-moving institutional change, as well as short-term variables of more dynamic change. Enhancing resilience means looking for sources of adaptive capacity and finding ways to support locally driven initiatives whose outcomes support a strengthening of the institutional context giving rise to them.

However, the trade-offs one often finds with local resilience is that what works to preserve social cohesion and social capital within a particular community may not have an upward impact, either on national governance or on surrounding regions of ongoing violence. Resilience at subnational levels is not guaranteed to counter national-level sources of fragility. In extremely fragile states, where there is a breakdown of law and order, where the central state suffers from a loss of legitimacy perhaps exacerbated by its lack of ability regain control, and where economic disparities are wide and worsening, there may actually be an inverse relationship between local cohesion and a national sense of we-ness. Dynamics of insecurity force perception to local levels, and people's trusted social networks get narrower [24]. Adaptive strategies that people use to circumvent and navigate their difficult environment tend to revolve around local leaders, traditional sources of authority, and informal rules and relationships worked out underneath (or alongside of) central authoritative structures. At the same time, social cohesion experienced at local levels (when it reinforces divisions along class or ethnic lines) can impede the efforts of politicians and interest groups seeking to bring about reforms [25]. Thus, there is no easy answer to questions about whether community resilience is scalable. Resilience on the national level is controlled by both fast and slow variables: constitutional and structural changes in governance are (or should be) slower to change than community policing mechanisms. At the same time that these long-term change processes are underway, we can focus on enhancing resilience in local communities.

Resilience and conflict prevention are tied together conceptually. Conflict prevention is "defined by a focus on the strength and resilience of social and political networks and institutions that identify and mobilise responses to known tensions and stress factors."[13] Resilience and prevention can be examined at multiple levels of analysis. At the global level, an especially important conflict prevention norm is the Responsibility to Protect or R2P, which "explicitly obliges states to protect their populations from genocide, war crimes, ethnic cleansing, and crimes against humanity and, moreover, calls on the international community to take collective action if states fail to do so" [26]. Global norms of conflict prevention also include adherence to human rights laws, economic development, rule of law, and good governance.

Yet, however, robust conflict prevention norms appear in the realm of international policymaking, rendering them from the "realm of ideas to the realm of action" has been far more challenging.[14] In particular, implementing conflict prevention depends on political subtleties associated with the United Nations Security Council and General Assembly.[15] At the macro-level of fragile states, resilience to extremism and sectarian violence involves consolidating and implementing norms of conflict prevention, including efforts to minimize sources of instability and conflict before they arise, to prevent violence and to restrict the influence of dangerous non-state actors—broad goals with few associated operational strategies.

Perhaps it is therefore unsurprising that "the most recurring observation about the nature of conflict prevention has been that it is a profoundly 'local' effort".[16] Resilience thinking "places prevention within indigenous responses to known tensions or stress factors as enabled by local networks and institutions".[17] At a micro-level, resilience to extremism and sectarian violence is a process of managing the gradual escalation of sectarian violence. In times of uncertainty and crisis, fears can grow quickly about "the other", and people's behavior deteriorates to match their assumptions about how the other is likely to act. Advanced planning and early warning procedures are vital, as conflicts tend to escalate quickly.

This book is a starting point, not an end point, toward understanding the sophisticated and complex set of explanations for community resilience. It has simply proposed that conflict prevention in Baghdad neighborhoods depended less on the presence of international security and development organizations and more on local actors, social networks, ad hoc organizations, and community leaders: the allies and entry points for building conflict resilience in urban communities outward.

---

13 Ganson and Wennman.

14 Carpenter [27].

15 Ganson and Wennman.

16 Ibid.

17 Ganson and Wennmann p. 4.

References

1. Mahdi, Abdul Adel. 2013. Government is a failure and Iraqis are hostages. Al Adala Newspaper, 26 April 2013.
2. Lemay-Hébert, Nicolas. 2009. Statebuilding without nation-building? Legitimacy, state failure and the limits of the institutionalist approach. *Journal of Intervention and Statebuilding* 3(1): 21–45.
3. Azeez, Hawzhin. 2010. Reconstructing Iraq: Iraq state-building nation-building and violence. *Nebula* 7(4): 78.
4. Clark, Helen. 2012. Putting resilience at the heart of the development agenda. Speech given at Cambridge University, 16 April.
5. Lederach, John P. 1997. Building peace: Sustainable reconciliation in divided societies. Washingon D.C.: United States Institute of Peace, p. 29.
6. Culbertson, R. and Pouligny, B. 2007. Re-imagining peace after violent crime. In after mass crime: Rebuilding states and communities.
7. Jean Mendieta Jiménez and Enrique Pasta Muñuzuri. 2013. *Diplomado en Ciudadanía para la Paz y Resolución de Conflictos*. Acapulco: Universidad Loyola.
8. Cobb, Sara. 1994. A narrative perspective on mediation: Toward the materialization of the storytelling metaphor. In *New directions in mediation: Communication research and perspectives*, eds. J.P. Folger and T.S. Jones, Thousand Oaks, CA: Sage.
9. Cobb, Sara. 2004. Fostering coexistence in identity-based conflicts: Towards a narrative approach. In *Imagine coexistence*, eds. A. Chayes and M. Minow, Joseey Bass: San Francisco.
10. Ross, M. H. 2013. *The politics of memory and peacebuilding*. In Handbook of Peacebuilding. New York: Routledge, 91–102.
11. Buchanan, G. M., and Seligman, M. E. P. eds. 1995. Explanatory style. Hillsdale, NJ: Erlbaum.
12. Seligman, M.E.P. (1991). Helplessness: On Depression, Development and Death. Second edition. New York: W.H. Freeman.
13. Carver, C.S. 1998. Resilience and Thriving: Issues, Models and Linkages. *Journal of Social Issues* 54(2): 245–266.
14. Kumar, K. 1999. Promoting Social Reconciliation in Postconflict Societies: Selected Lessons from USAID's Experience. Center for Development Information and Evaluation, U.S. Agency for International Development. http://www.oecd.org/derec/unitedstates/35112635.pdf
15. Hoglund, K. and R. Sundberg. 2008. Reconciliation through Sports? The case of South Africa. *Third World Quarterly* 29(4): 805–818.
16. Paula Pickering, Paula. 2006. Generating social capital for bridging ethnic division in the Balkans: Case studies of two Bosniak cities. *Journal of Ethnic and Racial Studies* 29/1: 79I.
17. Ricigliano, Richard. 2012. Making peace last: A toolbox for sustainable peacebuilding. Boulder, CO: Paradigm Publishers, p. 35.
18. Miller, K. E., and L. M. Rasco. 2004. *An ecological framework for addressing the mental health needs of refugee communities*. The Mental Health of Refugees: Ecological Approaches to Healing and Adaptation: 1–64.
19. Kumar, Chetan. 2011. Building national infrastructures for peace: UN assistance for internally negotiated solutions to violent conflict. In *Peacemaking: From practice to theory*, eds. S. Nan, Z. Mampilly, and A. Bartoli, 385. Santa Barbara, CA: Praeger.
20. Anderson, Lisa. 2011. Demystifying the Arab spring: Parsing the differences between Tunisia, Egypt and Libya. Foreign Affairs.
21. Tedeschi, R., C. Park, and L. Calhoun. 1998. *Post-Traumatic Growth: Theory and Research on Change in the Aftermath of Crises*. Mahwah, NJ: Lawrence Erlbaum.
22. Bloom S. 1998. By The Crowd They Have Been Broken, By the Crowd They Shall Be Healed: The Social Transformation of Trauma. In *Post-Traumatic Growth: Theory and Research on Change in the Aftermath of Crises*, eds. R. Tedeschi, C. Park, and L. Calhoun. Mahwah, NJ: Lawrence Erlbaum.

23. United Nations Office of the High Commissioner for Human Rights. 2012. Independent international commission of inquiry on the Syrian Arab Republic. 20 Dec 2012.
24. De'Estree, Tamara. 2003. Dynamics. In *Conflict*, ed. S. Cheldelin, D. Druckman, and L. Fast. New York: Lexington Publishing.
25. Ritzen, J., Easterly, W., Woolcock, M. 1999. On 'good' politicians and 'bad' policies: Social cohesion, institutions and growth. World Bank Policy Research Working Papers.
26. Stanes, Paul B, and Vessey, John W. 2011. Partners in preventive action: The United States and International Institutions. Council on Foreign Relations.
27. Carpenter, A.C. 2008. *Rendering Idea to Practice: Development Assistance and Conflict Prevention in Guatemala*. Fairfax, VA: George Mason University Press.

Author Biography

Ami Carpenter is an Assistant Professor at the Joan B. Kroc School of Peace Studies at University of San Diego. Her research focuses on community resilience to violence and the criminal dimensions of political conflicts. Area studies have included research in Iraq, Guatemala, the United States, El Salvador, and Zimbabwe. Dr. Carpenter works on numerous initiatives as a mediator, facilitator, trainer, and conflict resolution consultant. She served as a Fulbright Specialist to assist the National Peace and Reconciliation Commission (NPRC) in Zimbabwe to set up the country's first academic program in peace and conflict studies. Currently, she is researching vulnerability and resilience to violent conflict in Iraqi, Guatemalan, and US communities, including engagement strategies with transnational gangs and criminal networks in the US and Mexico.

A. C. Carpenter, *Community Resilience to Sectarian Violence in Baghdad*,
Peace Psychology Book Series, DOI: 10.1007/978-1-4614-8812-5,

Index

A
Access to resources, 110, 115
Activated social networks, 121
Adhamiyya, 91, 93, 111, 114
Adhamiyya, 69, 84
Adaptability, 73*n*5
Adaptation, 70, 73, 75
    collective adaptation, 97
    narratives, 102–103
    positive adaptation, 104
    self-organized adaptation, 96
    sources
        through leaders, 96–98
        through media, 98–99
        through working trust, 99–100
    spaces for, 100–102
Adaptive capacity, 64, 67, 70, 71, 73, 75, 77
Adhamiyya, 9, 11, 11*t*, 14–15, 35, 59, 69, 87, 88, 98, 100, 103
Advocacy for violence prevention, 125–126, 128*t*
Al Anbar, 88*n*3, 116
Al Nil, 2–4
Al Qaeda in Iraq (AQI), 20*n*13, 49, 56 57–58, 59, 88
    attacks against Iraqi Security Forces (ISF), 50
    strategies, 43–44, 50
Al-Askari Mosque bombing, 51
Al-Dhubat, 11, 11*t*, 73, 100, 113, 125
Al-Sadr, Muhammad Baqir, 33
Al-Sadr, Muhammad Sadiq, 16
Al-Sadr, Muqtada, 33, 59
Al-Sistani, Ali Husain, 33
Al-Sunna, Ansar, 57
Amariyya, 84, 88, 103
Amariyya, 84
Amiriyya, 1, 11, 11*t*, 13, 14, 16, 59, 88, 92, 93, 97, 98
Amiriyya, 69
Al Nil, 5
Anbar Province, 50, 88, 108
"Anti-establishment" thinking, 33
Azar, Edward, 28

B
Ba'ath Party, 1, 15, 45, 46, 47, 48
Baathism, 43
Badr Corps, 50, 50*n*6
Baghdad, 2, 7, 8, 11, 13–21, 87, 90
    before major sectarian violence, 11, 12*f*
    living conditions, 138–139
    neighborhoods, 2, 5
        regime characteristics in, 68–69
    sectarian violence in, 137.*See also* Violenceafter violence in 2006, 11, 12*f*
Baghdad bridge stampede in 2005, 85
Baghdad Neighborhood without Violence, A, 2
"Baiji purifier" in Salah al-Din, 15
Battle of Karbala, 32, 59*n*6
Bayaa, 11, 17, 68
Bayati, Hamid, 1
Border monitoring, 126, 128
Bridging capital. *See* Crosscutting bonds
Bridging ties. *See* Crosscutting bonds
Buffer capacity, 70, 71

C
Capacity for adaptation, 75
Civil war, 21, 32, 42, 50, 70, 107, 110

A. C. Carpenter, *Community Resilience to Sectarian Violence in Baghdad*,
Peace Psychology Book Series, DOI: 10.1007/978-1-4614-8812-5,

Iraqi civil war, 20, 43
sectarian civil war, 58, 103
Syrian civil war, 135
Civilian casualties, 48, 59
Civilian identity, 34, 69, 90, 122, 128*t*
Coalition Provisional Authority (CPA), 48
Cohesiveness, 56–57
Collective action, 4, 74, 81, 82, 100, 120
Collective efficacy, 120, 121–123, 127, 128*t*, 134, 136, 138, 141
Communication, 75, 76, 95, 96, 135, 145
contribution of, 104
and information, 73, 74, 77
and information sharing, 100–102
sources
through leaders, 96–98
through media, 98–99
through working trust, 99–100
spaces for, 100–102
Communication management , 21, 120. *See also* Community competenceCommunication systems, 100
Community
relations of, 88
sense of, 89–100
schism, 100
Community competence, 73, 74, 75, 76, 77, 119, 120, 135
behavioral components of, 124–126
psychological components of, 121
collective efficacy, 121–123
inward orientation, 123–124
and regime characteristics, linkages between, 126–128
Community empowerment, 120
Community mediators, 125
Community polarization, 60
Community resilience, 1, 4–6, 20
strengthening, 136
collaborative and crosscutting projects, 140–142
spaces for visioning, 136–139
supporting peace leaders, 142–143
Conciliation Resources (NGO), 9
Conflict, 24–27, 32, 36
communal, 31
defensive, 36
escalation, 72
ethnic, 23, 28
group, 23
intergroup, 29, 30
management, 66
meaning, 23
narratives, role in, 26
resilience, 64, 77
modeling, 72–76, 76*t*
resilient communities, 70
sectarian, 22, 35
in Baghdad, 64
social violent, 28
Conflict analysis, 42, 142
USAID's CAP, 141
Conflict drivers, 40, 42
elite/individual level, 47–51
global and regional levels, 42–44
state-level resources, 44–47
Conflict escalation, 1–2, 5, 17–21, 64, 72, 73
and conflict resilience, 53
community changes and, 60–61
sectarian militia, 60–61
group changes and, 55–59
"life cycle" metaphor, 54
psychological changes and, 54–55
Conflict prevention, 5–6, 5*n*1, 136, 142, 146
definition, 5*n*1
Conflict resilience, 5, 21, 61, 63, 96, 100, 103, 104, 105
definition, 20
indicators of, 6
Conflict-resilient areas, 3, 100, 125
Conflict-resilient communities, 5, 70, 97, 98, 123, 136
Conflict-resilient neighborhoods, 26–27, 98, 124, 126
Conflict resolution, 3, 32, 42, 45, 83, 120, 125, 139, 140
Constructivism, 24–27, 29, 36
constructing normative structures, 25–26
interdependence structure, 25
social construction of reality, 24–25
Contemporary Conflict Resolution (Ramsbotham, Woodhouse, and Miall), 50
Coping, 65, 73, 142
Coping ability, 103, 139
Coping strategies, 8*n*2, 73
Cordesman, Anthony, 1, 58*n*7
Criminals, 108
Crosscutting bonds, 83–84, 87, 92
Cultural narratives, 98, 125
Culture, 28, 29, 31–33, 35, 36
cultural re-enactment, 32
definition, 32
Culture of "civilian identity", 35

D
Dartmouth Medical School, 73
De'Baathification, 113
Decision-making, 67, 74, 83, 97, 103, 120

Dehumanization, 55
Deindividuation, 55
Development aid, 140
Dhubat, 89, 91, 92
Diversity, 64, 70, 74
Dura, 84, 88, 92, 93
Dura, 11, 11*t*, 15–16

E
Economic and Geospatial Infrastructure, 6, 7
Economic development, 74, 117
  definition, 107
  and probability of civil war, 110
  and resilience, 107–108
Economic resources, 76, 107–109, 135
  mechanisms of influence, 113–115
  socioeconomic status, 109–110
    and resilience to violence, 111–113
  trade networks, 115–115
Efficacy, 121
  collective, 120, 121
  community, 120
Elite strategies, 47, 48
Emotional changes, 54
Empirical microanalysis, 9
Enclaves, 101, 102
Escalation, 53
Escalation of violence, 134, 146
Escalation prevention, 6
Ethnic conflict, 20, 23, 28, 47, 123
  Extremism , 23–24. *See also* Violenceconstructivism, identity, and conflict, 24–27
    identity conflict through constructivist, 27–31
  group identities in Iraq, 32–36

F
Facilitators, 8, 91, 101, 111
Fatima Al-Zahra'a, 86
Feedback loops, 70*n*3
Freedom, 107

G
Geospatial variables and violence, 4
  ethnic entrepreneurs, 4
Global War on Terror (GWOT), 42
Governance, 44, 49, 120
Group cohesion, 56
Group dynamics, 24, 31, 86
Group identity, 27, 32–36, 54
Group narratives, 56, 102, 104, 122
Group polarization, 56, 86, 130
Group trauma, 144

H
Hasan Kafir families, 87
Horizontal legitimacy, 47
Hostile attitudes, 54, 87
  effects of, 55
Human development, 107, 108
Human social system, 25
Hussein, Saddam, 47, 61

I
Identity, 24–27, 36
  socially constructed, 36
Identity conflict, 27–31
Images, 103, 104
In-depth interviewing (IDI), 7
Information, 66, 73, 74, 75, 76, 95, 96, 135, 139
  and communication, 73, 74, 77
  contribution of, 104
  freedom of movement, 95
  nature of danger, 95
  options for survival and recovery, 95
  sources
    from leaders, 96–98
    from media, 98–99
    from working trust, 99–100
  spaces for, 100–102
  word of mouth, 96
Infrastructures for peace (I4P), 142
Ingroup bias, 30
Insecurity, 44, 110, 124, 134, 145
Instrumentalists, 28, 29
  and primordialist camps, 27
Interaction effect, 65
Intergroup relations, 135, 136
International Crisis Group, 34
International Federation of the Red Cross and Red Crescent Societies, 71
International Security Assistance Forces (ISAF), 48
Inward orientation, 123–124
Iran-Iraq War, 43
Iraq, 1, 2, 7, 10, 11. *See also* Multicultural IraqIraq Body Count, 9, 17, 17*n*11
Iraq, group identities in, 32–36
Iraqi security forces, 50*n*5
Iraqi tribes, 68
Islamic Army in Iraq (IAI), 57
Islamic world vs. West, 42

J

Jaghori District, Afghanistan, 3, 130
JAM in Bayaa, 20*n*13, 34, 50, 55, 57, 59, 89, 92, 100, 112, 113, 116, 117, 122
Jordan, 88
Joseph, Braude, 1, 46

K

Karada, 11, 11*t*, 16, 17, 100
Karada, 89, 91, 93
Karada, 68
Kazimiyya, 14, 100
Kazimiyya, 73
Kuraiaait, 11, 11*t*
Kuraiaat, 11, 11*t*, 89, 100
Kuraiaat, 68
Kurait, 73
Kurdistan Workers Party, 43
Kyoto Protocol, 67

L

Leaders, 124, 125, 126, 127, 127*n*10, 130
Leaders and Community Organization, 6, 7
Leadership, 96, 97–98, 103, 120, 125, 127*n*10
Lederach, John Paul, 81
Levi's Transaction Cost Theory, 82
Local peacebuilding, 135

M

Mahdi Army (JAM), 20*n*13, 49, 59
Markets, 5, 7, 13, 42, 61, 84, 101, 134
Mass violence, 136, 137
Media, 98, 99
Media bias, 99
Model of resilience to conflict, 76*f*
Multi-communal societies, 28
Multicultural Iraq, 13
  Adhamiyya, 11*t*, 14–15
  Amiriyya, 11*t*, 13–14
  Bayaa, 17
  Dura, 11*t*, 15–16
  Palestine Street, 17
  Sadr City, 11*t*, 16
  Zafaraniyya, 11*t*, 16–17
Mutah wedding, 87

N

Narratives, 26, 27, 33, 102–103, 136, 138, 139, 145
  or collective interpretations, 21
  conflict dynamics, 26
  psychocultural interpretations, 26
National peacebuilding, 142
Nation building, 48, 135
Nikah wedding, 87
Nomadism, 35, 87

O

Old Baghdadis, 35, 69, 87
Organization of non-sectarian security groups, 124
Outcomes, 4, 6, 65, 71, 75, 76, 99, 104, 105, 109, 126, 145

P

Palestine Street, 11, 11*t*, 17, 45, 47, 68, 73, 89, 93, 100, 111, 111*t*, 124, 125, 126
Pashtun tribes, 3
Patterns of Resilience: Adaptive Capacity in Fragile States, 3
Peacebuilding, 135, 137, 140, 141, 142
Peace leaders, 136, 143
  supporting, 142–143
Perceptual bias, 54–55, 56
Performance, 44, 74, 121, 137
Persian Gulf War, 43
Place attachment, 82, 88, 91–92, 122, 124, 126, 128*t*, 136
Political and Social Structure, 6
Popular Army, 88*n*3
Positive imaging, 137
Post-conflict peacebuilding, 140, 141
Post-conflict prevention, 6
Poverty, 107, 108, 110, 112, 116
  and community resilience, 116
Prejudice, 30, 129, 135
Primordialists, 27
  and instrumentalist camps, 28, 29
Private authorities, 45
Process capacities, 6
Protection narrative, 113, 127
Psychocultural interpretations, 26, 36, 122
Psychological changes, 54–55, 72, 73, 112, 113, 125, 130
Psychology of communities, 31
Psychology of crowd, 31
Psychosocial vulnerability, 113

R

Reconstruction, 135, 144
Redundancy, 64, 70, 74
Regime resilience, 69, 70–72
Regime shift, 70, 71, 76

Regimes, 6, 64
  characteristics, 67, 76
    in Baghdad neighborhoods, 68–69
  political, 67
  resilience. *See* Regime resilience
  system's, 67
Relations between people, 83
  crosscutting bonds, 83–87
  overlapping ties, 87–88
Relations with community, 88
  citizen participation, 90–91
  place attachment, 91–92
  sense of community, 89–90
Relationship and choice, 4
Religious identity, 32–36
Resilience, 63, 64–67
  community, 64, 77
  conflict, 64
  and conflict, 5–7
    modeling, 72–76, 76*f*
  concept of, 4, 64
  economic aspects, 108
  and economic development, 107–108
  meaning, 2
  regime characteristics in Baghdad neighborhoods, 68–69
  social resilience, 108, 109
    economic structure and, 109
    SES and, 110
  structural indicators of, 75
  structural vs. relational approaches, 135–136
  systems resilience, 66, 77
  to violence, 2
    and SES, 111–113
Resilience management, 64, 72, 73, 73*n*5, 74
Resilience mechanisms, 135
Resilience resources, 128*t*
Resilience thinking, 6, 21
Resource robustness, 74
1920 Revolution Brigades, 57
Robustness, 74, 74*n*7
Rotter's Generalized Trust Framework, 82
Rule of relative advantage, 115, 128

S

Sabatier and Jenkins-Smith's Advocacy Coalition Framework, 82
Sadr City, 11, 11*t*, 16, 46, 50, 68, 84, 90, 108, 111*t*, 112
  culture in, 87
  demography of, 109
Saferworld (NGO), 9
Samarra bombing , 9, 51. *See also* Al-Askari Mosque bombingSayyid, 86
Sectarian conflict, 20, 35, 61, 64
  reasons for, 24, 36
Sectarian Militia Permitted (SMP) areas, 10, 11*t*
Sectarian Militia Rejected (SMR) areas, 10, 11*t*
Sectarian militias, 60
Sectarian violence, 2, 5, 7, 8, 9, 11, 14, 17, 20, 21, 24, 134, 137, 146
Sectarianism, 6, 10, 28, 126
  meaning, 41–42
Security dilemma, 44
Self-defense groups, 60, 120
Self-esteem, 103
Self-organization, 97, 100
Sense of community, 89–100
Sense-making activities, 97
Shakkuka families, 87
Shia, 26, 27, 31, 32, 32n11, 33, 34
Shia vs. Sunni Islam , 3. *See also* Shia; Sunni
  good relationships, 10
  International Medical Corps data, 11
  US invasion, 10
Shiite Imam Ali Mosque, 58, 58*n*4
Social agency, 25
Social capital, 72, 74, 75, 76, 77, 81–83, 100, 101, 104, 122, 128*t*, 135, 145
  and conflict resilience, 82
  definition, 82
  trust, 82
Social class, 109, 115
Social cohesion, 121, 122, 123
Social conflicts, 24
Social construction, 24, 29
Social control, 7, 36, 121
Social identity, 28, 30*n*9, 109, 111
Social identity theory, 30, 31
Social support, 83, 101, 122
Social trust, 5, 20, 136
Socioeconomic status (SES), 72*n*11, 109–110, 127, 128, 128*t*, 130
  and resilience to violence, 111–113
Socioeconomic variables and violence, 4
Sources of information, 21
Spaces for communication, 21
Specialized arrangements, 67
State building, 134, 135
Stereotypes, 30*n*10
Stressors, 64, 70, 72, 73, 75
Structural interventions, 135
Structural peacebuilding, 135
Structural variables and violence, 4
Sunni, 26, 27, 32*n*11, 33, 34

heir selection, 32
tribes, 36
Sunni Awakening Council, 33, 34
Sunni insurgency, the, 58
Sunni-Shia divide, 31
death of Muhammad, 31
Sunni-Shia marriages, 36
Sunni-Shia relations, 81
Supreme Council for the Islamic Revolution in Iraq (SCIRI), 34
Supreme Islamic Iraqi Council (SIIC), 34
Sustained competence, 64
Syria, 88, 142, 144
Syria civil war, 134
Systems resilience, 64, 66, 67, 77

T
Tajfel's social identity theory, 30*n*9
Taliban fighters vs. Jaghori fighters, 3
Third party interventions, 125
Third side, 125
Trade networks, 115–116
Transactional capacity, 141
Transformational capacity, 70, 71
Trauma care, 141, 144
Tribal affiliation, 87, 115
Tribal identity, 32–36
Tribes, 68
Tripp, Charles, 1
Trust, 99, 100

U
Understanding Iraq: Society, Culture and Personality (Wardi), 35
United States Agency for International Development (USAID), 3, 49, 140–142
Urban resilience, 2, 135
Urban Resilience in Situations of Chronic Violence, 71
Urban violence, 2
Urbanism, 35, 87
USAID. *See* United States Agency for International Development

V
Vertical legitimacy, 45
Violence, 27–29, 33, 54, 60, 70, 71, 134, 137–139, 144, 145
bombing of holy golden domed Shia al-Askari shrine, 59
brutality of, 29, 55
interethnic, 28
outbreak of, 73
political, 72
resilience to, 64, 66
sectarian, 61, 64, 77, 134, 146
sectarian, in Iraq, 24
in Baghdad, 24
social, 66
and war, 63, 65
Visioning, spaces for, 136–139
Visualization, 137
Vulnerability, 108, 110, 111, 112, 113
psychosocial vulnerability, 113
individual vulnerability, 117

W
Wardi, Ali, 1, 35, 36, 87
Well-being, 4, 54, 65, 109, 110, 141
"We-they" dichotomy, 29
Wikileaks, 9, 50*n*6

Y
YouGov, 8, 36, 111

Z
Zafaraniyya, 83, 85, 89, 90, 91, 101
Zafaraniyya, 10, 11, 11*t*, 16–17
Zafaraniyya, 46, 101, 112
Zero-sum, 55–56
Zero-sum perceptions, 56
Zero-sum thinking, 55

Printed in the USA
CPSIA information can be obtained
at www.ICGtesting.com
LVHW021926270823
756422LV00005B/280

9 781461 488118